Economics: Contemporary Issues in Canada

edited by

D. A. L. Auld

Holt, Rinehart and Winston of Canada, Limited

Toronto   Montreal

Distributed in the United States of America by Mine Publications, Inc.

D. A. L. Auld
Associate Professor
Department of Economics
College of Social Sciences
University of Guelph
Guelph, Ontario

Copyright © 1972
Holt, Rinehart and Winston of Canada, Limited
Toronto, Montreal
All rights reserved

ISBN: 0-03-928077-2

Distributed in the United States of America by Mine Publications, Inc.,
25 Groveland Terrace, Minneapolis, Minnesota, 55403.

Printed in Canada
1 2 3 4 5   76 75 74 73 72

Preface

Students have sometimes complained that introductory economics is not "relevant" in terms of the social and political issues facing Canadian society today. It is true that textbooks usually include some reference to these issues but such references are not of any great depth.

Economics is not easy, and much of the job of a textbook and instructor is helping the student grasp the basic principles or theory of economics. This, of course, means that any detailed examination of contemporary issues cannot be undertaken in the lecture hall or textbook. The student will have to do this reading on his own and if he or she does, it is likely he will discover that economics is at the heart of many social and political questions facing Canadian society.

This collection was prepared with a view to illustrating the above fact; that economics is an *important* aspect of much that is going on today in this country. It offers the student a relatively short collection of articles, book chapters, government papers, and briefs that highlight the relevancy of economics. The debate on the future of confederation, what to do about poverty, the persistence of inflation and unemployment, urban problems, pollution and foreign investment are widely discussed topics in Canada today. This book is about these issues.

An understanding of the economic content of these questions will hopefully help the student to evaluate critically policies that have been proposed by all political parties and other groups to deal with the problems.

D.A.L.A.
University of Guelph
September 1971

Contents

Part A
Federalism   1

Chapter 1
Federal-Provincial Grants and the Spending Power of Parliament
Pierre Elliott Trudeau   3

Chapter 2
Can Anything Be Done to Minimize Federal-Provincial Conflicts?
Claude E. Forget   11

Chapter 3
The Economic Implications of Separatism
A. A. Birchant   19

Part B
Poverty   39

Chapter 4
The Problem of Poverty
The Economic Council of Canada   41

Chapter 5
The Real Poor in Canada — And Why We Don't Know Who They Are
Walter Stewart   49

Chapter 6
The Negative Income Tax: How It Helps to Alleviate Poverty
Colin J. Hindle   55

Part C
Inflation and Unemployment   63

Chapter 7
The Trade-Off Between Prices and Unemployment
R. G. Bodkin, E. P. Bond, G. L. Reuber, T. R. Robinson   65

Chapter 8
Inflation, Unemployment, and Incomes Policies
John Young, H. G. Johnson, Richard G. Lipsey   71

Part D
Urban Economics   **85**

Chapter 9
An Introduction to the Problems of Urban Canada
N. H. Lithwick   87

Chapter 10
Project and Policy in Transportation Planning
David M. Nowlan   113

Part E
Pollution   **129**

Chapter 11
An Economic Analysis of Environmental Pollution
D. A. L. Auld   131

Chapter 12
Fiscal Instruments and Pollution: An Evaluation of Canadian Legislation
Leonard Waverman   139

Part F
Foreign Investment   **149**

Chapter 13
Development and Dependence: The Canadian Problem
Abraham Rotstein   151

Chapter 14
Foreign Investment in Canada: A Review
Grant L. Reuber   161

Contributors

D. A. L. Auld, Associate Professor, University of Guelph, Guelph, Ontario.

A. A. Birchant, Canada Committee, Montreal, Quebec.

R. G. Bodkin, Professor of Economics, University of Western Ontario, London, Ontario.

E. P. Bond, Assistant Professor, University of British Columbia, Vancouver, B.C.

Claude E. Forget, Economist, Private Planning Association, Montreal, Quebec.

Colin J. Hindle, Economist, Treasury Board of Canada, Ottawa, Ontario.

Harry G. Johnson, Professor of Economics, London School of Economics, London, England and the University of Chicago, Chicago, Illinois.

Richard G. Lipsey, Professor of Economics, Queen's University, Kingston, Ontario.

N. H. Lithwick, Professor of Economics, Carleton University, Ottawa, Ontario.

David M. Nowlan, Associate Professor, University of Toronto, Toronto, Ontario.

Grant L. Reuber, Professor and Dean of Social Science, University of Western Ontario, London, Ontario.

T. R. Robinson, Director, Planning Branch, Treasury Board of Canada, Ottawa, Ontario.

Abraham Rotstein, Associate Professor, University of Toronto, Toronto, Ontario.

Walter Stewart, Correspondent for Maclean's Magazine.

Pierre Elliott Trudeau, Prime Minister of Canada.

Leonard Waverman, Assistant Professor, University of Toronto, Toronto, Ontario.

John Young, Chairman, Prices and Incomes Commission, Government of Canada, Ottawa, Ontario.

Part A
Federalism

Although there is a great deal of emotional debate about Canadian confederation there are a number of basic economic issues involved, especially concerning what level of government should have what spending and taxing power. The first of the following three papers presents the Federal government's rationale for making grants to the provinces and what the provincial criticism of such grants is, as Ottawa sees them. The second selection examines the political economy of federal-provincial conflicts and how conflicts can arise given the allocation of fiscal powers in Canada. In the third selection, an attempt is made to identify the economic effects on Quebec if that province were to become a separate state. The paper concludes that a viable separate state needs a strong economy which would not be the case if Quebec separated from Canada, according to the analysis.

Chapter 1
Federal-Provincial Grants and the Spending Power of Parliament*

Pierre Elliott Trudeau

The Constitutional Conference decided, at its February 1969 meeting, to accord priority to "the study of the distribution of powers, in particular the taxing and spending powers," and directed the Continuing Committee of Officials "to give its immediate attention to this aspect of the Constitution." This Working Paper has been prepared pursuant to this decision: its purpose is to examine the use of the "spending power" by the Parliament of Canada; to consider the criticisms which have been made of its use; and to present a possible proposal for establishing under a revised Constitution a new procedure for the use of the spending power in respect of federal grants to the provinces.

The Spending Power: What it is and How it has been Used

Ordinarily one thinks of the "spending power" of governments simply in terms of the spending they do on particular programmes, under the authority of legislation passed by their legislative bodies. Constitutionally, however, the term "spending power" has come to have a specialized meaning in Canada: it means the power of Parliament to make payments to people or institutions or governments for purposes on which it (Parliament) does not necessarily have the power to legislate. The best example, perhaps, is the grants to provincial governments to assist in the provision of free hospitalization across Canada: Parliament does not have the power under the Constitution to establish general hospitals or to regulate them or their use; but under its "spending power" it is generally conceded that Parliament can make grants to the provinces to assist them in financing provincially operated hospitalization programmes.[1]

The importance of the spending power in Canada can be illustrated by looking at some of the programmes which are founded primarily upon it (as

*A working paper submitted to the Federal-Provincial Constitutional Conference in June, 1969, pp. 4, 6, 8, 10, 12, 14, 16, 18, and 20. Reproduced with the permission of Information Canada.

[1] This latter statement must be qualified both in legal terms and in terms of the generality of the support for this view of the Constitution. See pp. 6 and 7, *infra*.

opposed to being based upon Parliament's regulatory powers). *The equalization of opportunity for individual Canadians,* in the form of income redistribution between persons, has been based in no small measure upon this power. In particular, family allowances are paid to all mothers in Canada ($560 million in 1968-69), and the federal government pays to the provinces one half of the cost of social assistance payments to individuals in need (under the Canada Assistance Plan — costing over $400 million). In addition to these measures, Canada Pension Plan payments, Old Age Security payments, and Guaranteed Income Supplements are paid by Parliament under a specific section of the Constitution. Obviously too, the Income Tax Act of Canada, through its higher rates on the rich than on the poor, contributes substantially to income redistribution across the country.

The equilization of provincial public services — including health, welfare, education, and roads — is also accomplished largely because of the existence of the spending power. The Government of Canada makes revenue equalization grants to the governments of low income provinces for this purpose (over $560 million in 1968-69), and it contributes as well to specific provincial or federal-provincial programmes. Health care for individual Canadians is supported through federal grants to the provinces for hospital insurance (nearly $800 million), through a $500 million Health Resources Fund, and now through payments to provincial medical care plans. Higher education is supported, indirectly, through unconditional grants to provinces — grants based upon the total operating expenditures of universities and technical institutes (over $220 million in cash grants, and another $275 million in tax transfers and equalization payments). The Trans-Canada Highway, which finds its constitutional foundation both in the spending power and, because of its interprovincial character, in other provisions of the Constitution, was financed under a joint programme involving both the federal and provincial governments (over $700 million). And there have been other smaller programmes.

Equalization of opportunity for individual Canadians through regional economic development is also achieved in part through federal-provincial programmes involving Parliament's spending power. One example is the $300 million Fund for Rural Economic Development, which is financing a broad range of regional development measures, some of which are based upon the spending power alone. Another is the $125 million ARDA programme (Agricultural Rehabilitation and Development Act) which might have been managed directly by the Government of Canada, but which took the form of a federal-provincial programme. And the new Department of Regional Economic Expansion will have to rely, for its new measures, both upon Parliament's power to legislate and upon its spending power — as did its predecessors, notably the Atlantic Development Board.

Finally, *specific projects of national importance* have been possible, constitutionally, because of Parliament's spending power. Expo is the outstanding example. But many other projects or programmes could be listed (some of which relied in whole or in part upon this power) — Roads to Resources, the South Saskatchewan River Development project, and various other measures within individual provinces.

The scale of the payments made under the spending power of Parliament is another index of its importance. In 1968-69 the Government of Canada spent some $3.4 billion — 32 percent of its budget — on programmes which are based largely upon it, involving payments to persons, payments to institutions, and payments to governments.

Table 1

	Amounts ($ millions)	Percent of Federal Expenditures
Payments to Persons	$ 855.2	8.0
Payments to Institutions	77.3	0.7
Payments to Governments		
Conditional Grants	1,616.9	15.0
Unconditional Grants	865.0	8.1
Total	$ 3,414.4	31.8

The Spending Power and the Constitution

A "spending power" of the kind which is to be found in Canada is not unusual in federal states. The constitution of the United States of America, for example, provides the central government with very broad power: "The Congress shall have the power to levy and collect taxes . . . and provide for the . . . general welfare of the United States . . ."[2] Similarly *The Commonwealth of Australia Constitution Act* provides specifically that the central Parliament "may grant financial assistance to any State on such terms and conditions as the Parliament thinks fit."[3]

In Switzerland and West Germany, on the other hand, the terms of the spending power are more explicit and more limited. The Swiss Constitution gives the Confederation broad powers to act "for the welfare of the people and the economic security of the citizens," but provides that these powers "may be introduced only in the form of federal laws or federal decrees subject to referendum," and that the "cantons must be consulted before the enactment of [such] laws." The Swiss Constitution also provides that "the Confederation shall encourage financial equalization among the cantons."[4] The Constitution of West Germany has three specific heads relating to the spending power as we know it in Canada. On matters involving mixed jurisdiction (concurrent legislative powers) the Federation has the power to legislate where individual states (Laender) cannot act effectively by themselves, or where action by one state "might prejudice the interest of other Laender," or where the "maintenance of legal or economic unity, especially the maintenance of uniformity of living conditions beyond the territory of a [state]" requires federal action.[5] Secondly, if a federal law imposes addi-

---

2 Article 1, section 8 of the American constitution.
3 Section 96.
4 See Articles 31A, 32 and 42B of the Swiss constitution.
5 See Article 72(2) of the constitution of the Federal Republic of Germany.

tional financial obligations upon the states, the central government is required to compensate them. And finally, as provided in the Constitution, a federal law has been enacted to establish the formula and criteria under which financially weak Laender qualify for equalization contributions from financially strong Laender. The Constitution also permits supplementary grants out of federal funds.

The spending power provisions of the Constitution of Canada are less precise than those of other federations. They flow from, and are a part of the general distribution of powers, and can best be understood in this context. The British North America Act divides the power to legislate between the Parliament of Canada and the legislatures of the provinces, principally in Sections 91, 92, and 93 to 95, and gives to the Parliament of Canada the residual legislative power. It follows that there are certain specific heads upon which Parliament may not legislate, namely those in Sections 92 and 93, and others upon which provincial legislatures may not legislate, principally those in Section 91.

In addition to the powers of the Parliament of Canada to legislate, the Constitution as it has been interpreted by the Courts gives to it the power to spend from the Consolidated Revenue Fund on any object, providing the legislation authorizing the expenditures does not amount to a regulatory scheme falling within provincial powers. The constitutional basis for this spending power is to be found in Section 91 (3) of the B.N.A. Act, which gives the Parliament of Canada the power to raise money by any mode of taxation, and Section 91 (1A) which gives Parliament the right to make laws respecting public debt and property, the latter having been construed to include every kind of dominion asset, including the Consolidated Revenue Fund.

A judgment in the Supreme Court of Canada said of these provisions:

> ... Parliament, by properly framed legislation may raise money by taxation and dispose of its public property in any manner that it sees fit. As to the latter point, it is evident that the Dominion may grant sums of money to individuals or organizations and that the gift may be accompanied by such restrictions and conditions as Parliament may see fit to enact. It would then be open to the proposed recipient to decline the gift or to accept it subject to such conditions. As to the first point, it is also undoubted, I conceive, that Parliament, by properly framed legislation may raise money by taxation, and this may be done either generally or for the specific purpose of providing the funds wherewith to make grants either before or after the conferring of the benefit.[6]

On appeal, the Privy Council stated the general principle in this way:
> That the Dominion may impose taxation for the purpose of creating a fund for special purposes, and may apply that fund for making contributions in the public interest to individuals, corporations or public authorities, could not as a general proposition be denied.

The qualification of this general proposition was stated as follows:

---

[6] Reference re Employment and Social Insurance Act, (1936) S.C.R. 427, Duff C.J. at p. 457.

But assuming that the Dominion has collected by means of taxation a fund, it by no means follows that any legislation which disposes of it is necessarily within Dominion competence.

It may still be legislation affecting the classes of subjects enumerated in s. 92, and, if so, would be ultra vires. In other words, Dominion legislation, even though it deals with Dominion property, may yet be so framed as to invade civil rights within the Province, or encroach upon the classes of subjects which are reserved to Provincial competence.[7]

It cannot be said that there is universal agreement among constitutional lawyers in Canada as to the precise meaning of these and related decisions. Some argue that they mean Parliament may make conditional or unconditional grants for any purpose, even if the purpose falls within exclusive provincial legislative jurisdiction, providing only that the programme involved does not amount to legislation or regulation (see for example Bora Laskin and Gerard V. La Forest).[8] Others, such as Quebec's Tremblay Commission, argue that the qualifications the Privy Council attached to the spending power mean that Parliament has no power to make grants of any kind in areas of exclusive provincial jurisdiction — even unconditional grants.[9] Others seem to suggest, when discussing federal grants to provincial governments, that Parliament might properly make unconditional grants to the provinces, but not conditional grants.[10]

In fact, there seems to have been little disposition on the part either of the federal or the provincial governments to seek further judicial clarification of the matter. Federal governments consistently have taken the position that Parliament's power to spend is clear,[11] while provincial governments generally have limited themselves to cirticism of the *use* of the spending power by Parliament — in particular to its use to start new federal-provincial shared-cost programmes, or to terminate old ones, without the consent of the provinces.[12] Only governments of Quebec have advanced the more general proposition that it was constitutionally improper for Parliament to use its spending power to make grants to persons or institutions or governments for purposes which fall within exclusive provincial jurisdiction.

The Spending Power and Federal-Provincial Programmes: Provincial Government Criticisms

The governments of the provinces have advanced three criticisms of Parliament for its use of the spending power to establish new federal-provincial programmes:

[7] (1937) A.C. 355 at 366.
[8] Bora Laskin, *Canadian Constitutional Law* (Toronto: The Carswell Co. Ltd., 1966), p. 666; and Gerard V. La Forest, *The Allocation of Taxing Power under the Canadian Constitution* (Toronto: The Canadian Tax Foundation, 1967), pp. 36-41.
[9] *Report of the Royal Commission of Enquiry on Constitutional Problems*, II, 1956, pp. 217-223.
[10] See, for example, the reference in Jacques Dupont, "Le pouvoir de dépenser du gouvernement fédéral: 'A Dead Issue?'", in *Cahiers de Droit* (Laval University), 8, footnote 63.
[11] See in particular a speech by Prime Minister Louis St. Laurent in 1957. *Hansard*, January 29th, p. 754.
[12] See the Proceedings of Federal-Provincial and Dominion-Provincial Conferences of the past 10 or 15 years.

1. That the Government and the Parliament of Canada are deciding, without the formal participation of the provinces in such decisions, as to when federal-provincial programmes ought to be started.

2. That shared-cost programmes force upon provincial governments changes in their priorities.

3. That "taxation without benefit" occurs when the citizens of a province whose provincial government has refused to participate in a shared-cost programme are required to pay the federal taxes which finance the federal share of the programme.

Each of these criticisms is examined in the paragraphs which follow.

Provincial Participation in the Decision to Establish
Shared-Cost Programmes

It is argued by many provincial governments that the Government of Canada ought not to, or perhaps ought not even have the right to, initiate, change or terminate shared-cost programmes without first obtaining some kind of consensus among provincial governments in favour of doing so. The rationale for this argument is essentially this: where exclusive provincial jurisdiction is involved, federal-provincial shared-cost programmes can only be established and operated by the provinces; therefore, the Government of Canada ought not to proceed with any plan to contribute to such programmes without first obtaining some kind of agreement from among the provinces. (The counter-argument has been that no provincial government is constitutionally obliged to enter into shared-cost agreements with the Government of Canada; and that what really is being criticized, therefore, is the political pressure which is imposed upon provincial ministers to participate in Canada-wide programmes.)

Provincial Priorities

Secondly, the provincial governments point out that, because they feel obliged to enter into new federal-provincial shared-cost programmes, they are forced to alter their spending and taxing priorities. Moreover, because shared-cost programmes cost the provinces only fifty cents for each dollar they spend (the usual ratio), there is a greater incentive to allocate provincial funds toward these as opposed to purely provincial programmes, and a smaller incentive to economize in administering them. (The response to this argument has been that the very purpose of shared-cost measures is to achieve a country-wide priority for certain programmes, and that in the absence of some such vehicle common priorities across Canada would be highly unlikely.)

"Taxation Without Benefit"

Thirdly, some provincial governments are arguing that their citizens ought not to be forced to contribute toward the federal share of shared-cost programmes which do not operate in their province, by reason of the decision of their provincial government. Alternatively, it is argued, the federal government ought to pay over to the provincial government the equivalent of what the taxpayers in the province are contributing toward the federal share of the programme, or the equivalent of what they would have received in benefits had the province embarked upon the programme. (The counter-argument has been that the taxpayers of each province are represented in Parliament as well as in provincial legislatures, and that they have participated, through their M.P.'s and their Senators, in Parliament's decision to offer to spend from the Consolidated Revenue Fund for the purpose of contributing toward new shared-cost programmes.)

The Spending Power and Payments to Persons and Institutions

In addition to the arguments which are made concerning federal-provincial shared-cost programmes, the Government of Quebec, as has been noted, has generally argued against the use by the Parliament of Canada of its spending power for the purpose of making payments to persons and institutions. The rationale for this position is different, generally speaking, than that concerning shared-cost programmes. New provincial programmes are not required as a consequence of federal payments to persons or institutions; at most, adaptations might be called for in the related federal and provincial programmes to achieve the best results for the citizen. Provincial government priorities remain unaffected; again the most which might be called for would be programme adaptation (usually involving reduced obligations on the provincial treasury). Finally "taxation without benefit" does not occur.

The argument against federal grants to persons and institutions is based more upon a particular approach to the Constitution, and upon what might be called "the case for programme integration". The constitutional argument is straightforward: Parliament ought not to have the power to spend except where it has a specific power to regulate. The programme argument is that a single authority is better able to integrate different programmes in the same or related fields — for example income redistribution and social security — than are two authorities. Further, the single authority, if it is the provincial government, would be able to adapt every programme to the specific demographic, income and regional structure of the province, without taking into account the situation in the rest of the country. This approach is based on the assumption, of course, that a province would be put in the financial position, by Parliament, of being able to finance the federal programmes it took over, including, if it were a lower income province, higher equalization payments.

It is not possible to enter into a discussion of this particular proposition without considering the whole of the structure of Canadian federalism, including the totality of the distribution of powers. There are two reasons for this. First, programmes which involve payments to persons and institutions and which are excluded from Parliament's jurisdiction under the propositions submitted by the Government of Quebec, include income redistribution measures, possibly certain economic development programmes, contributions to Canada's cultural development, and research and technological development measures — all of which the Government of Canada considers to be important powers of Parliament. This view was advanced by the federal government at the first meeting of the Constitutional Conference, when it was argued that Parliament ought to retain explicit powers in these fields. Secondly, to achieve the programme and fiscal transfers called for in the Quebec propositions relating to these matters would be to weaken very substantially the powers of Parliament across the country, or to call for special status for the National Assembly of Quebec. In either case the structure of Canadian federalism would be fundamentally altered. For these reasons the Government of Canada does not believe it would be appropriate to discuss the Quebec propositions concerning federal payments to persons and institutions until all propositions concerning the distribution of powers have been received by the Secretariat of the Constitutional Conference, and until their effect upon the structure of Canadian federalism has been fully evaluated by all governments.

Chapter 2
Can Anything Be Done to Minimize Federal-Provincial Conflicts?*

Claude E. Forget

Causes of Federal-Provincial Conflicts

Many Canadians are becoming weary of seemingly insoluble intergovernmental squabblings and quarrels. As people everywhere, they are sometimes impatient of governmental muddling, but they have perhaps more reasons than most, or so it appears to them, to feel some resentment at largely artificial crises among their several governments and to be disillusioned with federalism.

It is therefore appropriate to ask: can constitutional reform help resolve or avoid intergovernmental crises and conflicts? Before we address ourselves to this question, we want to see whether anything useful can be said about the nature of the federal-provincial conflicts that have arisen under the present Canadian Constitution.

There obviously is no intention of suggesting that federal-provincial conflicts subsume all conflicts that have taken place in Canada. As in all pluralistic societies, occasions for conflict abound, ranging the whole gamut from abolition of capital punishment to suggested attitudes and policies towards the alleged U.S. domination of the Canadian economy. These policy conflicts are resolved (and sometimes avoided) by the normal political process so far as they may be amenable to solutions in any case. In most instances these conflicts are irrelevant to the federal character of our Constitution. In some cases, however, these broadly political conflicts have involved sectional or regional interests rather closely identified with a province and with the cultural duality that is basic to the fabric of the country and to its federal constitution. So-called minority rights and the wartime issue of conscription provide good examples.

Casting to one side all the political problems more or less common to all complex societies, we may for the sake of this discussion distinguish three kinds of genuine federal-provincial conflicts where the structure of government of this country has had definite and specific implications.

*Chapter 1 (pp. 3-12) of *The Power of the Purse in a Revised Constitution* by Claude E. Forget, published by The Private Planning Association of Canada, Montreal, 1970. Reproduced with the permission of The Private Planning Association of Canada.

A. The Regional Implications of National Economic Policies

This has been an area for conflicts between some provinces and the federal government as to the objectives of policy, especially in connection with commercial and transportation policies and their presumed impacts on regional income differentials. It is significant that, in the case of one partial remedy, which has become known as the principle underlying equalization payments, longstanding grievances and disagreements appear to have been largely put to rest by the development of objective norms of interprovincial redistribution. The principle underlying these payments has hardly been disputed over the last decade after some ninety years of squabbling over what "fairness" is about. It would be interesting to find out whether such a systematic and rational approach to problems of regional imbalance as a whole could lead to conflict resolution there as well.

More recently, overall short-term policies to combat inflation have attracted some considerable critical comment from the provinces, and especially from the provinces most severely affected by the resulting increase in unemployment. For all the learned discussions about the problems of fiscal and monetary policy in a federal state, very little progress has been made towards their solution.[1]

B. Straightforward Jurisdictional Disputes

Examples are easily come by here: the federal government's disavowal of provincial social credit legislation in the Prairies during the 1930s, recent Quebec claims to international status and representation, federal assumption of responsibility for grants to universities in the mid-1950s, problems of implementation surrounding the Columbia River Treaty, conflicting claims to offshore resources.

Several disputes in this category grew out of a divorce between constitutional powers and policy objectives. Even when the Constitution grants concurrent jurisdiction, it remains silent on the type of policy objectives that can properly be pursued by each level of government. For instance, the power over natural resources is a power to do precisely what? In one case the failure to specify a purpose (i.e., the federal power to regulate commerce) has led to a complete pre-emption of the intended constitutional authority by the attribution of the implicit objectives to other similarly vaguely worded "powers" held by the provinces. This style of constitution drafting has, moreover, helped to accelerate the obsolescence of the constitutional distribution of powers because technological and social changes are more likely to affect policy instruments than broadly defined policy objectives.

When objectives were clearly seen, there was some evidence to suggest that a formal allocation of jurisdictions was not long allowed to stand in the

---

[1] See, on this question, the chapter "The Public Sector and Economic Policy" in *Ontario's Proposals for Fiscal-Policy Coordination in Canada* a budget paper accompanying the Ontario Treasurer's budget statement for 1970. The Ontario government has also reprinted its own staff papers, prepared for various federal-provincial conferences, under the title *Intergovernmental Policy Co-ordination and Finance*, (Department of Treasury and Economics, Toronto, May, 1970).

way of a constructive agreement. This took place in the field of unemployment insurance in 1940 and in the field of old-age pensions in 1951.[2]

C. Revenue-Sharing Conflicts

It is important to distinguish between revenue-sharing conflicts and the first-mentioned conflicts that used to rage with respect to what we now call equalization. Larger equalization payments have been for many provinces an alternative to a larger share of the tax dollar, and this has contributed to a blurring of the distinction. The difference is, however, genuine and is well illustrated by the fact that Ontario — not a likely recipient of equalization payments — has on many occasions displayed quite a healthy appetite for a bigger share of tax revenues.

One can hardly say that there has ever been any fundamental or lasting disagreement in Canada — even as between different levels of governments — about where, at any time, real priorities were; in 1940, the requirements of national defence and of the war effort made agreement to the first tax-rental agreements relatively easy. In the after-war period, the needs of education, social welfare, and health services induced the federal government to underwrite financially part of the cost of provincial activities in these fields. The central and regional governments have therefore been able to agree about priorities. What is significant, however, is the circuitous route that has been taken in each case to effect a transfer of resources, first from the provinces to the central government, and since from the federal government to the provinces. In both instances the jurisdiction surrendering resources has insisted on keeping some kind of prior claims to them. Tax-rental agreements in one case provided the channel for asserting, perhaps weakly, this prior claim of the provinces. Shared-cost programs have performed, in a more effective way, the same role of asserting the central government's prior claims on funds spent by the provinces; this has been so even while the federal government went along with the provincial governments and their own expenditure programs and priorities.

For these reasons it seems apparent that revenue-sharing conflicts have little to do with differences about the expenditure side of government budgets, and yet they indisputably are the kind of federal-provincial questions about which Canadians have seen their several governments get into the most frequent, the most spectacular, and the most stubborn fights. The power to tax is at the root, and constitutes the main symbol, of political power, so there will perhaps be no surprise if all government units tend to consider their own power to levy tax monies as a kind of proprietary right. If implicitly agreed expenditure priorities are such that a particular unit of government has no choice but to restrain its own expenditure for the benefit of another unit, at a different level in the federal structure of government, it will do so, but at the same time it will seek to retain its title to the revenues devoted (or "distracted") to these priorities.

---

[2] The Constitution was amended both times — in 1940 by adding unemployment insurance as item 2A to the list of central-government functions of article 91 of the British North America Act and in 1951 by adding article 94A to the Act, giving Parliament power to legislate concerning old-age pensions. This was done with the unanimous agreement of the provinces.

In the probably inevitable competition for power between provincial and central governments in a federal system, whatever one level of government gains the other level must lose. In such a context, conflicts are bound to assume a particularly obstinate character.

The purpose of this commentary is to look critically at the papers prepared and published by the central government in connection with the constitutional conference and which bear on two of the most fundamental aspects of the central and provincial governments' competition for power, namely, taxing powers and the central government's grant-making power. In this task we shall mostly have in mind the revenue-sharing type of conflict described above; this author believes the other kinds of conflicts are of relatively minor significance to an understanding of the issues raised by taxing powers and intergovernmental grants.

Conflict Resolution and Social Objectives

Conflicts represent a social waste: conflicts are costly in terms of time and energy — not least intellectual energy — for immediate participants and strategists. In a democracy they are also costly in terms of the limited interest and attention that the average citizen can devote to public affairs because conflicts make news and easily pre-empt all that interest and attention to the detriment of substantive issues.

Although they are a waste, conflicts can never be entirely avoided. Their occurrence can be minimized, and conceivably, they can be resolved in more or less efficient ways. Conflicts typical of federalism can be eliminated if federalism itself becomes irrelevant as a style of government, because the distinct regional identities are submerged under a new and wider identity or because the federation is broken up. Neither alternative need be considered in the present context.

Conflicts can be avoided or resolved in several different ways.[3] Solutions can be found either at the expense of commonly preferred substantive objectives or in agreement with these objectives; conflict avoidance or resolution itself can take place with greater or lesser effectiveness. To what extent can a federal constitution avoid public policy outcomes that the same population would positively turn down in a unitary state?

Individual conflicts can be resolved either one by one or according to given rules and within given constraints. A proposition presently to be developed is that a constitution can provide — within limits — some conflict-restraining and -resolving rules. However, the determination of such rules is no easy matter, so that a revision of a constitution gives rise to a trade-off problem of a kind familiar to economists: a balance must be struck between, on the one hand, a struggle about the rules that may help in a number of specific future disputes and, on the other hand, a series of probable future struggles on the substance of these individual disputes. In striking such a balance, public officials might be excused for adopting a rather shorter time

---

[3] Conflict resolution has become a field of study in itself. For an excellent glimpse of the field, consult T. C. Schelling's book, *The Strategy of Conflict* (Cambridge: Harvard University Press, 1960).

horizon than other, more disinterested, observers would do. Disputes about the rules of the game may be distinctly less rewarding in advancing any party's advantage than are disputes about individual cases. There is also a considerable pressure on officials to achieve at least apparent success with the minimum amount of delay: this can be done only if the scope of the problem is kept as narrow as possible, even if the cost consists in not resolving fundamental issues. In reading the constitutional documents prepared by the central government, as well as the views and reactions of provincial governments, one may justifiably be concerned whether fundamental issues are not being ignored for the sake of a happy ending to a process of constitutional review in which no one appears to have a clear notion of the goal to be reached.

The Potential Contribution of a Constitution to Social Objectives

Public choices, resulting from a political process that rests on majority rule, always imply a "cost" for those voters ("the minority") who are outvoted and who must live with the consequences of choices they opposed. What is remarkable is that the defeated minority will, without coercion, generally bear that cost and accept the unfavourable outcome. Such a minority does not adopt this attitude because it likes the situation – it obviously cannot – but, in some sense, because it considers that its own defeat was proper, legitimate, in a word "constitutional."[4]

In any organized society, the law provides a set of rules to appraise behaviour. Legal considerations are not the only ones that can be brought to bear in this exercise: ethics, economics, sociology, psychology, all bring different aspects of behaviour into focus. However, legal criteria have about them an undoubted definiteness and a high operational relevance.

Constitutional law has an even higher claim to be considered as a paramount criterion, since it serves to appraise legislative behaviour itself.

Inevitably, appraisal by reference to definite rules cannot go on indefinitely, and the appraisal of constitutional law throws us back for reference to the wider and sometimes conflicting criteria governing policy making in a legally unconstrained environment. Of course, it is no explanation at all to say that the outcome of a political process will be accepted as non-dictatorial and non-arbitrary only if the rules that govern that process are "legitimate" or "constitutional" in the eyes of those whom this outcome concerns. We have to be able to analyze and explain the characteristics of political structures and behaviour that make people consider the use of power as legitimate or not.[5]

---

[4] Professor J. M. Buchanan has devised the notion of a two-tiered choice process for democratic institutions. The first tier has to do with the determination of the "rules of the game" (rules about voting, types of majority required for an affirmative vote, eligibility, periodicity of elections), while the second tier is concerned with decisions on specific issues of substance. The first tier is very much in the nature of a constitution. See J. M. Buchanan and G. Tullock, *The Calculus of Consent* (Ann Arbor: University of Michigan Press, 1962).

[5] Naturally, constitutions by their very existence and given reasonable stability (see further, pp. 17 & 18) can themselves provide an element of legitimacy without necessary reference to outside factors – that is to say, they serve as "focal points" in the resolution or avoidance of potential conflicts. See Schelling, *op. cit.*

15

In a brief critical essay such as this one, there can be no pretension of solving such a momentous question — perhaps the central one for political theory.

Instead of attempting an involved justification (which might well fail in any event), the present author will merely state — and briefly explain — the assumptions to be used in this commentary as criteria for a future federal constitution for Canada. It is not expected that these criteria will strike anyone as being self-evident principles for constitutional reform. However, they may be looked upon as hypothetical statements, potentially testable empirically, to explain attitudes about the appropriateness of a particular federal constitutional arrangement. As such they describe aspects of federal systems that must not only be real but must also be seen to be real by those who live under these systems.

The rules that circumscribe the use of power by any one level of government in a federal system must have three essential characteristics: they should be functional, restraining, and stable.

A. A Functional Distribution of Authority

To say that constitutional rules should be functional is not to suggest that modern management's techniques are necessary to the legitimacy of government. An inefficient government may still be a legitimate and firmly based one. However, the machinery of government should be such that its action can consistently and clearly be oriented towards some objective of policy that the governed deem important by itself, however inefficiently that objective may be pursued by a particular administration. People should have a reasonably clear notion of the objectives that their government pursues — not necessarily in terms of policy alternatives on particular issues but in terms of broad areas of concern on which government action can be brought to bear.

A federal constitution, because of its comparative complexity, introduces a possible confusion that can breed disaffection unless care is taken to clearly identify the different levels of government with distinct and meaningful objectives. The fine points about the subtle ways in which different programs and objectives interact may be well taken and offer scope for increasing the efficiency of government operations, but these factors should not obscure the fundamental point that the role of government is to get a certain number of things done and that there can be support for only one particular form of government — including the federal form — if the nature and extent of the powers of government at each level are seen to be functionally related to these objectives. If, in particular, it were believed that "everything crucially depends on everything else," it would be extremely difficult to justify anything but a centralized form of government.

B. A Restraining Allocation of Authority

At any one time, there prevails in a society some more or less agreed view on what governments can or should actually attempt to do. In this age, for example, very few societies any longer believe that government should try to enforce the observance of purely religious duties by its citizens; there is less complete but apparently growing agreement that quasi-religious values should likewise not be legally enforced, as we notice in the gradual relaxation of official censorship and legal abortion rules. More positively, other values are making slow progress, as evidenced by the gradual elimination of capital punishment. Whether inscribed in formal constitutions or (most often) not, these shifts in social values carry strong implications for the accepted scope of the power of the state. We who live at a time when these shifts are taking place, and in democratic societies where governmental authority is remodeled accordingly, may find it difficult to appreciate the basis for the legitimacy of government in the minds of those long under its rule. We may fail to recognize the extent to which this legitimacy rests on the general congruence between the scope of governmental authority and the kinds of issues over which any government is believed by the same people to be competent to act. In most countries, a legal obligation to attend Sunday mass would spur opposition directed not only at this specific (and, as such, really innocuous) measure but also against a whole conception of the nature of the state's role in men's lives, of which this particular measure would be taken as the symbol.

The foregoing remarks suggest that the powers of the state must be limited by what is considered, by those who are ruled, as the proper extent of government authority. The illustrations employed, derived from ethics and religion, should not be allowed to detract from the general point made, for similar limits exist in other respects: one need only refer to the private-sector versus public-sector controversy. In a federal constitution, the same considerations are valid for each order of government taken individually, but of particular relevance is the so-called "sense of community" argument used by advocates of central as well as of provincial powers. This is a vague expression which, as such, is hardly susceptible to confirmation or contradiction by facts. However, it represents more than just empty rhetoric. Assuming a more nearly operational version of the idea could be found, it could play a greater role in helping to define a realistic goal for federalism. In any case, whether it is well defined or not, there is an underlying political reality that conditions the legitimacy granted to particular governmental forms. Inevitably it remains a matter of opinion, but it cannot for that reason be ignored.[6]

C. A Stable Allocation of Powers

The political constitution of a country represents some kind of equilibrium among different sectional interests, distinct regional concerns, and even divergent motivations and values inspiring individuals or groups of individuals. The sense of legitimacy of a government working under a constitution could not long endure if there were some indication of an impending disturbance in that equilibrium: a disequilibrium in a more or less delicately poised balance must be seen as a threat to some segment or other of the population.[7]

---

[6] On this point see Donald V. Smiley, "The Two Themes of Canadian Federalism," *Canadian Journal of Economics and Political Science*, XXXI, No. 1 (February, 1965), pp. 80-97.

[7] In the 1950s some Western countries became alarmed, rightly or wrongly, at the possibility of "subversion" by domestic groups using democratic methods to further what were, in their estimation, undemocratic objectives. In some cases, normal "constitutional" rules were felt to be no longer proper and were accordingly modified. For instance, the United States and West Germany legislated their respective Communist parties out of (licit) existence.

Our epoch is perhaps more aware of social change and of possibilities for change than were earlier ones, and there has been a greater concern in this century with social biases that political institutions may strengthen or that they may help neutralize. As the role of the state has increased in the economic and social spheres, human and civil rights movements have grown and have led to the institution of new objectives for, or constraints upon, the use of power, thereby restoring some kind of balance between the competence of the individual and that of the state.

Federal constitutions possibly constitute the most delicately balanced of all political institutions.[8] Given the widespread expectation that change is pervasive and inevitable, chances are large that some sectional interest or group, upon whose existence federalism depends, would consider some or any change as a threat. There is nothing that anyone can do about vague fears of still unknown events except avoid compounding the fears. A constitution can help in this way at least by being, as far as its institution and procedures are concerned, neutral towards change as among alternative outcomes, such as becoming rather more or less centralized. Constitutional change should not be left to look after itself, as an indirect outcome of a piecemeal process. A totally unbiased constitution — in this sense — probably is a pipe dream; the present must, by necessity, pre-empt the future to some extent, but this particular case of "spillover" should be kept to a minimum.

Many modern contributions to constitutional discussions stress the rapidly changing nature of many questions and the fast pace of technological and cultural change. While these observations are, of course, sensible enough, they often lead to the false conclusion that what is needed is a constitution that would try to be so flexible as to allow for any and all adaptations. Such a constitution could have little value, as it would provide virtually no constraint to political behaviour. The challenge that change offers to any normative behaviour rule will not be met by erosion of the rules. This challenge must be met squarely by the development of procedures for achieving a smooth changeover from one set of obsolescent rules to a new set.

It may be that the cost and frustration involved in reaching agreement on the "rules of the game" (i.e., in amending a constitution) are an inevitable accompaniment of the playing of an ever changing game. A point must, however, be reached when these costs and frustrations are no longer worth anyone's while and when rules for settling potential conflicts are not worth having at all. This point is reached when changes in a constitution would create more and more frequent problems than having any given constitution could help solve. The fundamental point is that a constitution should enable a complex society to economize on efforts at consensus formation in specific cases by applying general guidelines that can substitute for agreement. If the guidelines are subject to too frequent change, this economy is lost, and the guidelines themselves become pointless. Paradoxically, we therefore find that, whether a constitution is written or not, its stability is of the essence. If it changes too frequently, in either case, its authority is jeopardized and so is its usefulness.

---

[8] On the relative instability of federal constitutions see R. J. May, "Decision-Making and Stability in Federal Systems," *Canadian Journal of Political Science*, III, No. 1 (March, 1970), pp. 73-87.

Chapter 3
The Economic Implications
of Separatism*

A.A. Birchant

Separatism is a French Canadian psycho-sociological phenomenon peculiar to Quebec. For all it has in common with the regional "nationalisms" of other Canadian Provinces such as British Columbia, Alberta and Ontario, it must be considered unique in the Canadian experience because certain characteristics make it distinct from those other regionalisms. Separatism is based on a psycho-cultural state of mind, rooted in a rejection of some, or all, of the consequences of history and geography by a still very small intellectual and professional minority of the French-speaking population. It is thus primarily a manifestation of its followers' alienation, whether conscious or not, from the Canadian and indeed North American realities.

This last qualification is important as all French-speaking Canadians, both inside and outside the Province of Quebec, who do not share the views of separatism's leaders are denigrated as "lost" or "having sold out" to the "anglo-Saxons." The lack of interest most Quebec separatists have in their fellow French-speaking Canadians residing in other Provinces reveals in a bleak light their basic disinterest in francophonic institutions and in the geographical expansion of the French fact throughout Canada.

If, today, a minority of separatists is beginning to discover those French Canadians, it is attributable not to a burning love for the French cultural tradition but to the acceptance of an irredentist element in their political program.

The separatists, however, are finding it expedient to "move, live and have their being" within the framework of the realities which they wish to reject, for those realities cannot be either obliterated or ignored if they would achieve their ultimate objective — power.

Tactically, therefore, separatism has sought to incorporate within its "doctrine," such as it is, for it is still evolving, various perfectly legitimate economic and cultural aspirations that have come to assume a great importance for various segments of the Quebec electorate.

There are thus aspects within the content of separatism's doctrine that can only disappear as all of Canada comes to recognize French Canada's

*Chapter 3 (pp. 25-42) of *Option Canada* by A. A. Birchant, published by The Canada Committee, Montreal, 1968. Reproduced with the permission of The Canada Committee and the author.

cultural goals through the implementation of the recommendations of the Royal Commission on Bilingualism and Biculturalism. French Canada's economic objectives will be achieved through the continued integration of professionally-trained French Canadians into the nation's, and the continent's, economic mainstream. It also becomes clear, therefore, that separatism and French Canadian linguistic and cultural nationalism are by no means one and the same thing, and that it is possible to reject the first while recognizing and accepting the validity of the claims of the second.

Separatism as a doctrine also contains a number of less-legitimate idealogical strands that set its followers apart, in varying degrees, from traditional politically-oriented movements in Quebec and the rest of North America. As these strands have not been thought through to their logical conclusions, they should be viewed as general tendencies within the doctrinal body of separatism. Among these are four which explain in large measure the appearance, in Quebec, of a political climate that could prove decisively harmful to the Province's future economic stability and well-being.

1. A deep rooted belief in the necessity and efficacy of an "interventionist" *(dirigiste ou volontariste)* role for the state in economic, social and cultural affairs. This manifests itself in an emphasis on the collective instruments rather than on individual initiative.

2. An economic philosophy that seeks a redistribution of wealth well beyond anything attempted, or generally desired, throughout North America.

3. A cultural folk-myth that can conceive of survival only in collective terms.

4. A political nationalism, Quebec centred, to provide an emotional justification to the electorate for its support.

Separatism in Quebec is thus essentially a messianic theology of rejection, whose "god" is the myth of a powerful interventionist state, and whose "paradise" is a society predominantly nationalistic and collectivistic. As such, it can clearly hold few attractions for serious investors and entrepreneurs both inside and outside the Province.

Separatism — The Main Credos

Separatism currently manifests itself in three main credos which may be defined as

1. the independence or *"independantiste"* movement that is presently promoted by Pierre Bourgault et al;

2. the "sovereignty-association movement" that was founded and is now led by René Lévesque; and

3. last but not least, the "ultra-autonomy" or "special-status-for Quebec" movement which at its most extreme has a fundamental posture that is remarkably — and, to some, uncomfortably — similar to that of partisans of sovereignty-association.

In terms of their immediate significance not all three credos are of equal import. This may not be the case in the future, and one would seem to be justified in examining the possible economic implications, for the Province, of the attainment of its objectives by each. Caution is needed, however, in interpretive projection. The "answers" suggested here should be viewed more as "questions" than as conclusions having a predictive value. The imponderables — and perhaps as yet "unborn" factors — that will influence the future course of politics in the Province make any other evaluation impossible.

A. The Independantiste Movement

Fundamentally split in their economic doctrine, the independantistes seem to be composed primarily of persons who have chosen to ignore the economic implications of independence for Quebec, principally one suspects because of their profound ignorance of the subject, but also because they recognize that a precise intramural examination of the question might split their ranks. They choose, apparently, to gloss over these "difficulties" and to seek solace in such vague and reassuring pronouncements as Jean-Marc Leger's "the economic risk of independence is minimal." At the other end of the spectrum, a more sophisticated minority believes that "political" independence is illusory if it is not accompanied by "economic" independence. Madam Andree Bertrand-Ferretti, Vice-President of the Rassemblement pour l'Indépendance Nationale (R.I.N.) expressed this basic conviction in a bitter speech at the December 12th, 1967 meeting of her Party: "We are doubly colonized and exploited, as Quebecers and as workers, and only a national revolution, which is at the same time political and socio-economic, may liberate us from this double domination."

If, what is clearly an extreme-socialist-oriented independence party gained power in Quebec, it is relatively simple to estimate the ultimate consequence of economic policies such as those expressed by Madam Bertrand-Ferretti's. At worst, they suppose the immediate expropriation of non-Quebec-owned companies and, at best, the establishment of rigid Government controls over all privately-owned business firms, including those belonging to Quebecers. In view of the Province's total dependence on the outside world, these policies could only prove disastrous.

No amount of external economic assistance, assuming aid of the magnitude required were readily available and allowed to reach Quebec (two assumptions that would be unrealistic in the current international context), could cancel out the huge economic losses that would result from the mass flight of capital and people from the new state. The latter's complete economic and political isolation would inevitably accompany the advent to power of what can only be described as the lunatic fringe of the independantiste movement. The early economic demise of the new state would thus be assured.

The majority of independantistes, however, are not as *doctrinaire* for the simple reason that they have not been aware of the importance of the economic implications of their political program. It is only since the appearance on the political horizon of René Lévesque's sovereignty-association thesis that they began to realize that they had neglected a most critical and vital aspect of any coherent political program. In the unlikely eventuality that they came to power through a vote in favour of independence, by a majority of the electorate, the consequences could be far reaching.

It is probable that the border regions which have close relations with areas adjoining them in other Provinces, or the United States, would refuse to leave Confederation for a nebulous future within an "independent and sovereign" state of Quebec. It is probable too that Montreal would join these regions in this refusal and elect to retain its links with the rest of Canada, perhaps under a free port status, while the St. Lawrence River became an international waterway through which passage was assured. It may also be questioned whether Canada would permit the rump state of Quebec that emerged from such a vote for independence, (*ex* Montreal and the border regions) to keep those portions of its present territory assigned to the Province since Confederation. Such a series of developments would almost certainly lead to the collapse of the new state.

At the present time, in the completely unlikely and unrealistic eventuality that the majority of the population in all major regions of Quebec, including Montreal most particularly, voted in favour of independence, the question of the economic implications of separatism becomes more complex. We saw earlier that for every dollar of merchandise that the Province exports, it imports goods having a value significantly in excess of that amount (René Lévesque's estimate is from $2.50 to $3.00), including two thirds of its food products consumption, 100 percent of its petroleum requirements, etc. We also saw that this excess of imports over exports has been paid for on the one hand by a net capital flow into Quebec that is principally American in its origin and on the other by the Province's favourable "external" balance of trade in the service industries sector.

This net capital inflow to the Province has combined with the heavy and steady re-investment of profits generated within its boundaries to create the hundreds of thousands of new jobs (104,000 in 1966 alone) that have enabled Quebec Canadians, French and non-French alike, to stay and earn their living in the Province. In the event of independence for Quebec, therefore, one should ask what would happen to this well-established pattern of economic activity.

In a learned conference already referred to earlier which he gave to the St. Laurent Kiwanis Club on September 27, 1967, Robert Bourassa examined several of the possible economic implications of independence for Quebec, and although he did not go far enough in his analysis (this was not his intention, as he made clear), the speaker made some telling points. Most of them ultimately revolve around the creation of a Quebec currency and the resulting negative effects, certainly immediate and possibly enduring, this would have on the new state.

> In such circumstances, through fears of foreign exchange controls and in view of the conservatism of financial circles, the temptation would be great for holders of Quebec Securities (provincial bonds) to withdraw them from that territory either to deposit them abroad, or to bring them back once political and monetary stability had been attained, or to demand repayment at maturity in Canadian dollars since those securities were issued originally in that currency; in addition, they might also sell them before they came due, a development which would have a number of adverse effects, among which would be its negative impact on the borrowing ability of such Quebec bodies as the state of Quebec, the city of Montreal, Hydro-Quebec, etc.

In short, owners of Quebec securities whether or not they acted in unison, "would have the power to force us to devalue our currency." What this would mean for Quebec's external debt position can easily be imagined, continues Monsieur Bourrassa, if one considers the situation that would arise as Quebec became independent.

The new State, for example, would have to absorb its share of Canada's national debt, a share that on a per capita basis stood at over $6 billion, at the end of 1967. To repudiate that debt would clearly be impossible if only because to do so would be to repudiate a debt owed in large measure to investors whom the new State would have to approach for its future borrowing needs.

If one adds to Quebec's share of Canada's national debt, the debt of the Quebec and Municipal Governments as well as other state-owned institutions such as Hydro-Quebec, Autoroute, etc., which totalled at least another $6 billion at the end of last year and a substantial portion of which is owed outside Quebec, he will conclude — as Monsieur Bourassa seems to do implicitly — that the new State would be bankrupt externally (i.e. in terms of its foreign reserve position and requirements) the day it became independent and that it would be unable therefore to borrow sorely-needed funds in foreign capital markets.

The situation could only be made worse by the maintenance of restriction on U.S. capital outflows and competition from the rest of Canada for available funds. In addition, the uncertainties, external and internal, attendant on the emergence of any new state would be bound to affect the flow of private investments from other countries (principally the U.S.) as well as the willingness of firms with facilities already established in Quebec to reinvest their profits.

It cannot be forgotten that companies that have a "product" (goods or services) that is sold abroad can choose to repatriate only that part of the proceeds from that product's sale essential to the continued operations of their facilities located in the exporting state. The forced repatriation of all profits would only create new problems. For all these reasons it is certain that Quebec's present favourable external as well as internal capital position would deteriorate after independence.

This deterioration would in turn have a profound impact on the new state's ability to finance its excess of imports over exports in its merchandise balance of trade. It will also be remembered in this connection that the tentative conclusion was reached earlier that Quebec depends to some degree on the foreign exchange earnings of the other Provinces of Canada to pay for its imports from foreign countries. Independence for the Province would mean the disappearance of that source of foreign exchange and a further weakening of the new state's international economic position. From the other Canadian provinces' point of view, however, if this conclusion is correct, the elimination of the foreign exchange "burden" Quebec represents today would lead to the strengthening, of the Canadian dollar and to an increase in the latter's attractiveness for foreign lenders and investors, relative to the new state's currency.

Further, is it reasonable to assume that Quebec's situation vis-a-vis its present trading partners would not be affected by independence? Thus, new tariff walls might well effectively shut out many Quebec-manufactured goods. So far as the United States is concerned, Monsieur Bourassa points out that "we have few aces up our sleeve to negotiate with foreign business-men, especially American, in view of the very small importance of Quebec markets for overall American exports." This importance, such as it is, would vanish if Quebec attempted to pay for goods with a debilitated and virtually worthless currency.

Nor should it be forgotten that Quebec's exports to the United States consist principally of primary industrial products (pulp and paper, minerals, primary metals) which are readily available from sources other than the Province. The new state could never be sure that it would continue to keep its present share of the markets for these products.

What of Quebec's exports to the other Canadian Provinces? It may be doubted that Monsieur Bourassa is right to state that those exports would probably not diminish because "we import *so much* from the other Canadian Provinces and notably from Ontario." First of all, exports from Quebec both to Canada and to other foreign countries would decline in any case because of the new state's inability to pay for many of the imports that contribute a major share of those exports' "content" — *directly* in the form of raw materials and semi-finished goods and *indirectly* through the value-added made possible by production equipment.

Then again, even if no measures were taken by Canada to hinder the flow of Quebec-made goods into its territory, it remains true that as the Kennedy Round agreements are implemented, a considerable portion of these goods would have to compete with substantially similar products from other countries. It may be doubted that the Government of a Canada-*ex*-Quebec would be psychologically predisposed to intervene directly, or that the Canadian population would go out of its way, to protect Quebec's present share of the market for these products in the Canadian Provinces. The establishment of tariff walls would, of course, only compound the problem. Thus, as the new state found itself selling less to the Canadian Provinces, it would be forced to purchase even less from them in the absence of adequate foreign exchange earnings and reserves.

In the segment of the service industries sector in Quebec that is external-ly oriented, the departure of the many national companies which now make their home in Quebec would also unquestionably affect adversely the new state's internal balance of payments. These companies include, as Mr. R. B. MacPherson of DuPont of Canada rightly points out, many manufacturing firms which have plants in both Quebec and the rest of Canada and which provide "services" (e.g. in the areas of management, marketing, information gathering, etc.) to their facilities located outside the Province.

One might also ask what effect independence would have on the port of Montreal. It is conceivable, for example, that companies which ship their products via the city would choose to bypass it. Quebec would have little to say in the matter, as a realistic appraisal of the post-independence situation would lead to the conclusion that the St. Lawrence Seaway and River would become a fully-internationalized waterway.

Finally, the question arises whether Quebec's economy would be able to function following the flight from the state of much of the short-term capi-tal currently available to business for working capital. Would Quebec at-tempt to solve the problem by printing new money, the value of which was assured by the majesty of the new law and the long arm of the new Govern-ment?

The cumulative effect of any or all of these developments, whether they took place simultaneously or successively, would be to create rapidly increasing unemployment, economic distress and social discontent. Then an already interventionist Government would be obliged to impose further controls upon the already constricted economy of its territory. If history is any guide, this accentuated "statism" would be accompanied by a stronger and more vociferous linguistic and cultural nationalism, with English-speaking North America the predestined scapegoat.

What might be the reaction of non-separatist Canadians? So far, this has been ignored by the independantistes, by the followers of René Lévesque, and by those demanding a special status for Quebec. This reaction is important, for non-French Canadians effectively control Quebec's economy. This "control," it must be emphasized, is not solely related to the fact that ownership of the predominant majority of business enterprises in the Province is in their hands. It is more a function of the fact that they include a "class" of business-oriented, professionally-trained and experienced individuals, whose specialized knowledge of American management and business techniques, awareness of current development in science and technology and whose longstanding personal relationships with the individuals forming the external commercial and financial world are so vital to the economic prosperity of today's Quebec.

How then would non-French Canadian residents in Quebec react to independence for the Province? Would they stay on in the new state? Certainly, they could not be prevented from leaving if they chose to so do. Many undoubtedly would depart with the national companies for which they work as the latter moved their headquarters from Quebec. In addition, as the economic situation deteriorated and the Government sought to exercise an ever-increasing degree of control, an exodus of the population, both French and non-French Canadian would be set in motion that would drain the state of its most able and dynamic inhabitants. The reaction of the new and fast-growing class of professionally-competent and bilingual French Canadians who have become integrated in North America's economic life would be similar to that of non-French Canadians both groups could elect to leave Quebec because they wished neither to perish economically nor to suffocate culturally.

What of those non-French Canadians who attempted to stay on in the new state? What would their status be? Could they reasonably be expected to surrender their Canadian citizenship in favour of Quebec's?

If they refused to do so, would they agree to remain in a state in which they contributed a substantial share of fiscal revenues without demanding a voice in the councils of Government? Would the problem be solved by offering them dual citizenship? Then again, how would they react to the forced Gallicization of a society located in an otherwise English-speaking continent from which they were becoming increasingly isolated? Would they agree to subordinate their spirit of individual enterprise and their personal aspirations to the wishes and commands in the economic sphere of an increasingly-collectivistic and interventionist Government? To ask these questions is to answer them, as the attractions of an existing alternative, that is, to seek out a new future in the rest of the North American continent, would undoubtedly prove irresistible for many.

By now, an independent state of Quebec would be faced with the prospects of economic collapse and possibly a revolutionary state of affairs within its borders.

B. René Lévesque's "Sovereignty-Association" Movement

It is to René Lévesque's credit that he has foreseen these difficulties and sought to obviate them by proposing sovereignty-association for Quebec. In this he has followed many French-Canadian nationalist and not so nationalist thinkers and writers on the economics of the Province. What his proposal attempts to accomplish, what it means and what it might involve are indicated by the following extracts from his public statements.

1. Assumptions and Goals of Sovereignty-Association†[1]

We are Quebecers. What this means first of all and before everything else, and perhaps even exclusively, is that we are attached to this only corner of the world where we have the possibility of being fully ourselves, this Quebec which, we feel deeply, is the only place where it is possible for us to be fully at home. To be ourselves is essentially to maintain and develop a personality which has existed for three and a half centuries. At the core of this personality is to be found the fact that we speak French. All the rest hangs on that essential element, flows from it, or brings us back to it. We are the children of that society of which the *"habitant,"* our father or our grandfather, was still the central citizen. Whoever does not feel this at least once every so often is not, or no longer is, one of us.

We are economically, a colonized people whose three daily meals depend too often on the initiative and goodwill of foreign employers. [To change this state of affairs, we have already taken a number of steps.] In the area of economics, through the nationalization of electricity, the creation of the Société Générale de Financement, of Sequem, of the Pension Fund, we have laid the first foundations of that collective control of a certain number of essential "instruments" without which no human community can feel truly at home.

[On the road to further progress, however], we face a prime obstacle which is becoming increasingly flagrant these days – the political system under which we have lived for 100 years. What is important for today and tomorrow is that both sides realize more clearly every day that the system is obsolete and that it is urgent either that it be profoundly changed or that a new one be erected in its place.

[To assure] once and for all . . . the security of our collective personality . . . we [must] have the power to act without restrictions – this does not mean without co-operating – in such fields as citizenship, immigration, labour, the main instruments of mass culture [cinemas, radio and television], and external relations.

---

†[The parenthetical inserts in the following quoted passages are included by A. A. Birchant, not myself: D. Auld.]

[1] Written prior to publication of Lévesque's "Option-Quebec."

Mr. Lévesque then goes on to quote with approval the following statements by three Quebec Labour Unions (Confédération des Syndicats Nationaux, Fédération des travailleurs du Québec, and Union des Cultivateurs Catholiques):

> ... the Quebec Government will have to exercise its powers on the general direction of the economy ["dans l'orientation de l'économie"], the rationalization of marginal industries, the development of the secondary industrial sector, etc. The Government of Quebec will have to promote an economic policy that is clearly favourable to its population and more demanding vis-a-vis capitalist interests, for it is no longer enough to seem to be governing in the people's best interest in this field. This Government, specifically, will have to derive out of the exploitation of natural resources the maximum benefits and royalties that it can reasonably expect to obtain.

In short, concludes Monsieur Lévesque, the new powers of the state of Quebec will have to be exercisable over

> industrial and commercial enterprises, savings and fiduciary institutions, all the internal instruments of development and industrialization, as well as [include] the power to manage ["régir"] the direction and investment of our capital. [Finally, there will have to be effected] a massive transfer [from the Federal to the Quebec Government] of the fiscal resources that are necessary to the undertaking of all those tasks to which our state of Quebec must devote itself in our name. [Thus] we have here what is, for us, truly a minimum.

2. Ways and Means of Achieving These Goals

If the goals outlined above represent "truly a minimum," continues René Lévesque,
> to believe that, for the rest of the country, they could represent something other than a maximum [which is] both astounding and totally unacceptable, would be to dream. [For to attempt to reconcile what in the final analysis are] two ways of life, with their separate needs and aspirations, [is ultimately to waste one's time and energy, and the conclusion must inevitably be reached that] we must rid ourselves of a Federal System that is completely obsolete, and start anew.

> How do we start anew? The answer is clearly set forth, in our opinion, in the two great trends of our age: those of the freedom of peoples and of economics and political associations freely agreed to. This means that Quebec must become a sovereign state as soon as possible. We will find in this, at long last, that security for our collective "being" which is vital, and which, otherwise, could remain only uncertain and crippled. In this also we will have at last the opportunity — and the obligation — to devote the best of our energies and talents to the resolution ... of all the important questions which concern us.

Since it would be foolhardy for both Canadian majorities to liquidate the existing network of economic relations that makes them so interdependent, the two should agree to the establishment of an economic "association" between a sovereign Quebec and a sovereign Canada-*ex*-Quebec that would assure the preservation of the economic benefits they derive from their present interdependence. Such an arrangement might include

> a monetary union, a customs union, a postal union, the management of the public debt and the co-ordination of fiscal policy.

> We propose, in short, a political system ["un régime"] in which two nations, one whose home would be Quebec, the other, which could restructure as it saw fit the rest of the country, associated freely in an original adaptation of the now-current Common Market Formula, [thereby] forming a whole which could be called, for example, and very exactly, the Canadian Union.[2]

3. Structure of the Proposed Canadian Union
(as translated from René Lévesque)

> *Monetary Union.* That there be estabished a central bank which exists as a (public) corporation, the capital of which ($5 billion) is currently under the guardianship of the Federal Minister of Finance.
>
> Two associated states decide to turn it into a joint venture in the in the following eminently practicable way: the Board of Directors, 12 members' is evenly split between the two states, each of which owns 50 percent of the bank's capital stock.
> - The Quebec Deputy Minister of Finance joins the corresponding Canadian official on the Board who is already a member without voting rights.
> - The Bank's articles of incorporation stipulate that the positions of Governor-President and Deputy Governor-Vice-President alternate between the two states.
> - A proportional distribution of the senior positions is carried out during a reasonable period of adaptation [to the Bank's new joint status].
> - And this Bank issues and protects a common currency, administers on a joint basis the reserves and the [public] debt and ensures the stability of the two states.

> *Common Market.* Here, both states maintain the present absence of borders from the point of view of reciprocal imports and exports. But for the establishment of new tariffs or changes (in the existing tariff structure) vis-a-vis the outside world, it will be necessary for the two ministers of finance to consult each other on an equal footing and that there be an accord on the advantages of modification. In that instance, as well as in the matter of fiscal co-ordination which flows from the former, it would be necessary to form permanent mixed commissions composed of civil servants appointed by the two states; commissions to which would be added, right at the beginning, other similar committees on corollary questions that required co-ordinated, joint and parallel programs — e.g. the St. Lawrence maritime route, minorities, radio and television, citizenship and move-

---

[2] Lévesque – "Nous sommes des Quebecois," 15th September 1967.

ments of labour — without excluding, it goes without saying, regular meetings of joint councils of ministers, or more or less frequent gatherings of delegations from both Parliaments. And that is all. And that is enough.[3]

This arrangement would remain in force for a transition period of perhaps five years, according to René Lévesque. Then, both associated states would take a fresh look at what has been accomplished and adopt any necessary amendments.

4. Some Further Selections from René Lévesque's Concept of the Economic and Social Policies of an Independent Quebec

At a conference given at the University of Montreal in November 1967, René Lévesque was quoted as saying that

> it is necessary to bring about to the fullest extent possible the economic growth of Quebec and to accomplish this within the context of the real collective mobilization of our resources and through making the State the moving force behind this growth. In the social field, it will be equally necessary to have recourse to collective instruments and for all social policies to aim at reducing, in the maximum degree that is humanly possible to do, the gap which exists between the wealthiest people and the poorest.

On Quebec's Need for Outside Capital

In an interview given to *U.S. News and World Report,* issue of January 15, 1968 *(The Case for a Free Quebec)* René Lévesque, on being asked whether capital from the outside world would be essential to the survival of an independent Quebec, answered that this would obviously be the case. He then went on to say that he expected at least a slowdown in the current flow of investment capital from the United States, but that he hoped European capital (particularly from France and Belgium) as well as capital expenditures by the Government of an independent Quebec would compensate for this slowdown.

On the Status of English-Speaking Minorities in a Sovereign Quebec

During a panel meeting at McGill University René Lévesque was quoted as stating that

> the problem of the English-speaking population, [in an independent Quebec], would be the normal one of a minority having rights and not privileges. That section of the population has benefited from privileges for years [but those privileges will be stripped away] and it will remain only a respected minority, [that his] movement would end the domination of Quebec's economy by about 60 old-line English speaking families.

[3] Lévesque — "Comment y arriver? Comment faire face à la periode de transition" 1967.

In a speech in Sept-Îles, Monsieur Lévesque specified further that

> the elements of the English-speaking minority of Quebec, which have
> forgotten that they are a minority here, will have to learn to respect
> us. So far as immigrants are concerned, they will have to become
> integrated into the French-speaking majority.

On the Recommendations of the Royal Commission on Bilingualism and Biculturalism

René Lévesque's spontaneous reaction to the release of the Royal Commission's report was to say, among other things, that the latter's recommendations constituted an "illusory and expensive attempt to build a country,
'(and)', indeed dust that is being thrown into the eyes of Quebec to appease
it." He further added that "nothing would be able to plunge Quebec back
into the sleep from which it has just emerged."

More recently, however, in the *U.S. News and World Report* interview
already referred to, he expressed the following additional thoughts on the
recommendations of the Royal Commission:

> This thing about biculturalism from sea to sea would mean building a
> more or less separate-but-equal school setup. In the first place, it is
> too costly, because right now, even based on present conditions, we
> need hundreds of millions more for education. So would it be sensi-
> ble to build a parallel system? We know what happened to "separate
> but equal" in the United States.
>
> This is just as absurd — even more so. Outside of next-door New
> Brunswick, where French Acadians are close to 40 percent of the
> population, you must not forget that French Canadians count for
> less than 4 percent of Canada!, *ex* Quebec.

On the Condition of Quebec's French-Speaking Human Infrastructure

In the same interview with *U.S. News and World Report*, we read of the
following statements.

> Now, for a long time we were largely an uneducated population with
> a small elite. But in the last fifteen or twenty years we've been
> widening our educated population by leaps and bounds. Quebec's
> "revolution" is basically an educational revolution. Quebec used to be
> a sort of inner colony of Canada — patient people without much
> education, with small jobs and limited horizons. Education has
> changed that, with results that are felt especially in Politics. We
> suddenly found out, that once you have available competent people
> in your own society, you can do your own job better than anybody
> else can do it.

The Sovereigntist Thesis and the Realities

As the lengthy extracts from René Lévesque's words that have been cited
make clear, Lévesquism represents an attempt to reconcile an amalgam of
nationalistic, atavistic, collectivistic and statist *[sic]* myths with the Canadian
and indeed the North American realities.

Do the doctrine's "ideals" have in them the potential of appealing to the majority of the French-speaking electorate in Quebec?

Are its programmatic, political, and economic theses sufficiently realistic to ever be successfully implemented?

While only the future can give a final answer to the first question, it is to be hoped that the average Quebecer's sound realism and common sense will cause him to reject this simplistic and utterly unrealistic political mythology. There is no doubt, and this René Lévesque readily admits, that the overwhelming majority of the population of the Province would refuse to "go-along" today.

An answer to the second question is reached more easily. For, as will be shown below, Lévesquism's much vaunted realism ends at precisely the point at which its "practical" program starts — viz. at its unequivocal and clearcut recognition that an independent Quebec could not "go it alone" economically and hope to maintain the Province's standard of living.

Two major, inextricably intertwined and insurmountable obstacles stand in the way of Lévesquism's successful implementation. The first is psychological, the second "technical."

Psychological

There is a psychological unsoundness and unreality in the sovereigntist "no-yes" approach to relationships between French Canadian in Quebec on the one hand and all the other Canadians both in and outside Quebec on the other. French Canadians in Quebec are thus being asked to reject "English" North America, its cultural traditions, its openness, its spirit of individual initiative, its acceptance of the fundamental tenets of the free enterprise system, its relative political, ethnic and cultural tolerance, and its political and legal institutions. They are offered an inward-looking, atavistic, narrowly parochial, unilingual, territorialized nationalism, a collectivistic conception of life, and the prospect of direct governmental intervention and controls in the economic, social, cultural and, no doubt, political affairs of the nation. At the same time, they are told to deal with the rest of English-speaking North America as if there had been no rejection. English-speaking North America, however, is asked to agree to being rejected while it is simultaneously asked to continue to do business as usual.

Technical

The technical objections are more simple to define. The sovereigntist philosophy assumes intervention by the state in economic affairs. This contradiction of the North American ethos would assure the fright-transfer of any mobile capital out of Quebec. The retention of a common currency with the rest of Canada would allow the eventual exportation of capital generated from immobile fixed assets.

A significant increase in taxes would become imperative to compensate for the decline in fiscal revenues. Customs duties on imports from outside could not be raised without the consent of Canada.

This consent would not be forthcoming in view of current trends towards tariff-reduction.[4]

The new state's external borrowing power would disappear because of the internal economic crisis and because of Canada's certain refusal to accept any increase in such *jointly managed* external public debt. Or, are we to assume that this debt would not be a *joint responsibility?* In the absence of such a joint responsibility Canada would never agree to allow Quebec an equal voice in the management of the monetary union's reserves, banking policy, public debt and fiscal policy.

The sovereigntists assume access to European governmental and quasi-governmental capital sources to finance development. Funds of the necessary magnitude, however, do not exist. In the context of the present international monetary situation, moreover, and increasing pressures on the dollar, such funds as might become available would hardly be invested in Quebec.

The sole remaining source of capital would be possible U.S. economic aid. Needless to say a Quebec which maintained increasingly close relations with France would be seen as a French bridgehead on the North American continent. In itself, this would be negative given France's present policy orientation. If in addition the dollar ceased to be convertible, in part due to France's intransigent stand in favour of an "eternal" link between gold and national currencies, Quebec could expect no American aid.

Canada and the Sovereigntist State

To implement its ideals, Canada would have three alternatives:

1. To refuse its consent to independence for the Province and enforce its decision by a political and economic blockade of Quebec as well as by force if this became necessary;

2. To refuse to have anything to do with the new state, but to secure, in all likelihood jointly with the United States, free and innocent passage through the St. Lawrence Maritime route by ships of all nations, and to obtain as well as to guarantee the rights of English-speaking minorities and other French Canadians living in Quebec.

3. To agree to negotiations on the establishment of an economic association between itself and Quebec.

The first two alternatives are not within our terms of reference, the third is pertinent.

Canada's reaction to René Lévesque's specific proposal, in its present format, for a customs and monetary union between the two states would without question be negative, if only — and perhaps only — because of provisions giving Quebec and Canada an equal share in the union's basic decisions and an equal vote in the management of its affairs. Even under the present conditions when Quebec's share of the country's gross national product is only some twenty-five percent (25 percent) of the total, such provisions would be rejected out of hand. This would be even more the case in

---

[4] Kennedy Round Agreements, vs – Canada Auto Parts Pact.

the wake of the exodus of people, business enterprises and capital that would precede, accompany and follow the coming to power of men whose public utterances reflected sentiments similar to the following.

"We are two nations in one country; that also means, in reality, two majorities, two societies complete and quite distinct"; "the elements of the English-speaking minority of Quebec, which have forgotten that they are a minority here, will have to learn to respect us"; "the Government of Quebec will have to exercise its powers on the general direction of the economy [and on] industrial and commercial enterprises, savings and fiduciary institutions, all the internal instruments of development and industrialization, as well as [have] the power to manage the movements and the investments of our [!] capital"; "the economic growth of Quebec [must be accomplished] through the collective mobilization of our resources and through making the State the moving force behind this growth."

Would Quebec be prepared to go along with a counterproposal whereby, subject to only certain pre-determined guarantees, Canada would have the power to act alone on behalf of both States? While this is highly unlikely, it may be of interest to consider what might happen to the two states' economies under such circumstances. If one assumes, therefore, that some understanding were arrived at that led to the establishment of a customs union between Quebec and Canada, within the context of a monetary arrangement allowing Quebec to use Canada's currency as its own, Canadian, American and other foreign investors might well look with favour upon such an accord if it meant that they could gradually pull their capital out of the former's territory while continuing to sell in it their own goods, and services.

A decreasing purchasing power in Quebec would lead to a gradual diminution of Canada's exports to its former province and thereby force basic changes in the direction of the former's foreign trade, lessening its dependence on Quebec as a major market for its goods and services. Many of the consumers, comprising that market, would have already moved, or would soon move, to Canada. As an independent Quebec would not be able to replace both the job creating capital ($4.5 billion in 1966 in long term investments alone!) and the experienced people required to keep its economy viable, a customs and monetary union between itself and the rest of Canada would destroy, more effectively than any temporary attempt at complete independence along the lines of the independantists' movement, the very foundations of the new State's existence.

Sovereignty-Association: History Misread

The great lessons of the economic history of the last one hundred and fifty years have clearly been lost on Monsieur Lévesque, even though he freely refers to the European Common Market and the 1905 separation of Norway and Sweden and their subsequent economic interdependence as "proof" that the sovereignty-association thesis is a sound and practicable one. Perhaps his understanding of these events is not sufficiently profound. Otherwise he would surely recognize:

1. That any economic association between two or more States, of the type envisaged by René Lévesque presupposes that its various members are themselves relatively well-integrated economically and that a certain balance of

economic power exists among them. We saw earlier, of course, that Quebec is *not* an integrated economic region and that the Province in 1966 accounted for only some twenty-five percent (25 percent) of Canada's gross national product.

2. That economic interdependence of two or more regions (or nations) is not the same thing as economic solidarity between them. That such interdependence, in the absence of a supra-regional (or supra-national) authority serving as a mechanism of adjustment, may result in the impoverishment of one and the enrichment of the other(s). It cannot be doubted that a Canada-*ex*-Quebec would refuse to agree to the establishment of such a supra-national authority having the power to help its former Province pass through the difficult period that would result from an exodus of its population, business enterprises and capital.

3. That, in the absence of a general determination to make viable decision-making institutions common to two or more economic regions (or nations), any economic union will not last. The European Common Market has endured for almost eleven years only because — up to 1967 at least — *all* the members of that Community were determined to make its institutions work. There is every reason to doubt that Quebec's will-to-separation would be conducive to the creation of a psychological climate favourable to successful negotiations for a customs and monetary union between itself and the rest of Canada.

4. That the conditions just described, if they were accompanied by the cessation of the flow of foreign private capital into Quebec that would be the inevitable consequence of a lack of harmony or parallelism between antithetical social and economic systems, would transform a customs and monetary union between Canada and Quebec into an economic association in which the weaker of the two partners would soon find itself facing a growing and irreversible economic crisis.

5. That the swing towards economic authoritarianism which would inevitably result from the breakdown of sovereignty-association would produce a situation in Quebec similar to the dire economic consequences, described earlier, of the coming to power in the Province, of a leftward-oriented independantiste party.

C. Economic Consequences of a "Special Status" ("Un Statut Particulier") for Quebec

The term "special status", which has been bandied around in recent years by certain intellectual and political groups in Quebec serves today as a "catch-all" phrase with a bewildering and almost infinite variety of connotations. It has been used, for example, in connection with political and economic programs that actually reflect centrifugal tendencies which are present in the entire Canadian body politic. Thus, Mr. Eric Kierans in his recently published *Challenge of Confidence* found it possible to write:

> The appropriate distribution and use of revenue is of equal importance, and this responsibility, except in the areas of Federal author-

ity, should be left with the provinces. When the electors vote provincially, the distributions of that wealth, the priorities and the particular objectives, which each province or region stresses in fields like education, health, welfare, and cultural affairs should be the paramount issues. It is here that particular responses, a particular status, emerge.

So far as this writer is aware, the term "special status" has never been used by such distinguished Canadians as Monsieur Marcel Faribault whose profession of faith in the necessity for a major revision of the British North America Act and a further devolution of Federal powers through the provinces, (to all provinces it must be stressed), is well known.[5] Nor was it even mentioned by Premier Daniel Johnson at the November 1967 Conference of Provincial Premiers on the future of Confederation. The entire question of the distribution of legislative power between the Federal authority and the Provinces should thus not be confused with that of a "special status" for Quebec. For the latter, whatever its reality may ultimately become, implies by its very meaning the acceptance by a "reformed" Canadian Constitution of a "status" within Confederation peculiar to Quebec which would set the Province apart from the other Canadian Provinces in certain fundamental and essential respects. What those would be is suggested by trends that have become manifest in the last few years, and more particularly in 1967, in the published work of French Canadian intellectuals who have concerned themselves with the question of a "special status" for Quebec.[6]

In the "cultural" arena one can discern a clear trend towards demands for a more complete Gallicization of life in Quebec through direct Provincial Government intervention and control of immigration and citizenship and the broader use of the French language in Quebec. A constitutional justification for such a development is found by Jean-Charles Bonenfant who states that the Quebec Act (1774) implicitly, and the British North America Act explicitly recognized the special status of Quebec in assuring the survival of the French language and the Province's French character.[7] Thus to quote Jean-Charles Falardeau,

> it is the right of the State of Quebec only, in its capacity as the historical home and political framework of the French Canadian Nation, to concern itself with the destiny of that nation's culture. It is that state which must take the measures that can facilitate this destiny if not to direct its orientation. By culture, we understand the sum total of the technical, institutional, and mental and spiritual patrimony of a society.[8]

---

[5] Monsieur Faribault's views on the distribution of powers within a "reformed" Canadian Constitution are not without interest. For if he says on the one hand that the residuary powers should be ascribed to the provinces or at least removed from federal jurisdiction, he also specifically states on the other hand that this jurisdiction should include "all those questions which are of Federal concern and the usual subject matter of treaties, namely, trade and commerce, monetary policy, war and peace, citizenship, immigration, customs, telegraph, shipping, navigation, etc." Source: *Why Confederation?* In addresses 1966/67: The Empire Club of Canada (Toronto, 1967) pp. 106-124, *passim.*

[6] "Le Quebec dans le Canada de Demain" Nos. 1 and 2, *Le Devoir*, 30th June 1967.

[7] *Idem.*, pp. 50-57.

[8] *Idem.*, pp. 146.

Quebec has become involved with economic planning, in social security programs and in a gigantic effort to provide a sound education to all age groups. These efforts, especially in education, will be futile if they are not, at the beginning as well as at the end, inspired by bold cultural planning.[9]

In the areas of politics and law, there is talk of replacing Parliamentary institutions with a Presidential system; and the criminal Common Law by the French Penal Code. In external affairs, it is assumed that Quebec's personality should be allowed to play an increasingly important role, at least in cultural, economic and related affairs. A conviction exists that social policies must originate and be managed in and by, Quebec, and that the Province must be given the powers it needs to develop its economy in accordance with what it considers to be the "real" needs of its population. Therefore Quebec must have the power to plan and control its economic development as well as to play a direct role in the future economic growth of the Province. All these concepts take for granted the transfer of Federal tax revenue and other federal powers.

Whatever else this assortment of demands may lead to, it is clear that their acceptance by Canada would result in the emergence of a Quebec having a "personality" essentially different from the one it has today and from that of other Canadian Provinces. It is also clear that if these concepts were carried to their logical extremes, the "new Quebec" that emerged there from would resemble the "sovereign" Quebec that René Lévesque seeks to create.

This Quebec would be faced with problems not essentially dissimilar from those encountered by either an "independent" or a "sovereign" state of Quebec. The English-speaking minorities in the Province of Quebec today are not true minorities being part of the English-speaking majority in the North American continent. They could find themselves in an increasingly hostile cultural environment as well as in an economic and psychological climate unfavourably disposed towards the free enterprise system. Thus, as Quebec's status became more "special," it would be accompanied or followed by developments similar to those that would confront both an "independent" as well as a "sovereign" state of Quebec.

Separatism: Summary and Final Comments

Separatism in its three, or perhaps four, principal manifestations can be seen to have essential attributes that make it a unique political phenomenon in the history of the North American continent. As a political and ideological movement, it was analysed as basically opposed to the North American ethos.

It was found to express itself, however, in "affirmations" which if implemented, would imply the rejection by French Canadians in Quebec of the historical and geographical realities which have moulded their province.

[9] *Idem.*, pp. 150.

The implications of the various credos, in separatism, were examined and found basically self-destructive and economically unsound. For without a viable economy the Province's francophonic cultural and other legitimate aspirations could not expect to be realized.

One can perhaps accept as a final judgment on separatism the general comments made by Henry Cabot Lodge in his Class report at his 25th Reunion at Harvard University:

> My experience has convinced me that the interests which men have in common and which bind them together are more numerous and important that those which drive them apart. The really evil politician is he who seeks to stress the things which divide. . . . Because a united people can overcome all obstacles, it is a public servant's job to find the common ground and to unite. A public servant who seeks to divide the community is like a doctor who is trying to kill his patient.

Part B
Poverty

Since the publication of the *Fifth Annual Review* by the Economic Council of Canada in 1968, poverty in Canada has become a widely debated issue. The first selection here is the introduction to Chapter 6 of the *1968 Review*, which defines the poverty line and measures the extent of low incomes in Canada. The second selection is an indirect criticism on the Council's conclusion. This criticism is based on how Canadians feel about poverty and their overall well-being, instead of using actual income data. The debate on poverty has also raised questions about how to deal effectively with raising people's incomes above the poverty line. One of the suggested solutions is the negative income tax, the operation of which is outlined in the third selection.

Chapter 4
The Problem of Poverty*

The Economic Council of Canada

Poverty in Canada is real. Its numbers are not in the thousands, but the millions. There is more of it than our society can tolerate, more than our economy can afford, and far more than existing measures and efforts can cope with. Its persistence, at a time when the bulk of Canadians enjoy one of the highest standards of living in the world, is a disgrace.

What is poverty in Canada? Those who have seen it, felt it, experienced it — whether as its victims or as those trying to do something about it — can supply some telling descriptions. But one of the notable characteristics of poverty in modern times is that it is so located in both city and country, and often so disguised (it does not, for example, invariably go about in rags), that it can pass largely unnoticed by those in happier circumstances. An occasional glimpse from a car window; a television show or Saturday supplement article — these may be the only manifestations of it which touch many a middle-class consciousness. Yet the figures — even the conservative, rather tentative estimates in this Chapter — show indisputably that it is there, almost everywhere in Canada, on a larger scale than most Canadians probably suspect.

One reason for poverty's partial invisibility is that the poor tend to be collectively inarticulate. Many of them lack the education and the organization to make themselves heard. For example, most of them are outside the ambit of the trade union movement. They have few spokesmen and groups to represent them and give voice to their needs.

Another difficulty is that it is all too easy, in Canada, to file poverty away under the heading of certain other long-standing national problems, and in this way to lose sight of it as a major problem in its own right. Thus many Canadians may assume that the problem of poverty is close to identical with the problem of low average incomes in the Atlantic Provinces and Eastern Quebec (especially their rural areas) and among the Indian and Eskimo populations. But this is an inaccurate impression. The *incidence* of poverty — the chance of a given person being poor — is certainly much higher in the areas and among the groups just mentioned. But in terms of absolute

*Chapter 6 (pp. 103-110) of *The Fifth Annual Review: The Challenge of Growth and Change* by the Economic Council of Canada, 1968. Reproduced with the permission of Information Canada.

numbers, between a third and a half of the total poverty in Canada is to be found among the white population of cities and towns west of Three Rivers. The resident of Montreal or Toronto need not travel far to see poverty first-hand; a subway fare will suffice. Much rural poverty, too, is to be found dispersed through areas where *average* income, by rural standards, is relatively high.[1]

There are two major problems in defining poverty. First, it is a *relative* concept. Second, while the availability of relevant statistics compels it to be discussed here largely in terms of low incomes, it means something more than simple income deficiency.

Let us deal first with the problem of relativity. It is of course true that generally-agreed-upon concepts of poverty alter through space and time. Thus, the situation of those Canadians whom the majority of their fellow citizens would deem to be suffering from poverty is hardly to be compared with that of the street-sleepers of Calcutta. And if a typical 1968 "poverty line," defined in terms of real income, were extended back through time, most Canadians during the Depression of the 1930's, and perhaps even most Canadians of the 1920's, would be found to have been living below that line.

But neither of these facts makes poverty in Canada in 1968 any less real or painful. To feel poverty is, among other things, to feel oneself an unwilling outsider — a virtual nonparticipant in the society in which one lives. The problem of poverty in developed industrial societies is increasingly viewed not as a sheer lack of essentials to sustain life, but as an insufficient access to certain goods, services, and conditions of life which are available to everyone else and have come to be accepted as basic to a decent, minimum standard of living.

Poverty, thus defined, is not quite the same thing as low income. A statistician would say there is a very strong association between the two, to the extent that one can often be used as a rough-and-ready substitute for the other. They are not, however, identical. For example, the low-income population of Canada includes a small proportion of people such as the university student who gets by on $1,500 a year, but does not feel himself irrevocably poverty-stricken, first, because he has a family to fall back on if necessary, and second, because much better income prospects lie a short distance ahead of him. Much more serious and more widespread is the kind of low-income situation that carries with it a sense of entrapment and hopelessness. Even the best statistics can only hint at this. They cannot capture the sour atmosphere of poor health and bad housing — the accumulated defeat, alienation and despair which often so tragically are inherited by the next and succeeding generations.

We believe that serious poverty should be eliminated in Canada, and that this should be designated as a major national goal. We believe this for two reasons. The first is that one of the wealthiest societies in world history, if it

[1] "... the problem of low rural incomes can be associated to a degree with the problem of poor regions, but if this association is overemphasized, attention may be unduly diverted from the dispersed, but in absolute numbers still very substantial, poverty problem in prosperous regions. Although one third of the 'poor' farms in Canada were located in areas where their proportion was so high that the areas themselves could be classified as poor, almost another third of the poor farms were located in areas where the opposite was true." Helen Buckley and Eva Tihanyi, *Canadian Policies for Rural Adjustment.* A Study of the Economic Impact of ARDA, PFRA, and MMRA, Special Study No. 7, Economic Council of Canada (Ottawa: Queen's Printer, 1967).

also aspires to be a just society, cannot avoid setting itself such a goal. Secondly, poverty is costly. Its most grievous costs are those felt directly by the poor themselves, but it also imposes very large costs on the rest of society. These include the costs of crime, disease, and poor education. They include the costs of low productivity and lost output, of controlling the social tensions and unrest associated with gross inequality, and of that part of total welfare expenditure which is essentially a palliative made necessary by the failure to find more fundamental solutions. It has been estimated in the United States that one poor man can cost the public purse as much as $140,000 between the ages of 17 and 57.

It should also be noted that in recent years there has been a burst of improvement in the available weaponry against poverty. Not only have new weapons been devised or proposed, but there has also been a development of techniques of evaluation by which the effectiveness of both old and new weapons can be assessed and enhanced. Much of this improvement has occurred since the U.S. Government declared formal war on poverty with its Economic Opportunity Act of 1964. (The term "war on poverty" is appropriate in more than one sense, for, ironically enough, some of the techniques of policy planning and evaluation now being applied in the field of poverty originated within the military and defence planning establishments.) There have also been some extremely promising developments in Canada and some overseas countries. We would not wish to paint an overoptimistic picture, nor to suggest that much further experimentation and improvement are not required. But it is undoubtedly the case that the prospects for mounting a powerfully renewed offensive against poverty, with clear performance criteria and appropriate feedbacks of information on actual results obtained, and with a greater sense of involvement on the part of the poor themselves, are considerably better today than they would have been ten years ago.

In the remainder of this Chapter, some income statistics are first presented in order to give the reader some sense of the overall magnitude of the problem of poverty in Canada. Some broad characteristics of low-income families and individuals are also examined—characteristics significant for the planning of anti-poverty programs. A brief reference is made to the special characteristics of poverty among Canada's Indian and Eskimo populations. This is followed by a sketch of the U.S. war on poverty and some useful lessons from that experience. There is also some reference to the highly interesting techniques of anti-poverty planning recently used in the Gaspé and Lower St. Lawrence areas of Quebec. Finally, the concluding section of the Chapter puts forward some proposals that would help to lay the basis for a well co-ordinated and effective Canadian war on poverty.

The Extent of Low Incomes in Canada

In popular discussion of the problem of poverty, a traditional opening question has been, "Are the rich getting richer while the poor get poorer?". In other words, poverty has been viewed in terms of trends in the distribution of income through society as a whole. This is not a particularly useful way of coming to grips with poverty as it is defined here. Nevertheless, recent trends in the distribution of income are taken as a starting point in order to clear the ground for what we regard as a more fruitful approach.

43

Table 1

Distribution of Nonfarm Family Income Before Tax

	Distribution of Total Income			Average Income per Family
	1951	1961	1965	1965
	(Percentage)			(Dollars)
Lowest-income fifth of families	6.1	6.6	6.7	2,263
Second fifth	12.9	13.4	13.4	4,542
Third fifth	17.4	18.2	18.0	6,102
Fourth fifth	22.5	23.4	23.5	7,942
Top fifth	41.1	38.4	38.4	13,016
All families	100.0	100.0	100.0	6,669

Source: Based on data from Dominion Bureau of Statistics.

As may be seen from Table 1, there has been relatively little change in the distribution of family income in Canada over the last fifteen years. In particular the share of total income received by the bottom fifth of families has altered only fractionally. Breaks in the statistics make it difficult to extend these comparisons further back in time, but it appears that there may have been a trend towards greater income equality between 1931 and 1951, with the share received by the bottom fifth showing an appreciable increase. Between 1951 and 1965, however—a period over which average family income increased very rapidly—little shift in percentage shares was apparent. (It should be noted that the distribution of family income in Table 1 is *before tax;* exactly corresponding figures of income *after tax* are not available, but Table 2 gives some idea of the effective rates of income tax applying to various income groups in 1961.)

The lower fifth, or lower third, or any other fraction of an income distribution, makes a poor statistical substitute for poverty as we have defined it. It bears no necessary relation to the needs of the poor—to their degree of access to certain goods and services regarded as basic to a decent standard of life at any point in time. The proper object of an attack on poverty should be the careful identification and aiding of those whose circumstances do not permit them to achieve such a standard. Ultimately, the object should be the elimination of poverty.

In a later section of this Chapter, we shall recommend thorough-going procedures for the setting of minimum living standards and the estimation of the amount of poverty in Canada. Here, operating without the benefit of such procedures, we nevertheless feel it necessary to give the reader some general notion of the size and character of the poverty problem which proper estimates would be likely to reveal. The tentative and broadly illustrative character of the figures should be strongly emphasized. It would be most distressing to see them taken up as fixed, precise and authoritative measures of poverty in Canada: rather, they should be superseded as soon as possible by better and more informative figures. To underline this point, two alternative estimates of "total poverty" are presented.

Table 2

Classification of Nonfarm Families and Persons Not in Families, by Income Group, 1961

Income Group	Number of Families	Number of Persons Not Living in Families	Average Income Tax as a Percentage of Income*
	(000)	(000)	
Under $1,000	137	306	—
$1,000–$1,999	275	192	1.5
$2,000–$2,999	356	157	3.2
$3,000–$3,999	524	150	4.6
$4,000–$4,999	583	71	6.0
$5,000–$5,999	500	35	6.5
$6,000–$6,999	365	17	7.1
$7,000–$7,999	260	9	7.4
$8,000–$9,999	296	8	8.5
$10,000 and over	331	10	16.5
Total	3,627	955	8.1

* Applies to families and persons not living in families.
Source: Based on data from Dominion Bureau of Statistics.

The two estimates are derived from a special study of the low-income population of Canada, carried out by the Dominion Bureau of Statistics on the basis of the 1961 Census.[2] Low-income families were defined as families with incomes insufficient to purchase much more than the basic essentials of food, clothing and shelter. An examination of data on family expenditures, collected from a sample of about 2,000 families living in urban centres with populations of 15,000 or more, showed that, on average, families allocated about half of their income to these needs. It might therefore be concluded that where a family was using up a good deal more than half its income on essentials, that family was likely to be in straitened circumstances, having little money left over for such things as drugs, medical care, education of children, recreation, savings, etc.

For purposes of the first estimate, low-income families and individuals were defined as those using 70 percent or more of their incomes for food, clothing and shelter. On this basis, low-income families and individuals would include single persons with incomes below $1,500, families of two with less than $2,500, and families of three, four, and five or more with incomes of less than $3,000, $3,500, and $4,000 respectively.

As of 1961, some 916,000 nonfarm families plus 416,000 individuals were living below these levels.[3] The total number of persons involved was about 4.2 million, including 1.7 million children under 16 years of age. In all, they accounted for some 27 percent of the total nonfarm population of Canada.

[2] J. R. Podoluk, *Incomes of Canadians,* Dominion Bureau of Statistics Census Monograph (1968).
[3] Average incomes of low-income families in 1961 were:

Two persons in family	$1,427
Three persons in family	$1,851
Four persons in family	$2,347
Five or more persons	$2,707

There are a number of special difficulties in defining and estimating the incomes of farm families, and the figures in this area are not much more than educated guesses. It would appear that, in 1961, roughly 150,000 farm families,[4] comprising perhaps 550,000 persons, may have been living below the income levels set forth above. The addition of these people to the non-farm group would have brought the low-income percentage for all of Canada, including farms, to just under 29 percent on the basis of the definition employed.

The Canadian economy has of course undergone a vigorous expansion since 1961, sufficient to lift the incomes of a good many families and individuals above the low-income lines we have specified. No comparative figures are available for farm families or for nonfarm individuals, but it would appear that by 1965 the percentage of nonfarm families living below the specified levels (their incomes being expressed in 1961 dollars) has declined from 25 percent to 20 percent. This probably gives an exaggerated impression of the longer-term trend of improvement, inasmuch as in 1961 the economy was at a low point of the business cycle, with the ranks of the poor temporarily swollen by unusually large numbers of unemployed.

The above estimate is the more conservative of the two presented. Most readers who care to reflect on the income cut-offs on which the estimate is based, and to compare these cut-offs with their own personal income situations, will agree that living standards at or just above the cut-offs are likely to be modest indeed.

In the second estimate, the cut-offs are raised somewhat by the device of assuming that the expenditures of 60 percent or more (instead of 70 percent or more) of income on food, clothing and shelter by an individual or family indicates straitened circumstances. This brings the cut-offs up to $2,000 for a single person, $3,500 for a family of two, $4,000 for families of three and four, and $5,000 for families of five or more. Applied to the 1961 nonfarm population, these changes raise the low-income percentage from 27 percent to 41 percent.

At the beginning of this series of estimates, their "tentative and broadly illustrative character" was emphasized. They are not fully adequate measures of poverty. Such measures require among other things a thorough-going analysis of the needs and expenditure patterns of different types of families, and a consideration of assets, borrowing power, and income in kind as well as money income. It is useful also to distinguish between temporary and long-term poverty, and to allow for differences in living costs between different cities, towns, and rural areas.

But for all their shortcomings, the estimates presented here—particularly the first, more conservative set—suggest very strongly the existence of a major poverty problem in Canada. The statement that at least one Canadian in every five suffers from poverty does not appear to be a wild exaggeration. It is almost certainly close enough to the truth to be taken as one of the most serious challenges facing economic and social policy over the next few years.

---

[4] The *total* number of families primarily dependent on farming for a livelihood in 1961 was in the order of 275,000. Thus more than half these families were below the income levels used here.

Table 3

**Selected Characteristics of All Nonfarm Families and Low-Income Nonfarm Families
Year Ending May 31, 1961**

	(1) Number of Nonfarm Families	(2) Number of Nonfarm Families	(3) Incidence of Low Income
	All Families	Low-Income Families	(2) as a percentage of (1)
	(000)	(000)	
Nonfarm Families	3,627	916	25
Place of Residence			
Metropolitan	1,901	314	17
Other Urban	959	250	26
Rural	767	352	46
Region			
Atlantic	349	158	45
Quebec	988	276	28
Ontario	1,363	254	19
Prairies	556	150	27
British Columbia	368	78	21
Sex of Head			
Male	3,344	795	24
Female	283	121	43
Age of Head			
Under 25	149	43	29
25-54	2,509	554	22
55-64	491	109	22
65 or over	478	210	44
Size of Family			
Two	960	280	29
Three	734	148	20
Four	758	157	21
Five or more	1,175	331	28
Number of Children under 16			
None	1,383	330	24
One	699	143	21
Two	679	156	23
Three or more	866	287	33
Labour Force Status of Head			
In current labour force	2,996	573	19
Not in current labour force but worked during year	100	49	49
Did not work	531	294	55
Education of Head			
No schooling or elementary only	1,681	625	37
Secondary, 1-3 years	1,068	208	20
Secondary, 4-5 years	551	62	11
Some university	137	13	9
University degree	190	8	4
Number of Earners in Family			
No earners	268	217	81
One earner	1,870	529	28
Two earners	1,114	142	13
Three or more earners	375	28	7
Major Source of Income			
Wages and salaries	2,909	533	18
Self-employment	306	76	25
Transfer payments	271	245	90
Investment income	75	26	35
Other income	55	25	45
No income*	11	11	100

*This relatively small group includes such people as recent immigrants and recently widowed women who had received no income in Canada over the period covered.

Source: Based on data from Dominion Bureau of Statistics.

Some Statistical Characteristics of Low-Income Families and Individuals

Statistics cannot adequately describe poverty. But used with care they are capable of furnishing important clues to types of policies likely to be effective against poverty. With this end in view, some further information is set forth here concerning the nonfarm low-income families and individuals included in the *first* of our estimates of the extent of poverty in Canada.

Two important warnings must be issued at the outset. Statistically, low-income families and individuals differ noticeably from the total Canadian population in respect of a number of things besides income. Certain characteristics of age, family size, place of residence, education, relationship to the labour force, and occupation, are more commonly found among them than among the population at large. Put another way, where these characteristics are present, the chance of a family or individual having a low income (the *incidence* of low income) is high. These high rates of incidence are often significant as policy guides to particular kinds of poverty problems.

Chapter 5
The Real Poor in Canada-
And Why We Don't Know Who They Are*

Walter Stewart

Canadians don't think of themselves as poor–the federal government does. Canadians don't measure themselves in dollars–the Economic Council of Canada does. The result is that we're creating a climate of psychological poverty in this country that has little to do with what is really going on; we're dismissing whole regions as poverty-bound and trying to convince the people of those regions that they are a collective failure, when they don't see themselves that way at all.

Those are the main conclusions drawn by sociologist Martin Goldfarb from the fifth *Maclean's–Goldfarb Report*, a study based on a statistically reliable sample of Canadians from all across the land. This report, which in many ways reinforces an earlier survey of Canadian attitudes on success *(Maclean's,* December 1970), suggests it is time we took an entirely new look at poverty, stopped measuring it in terms of arbitrary standards laid down by Ottawa bureaucrats and started viewing it in terms of the plight of real people.

Official Ottawa accepts an arbitrary definition of poverty, one laid down by the Economic Council of Canada in 1968. In its annual report for that year, the council suggested that the poverty line should be drawn for a single person at $1,500 annual income, for a couple at $2,500, and for families of three, four and five or more at $3,000, $3,500 and $4,000. Applying that standard, the council discovered that 4.7 million Canadians live on the wrong side of the poverty line. Its roll call of poverty includes 29 percent of the nation, more than half of all farm families, 45 percent of all families in the Atlantic region.

The figures are startling – the ECC called them "a disgrace" – and they have been quoted in almost every brief, article, brochure and book on poverty since they were issued; they are embedded in our thinking, enshrined in the federal government's regional approach to poverty problems.

But are they a fair measure of Canada?

*"The Real Poor in Canada – And Why We Don't Know Who They Are," (pp. 44-46) of *Maclean's Magazine,* January, 1971, from a report made by Martin Goldfarb Consultants of Toronto. Reproduced with the permission of Mr. Goldfarb and *Maclean's.*

Goldfarb says they are not, that they measure only a part — an important part, but only a part — of what it means to be poor. He does not minimize the human tragedy that poverty is — he calls for a more sophisticated understanding of how it marks the lives of its victims. "Poverty," he says, "is more than a physical thing, it's more than being deprived of dollars; it's an attitude, a sense of defeat, a loss of dignity. But when you probe Canadian attitudes, you don't find that defeat. You find a great many Canadians the ECC says are poor who don't accept that definition of themselves, who say, 'Dammit, I'm *not* poor.' You find such anomalies as the fact that more people in the $8,000-to-$10,000-a-year bracket consider themselves to be in poverty than in the $6,000-to-$8,000 income group."

In an earlier study on attitudes of Canadians to the United Appeal, Martin Goldfarb Consultants found that people on welfare would rather get food and help from the Salvation Army than from a community agency, because "Once you start on welfare, then you're poor . . . The Salvation Army has no questions to ask, no demands to make. You're not beholden . . . You may be down on your luck, but nobody has to classify you as poor to help you."

That's an important distinction, and one that most Canadians make, even if their governments do not. A Prince Edward Island lobster fisherman who supports a family on less than $3,000 a year often cannot buy the things he wants; but he lives by the sea in a surrounding he loves, he is his own boss,

Table 1

Would You Consider Yourself to Be in Poverty?

Percentage of Respondents	Yes	No
Total Respondents	10	89
Province		
BC	13	87
Prairies	12	87
Ontario	7	92
Quebec — English	11	89
— French	13	87
Maritimes	11	89
Age		
Under 25	6	94
25 - 34	7	93
35 - 44	10	87
45 - 54	13	86
55 and over	15	85
Education		
High School or Less	16	84
Completed High School	8	91
Completed University or Better	4	94
Language		
English	9	90
French	14	86
Income		
Less than $6,000	25	75
$6,000 - $8,000	7	93
$8,000 - $10,000	9	91
$10,000 - $12,000	4	96
Over $12,000	2	95

he has enought to eat, and a sense of pride in his own worth. An unemployed laborer in Toronto or Montreal may have roughly the same income, but may live in a slum, spin out his days waiting for a job, and find himself sinking in defeat and despair. There is no way to equate the two brands of poverty — yet the statistical approach does just that. The ECC's contention that nearly half of the families in the Atlantic area are below the poverty line reinforces the government's tendency to deal with poverty on a regional basis. This is underlined by the fact that we have a federal Department of Regional and Economic Expansion and in the way that department spends its money. Of 22 "special areas" that will receive $200-million in extra aid this year, 13 are in the Atlantic region, and one in Ontario. Yet, even by the ECC measure, there are more poor in Ontario than in the Atlantic area (254,000 families against 158,000).

"The implication," says Goldfarb, "is that areas such as Toronto should be penalized, and that is folly."

He does not suggest switching the aid from Halifax to Hamilton; he does suggest that some standard other than the dollar measure should be used to guide our choice of where and how to spend funds. Only by ascertaining people's attitudes toward poverty can we find out who are the truly deprived, he argues, and only when we do that will we end the myth that a man can be made poor by the stroke of a pen.

As [Table 1] indicates, only 10 percent of Canadians consider themselves to be in poverty, compared to the officially estimated 29 percent; only 11 percent of Maritimers regard themselves as poor, compared to 45 percent; and the rejection of poverty as a self-description is high among Canadians of every region and income group.

When Does Poverty Start to Hurt?

When Goldfarb respondents were asked to draw a poverty line, the bulk of them — 53 percent — set it between $5,000 and $6,000 annual income — higher than the Economic Council standards. But 12 percent of Canadians feel it is possible to get along on $4,000 or less, and another 5 percent put the figure at $3,000. The average of all the respondents' replies was $5,920. Apparently Canadians set a higher objective standard than the one they apply to themselves, because only 25 percent of those in the under-$6000

Table 2

What is the Minimum Income You Need To Stay Above the Poverty Level?

	% Respondents
$3,000	5
$4,000	12
$5,000	31
$6,000	22
$7,000	10
$8,000	8
over $8,000	12
Average: $5,920	

annual-income bracket consider themselves to be in poverty. A further break-down of this study reveals interesting variations: 27 percent of those who live on the prairies believe the cutoff point comes at $4,000, while only 14 percent of Maritimers accept that income level as sufficient. The standards vary with age, too: 26 percent of Canadians in the 25-44 age group draw the poverty line at $8,000 or higher, compared to 8 percent of those under 25.

Who Are the Poor?
Not Whom You Think

The fuzziness of our current approach to poverty appears very quickly when Canadians are asked to identify the underprivileged in society. There is an overwhelming tendency to pick out fishermen and farmers, lazy people, hippies, addicts, alcholics and Maritimers. The Economic Council of Canada, in its statistical approach to poverty, acknowledged that more than 83 per-cent of Canada's low-income non-farm families live outside the Atlantic area, and more than half of low-income families live in metropolitan zones, but the council's dollar yardstick argued that nearly one in every two Maritime families is poor, riveting attention to a single geographic area. The incidence of poverty *is* higher in eastern Canada, but in actual numbers there are more poor in Ontario, many more in Quebec, than along the Atlantic coast. Yet the image we have of a typical poor person is that of a fisherman, a logger or a farmer. What's wrong. Typically, Canada's low-income family lives in a city, and the head of the family has a job. Senator David Croll, Chairman of the Special Senate Committee on Poverty, has estimated that 68 percent of our poor are employed.

Because we have accepted a stereotyped out-of-work fisherman as our typical poverty case, Goldfarb argues, we have turned the Maritimer into a

Table 3

Who Make Up The Bulk of The Poor?

	Percent
Farmers	17
Fishermen	63
Steel Workers	1
Auto Workers	1
Civil Servants	3
Truck Drivers	5
Lumber Workers	9
Lazy People	44
Sick People	11
Old People	6
Invalids	5
Mental Retards	6
Unwed Mothers	2
Hippies/Addicts/Alcoholics	25
English	5
French Canadians	19
Italian Immigrants	9
Jews	3
German Immigrants	2
Maritimers	59

second-class citizen. "We have created a prejudice against these people, many of whom, while they don't have much money, are among the most independent, self-reliant, dignified people in the entire nation."

You're Poor When You Lose Your Pride

Almost as many Canadians consider poverty to be a way of thinking as a set of physical circumstances, and more people believe it is self-imposed than a product of outside circumstances. To researcher Goldfarb, this does not suggest that Canadians accept poverty, or think nothing should be done about it, but rather than "people don't measure their achievements by how many dollars they have to spend; what they're saying is that if you let yourself lose your pride, you're in a state of poverty."

Table 4

Is Poverty . . .	
A Natural, Physical Thing	52
A Way of Thinking	43
Did Not State	6
Is Poverty . . .	
Self-Imposed	50
A 'Can't Help Yourself' Thing	48
Did Not State	6

Chapter 6
The Negative Income Tax:
How It Helps to Alleviate Poverty*

Colin J. Hindle

Introduction and Rationale for a Negative Income Tax

Most persons are familiar with the nature and workings of the personal income tax. It is one of several taxes used by Canadian governments to raise the funds necessary to carry on their programs. At first sight the idea of a negative income tax seems absurd — a personal income tax working in reverse, tax payments being made by governments to persons rather than the other way about? On second thought, however, the notion is not so strange. Canadian governments have been making payments to persons, that is, transfer payments, for a long time. The best known of these transfer payments are, probably, provincial social assistance, family allowances, and old age security, but there are a number of others as well.

So a negative income tax is simply a type of transfer payment. Nevertheless, it is a transfer payment with certain special features which perhaps do bear more resemblance to an income tax operating in reverse than to more conventional transfer payment programs. Unlike family allowances and old age security, for example, negative income taxes are not paid regardless of an individual or family's income level. Just as the personal income tax takes more money from taxpayers with larger incomes than from those with smaller incomes, the negative income tax pays more money to individuals or families with smaller incomes than to those with larger incomes. Indeed, in the case of persons with incomes above some specified level no payments are made at all. Whereas provincial social assistance payments, to take another example, are virtually reduced dollar for dollar when welfare recipients acquire income from other sources, negative income tax payments are reduced more gradually so that persons receiving them can increase their total incomes by working and saving. And, unlike most provincial social assistance plans, being in a state of unemployment is not a necessary condition to receive negative income tax payments. Income and family status, that is, age

*This paper was especially prepared for this collection by Dr. Hindle. The author has been involved in the evaluation of income maintenance schemes for the Federal government, and the editor is grateful for his willingness to undertake the writing of Chapter 6.

and number of family members, alone determine the level of negative income tax payments.

Arguments used to justify transfer payments, such as negative income taxes, are usually based on the idea of inadequate personal income or economic poverty. The reasons why certain incomes are determined to be inadequate are complex. Standards of income adequacy or of economic poverty are relative – they vary over time and place. Poverty standards clearly do not depend so much on considerations of absolute physical minimum requirements for living as on the general standard of living which a society enjoys. In any case, if the rationale for transfer payments is poverty reduction, one might question if there are not other, better ways of achieving this objective. It is sometimes argued that inadequate personal incomes are best remedied through worker training and mobility programs or by means of schemes designed to improve or increase the plant and equipment used by workers. These kinds of "structuralist" programs combined with policies designed to ensure a strong demand for labour services, it is said, cure the causes of poverty whereas transfer payments merely alleviate the symptoms. But it must be clear that these measures are complementary rather than competitive ways of raising income levels. This is so because "structuralist" and "demand" policies normally require a fairly lengthy period of time to become effective whereas transfer payments can be made effective as soon as the need arises. It is also true that there is likely to remain a substantial number of persons that neither "structuralist" nor "demand" policies can assist adequately.

If a case can be made for transfer payments in general, it still remains to present an argument in favour of the negative income tax in particular. Why might a negative income tax be preferred to other kinds of transfer payments? Two considerations seem to be of greatest importance. The first is a matter of equity and the second involves unwanted behavioural effects. As a general rule, equitable treatment seems to imply that all of the poor should receive aid regardless of the source of their poverty. There may be some qualification placed on this rule in the case of persons who are capable of earning income but prefer not to, but on the whole it seems defensible. In this respect the negative income tax is superior to those provincial social assistance programs which require not only that persons be poor but unemployed besides. The effect of that particular kind of additional qualification is simply to exclude the employed poor from receiving any assistance. The second reason why a negative income tax might be preferred to other transfer programs is because it results in fewer adverse behavioural effects. As an instance, transfer programs that cause persons to work or save less by reducing the incentives for these kinds of behaviour are generally regarded to be less desirable than those which do not affect persons to the same extent in these ways. Again, as an example, most provincial social assistance programs leave very little incentive to work or save because these transfer payments are greatly reduced when earned income increases. The effect is to leave the total incomes of welfare recipients almost unchanged whether they work, save, or do nothing. Negative income tax systems, on the other hand, are usually designed so that recipients do not lose all of their negative income tax payments when they receive income from other sources.

Operation and Properties of a Negative Income Tax

So much for the rationale of a negative income tax, but what about the way in which it operates? With the use of simple algebra we can write down a negative income tax formula and then use this formula to investigate a number of properties of the negative income tax. One kind of negative income tax (several types are possible but most have the basic form shown below) may be written as follows,

$$N = (n \cdot A + m \cdot C) - t \cdot Y \geqslant 0$$

where the algebraic symbols have the following definitions,

N = negative income tax payment
n = number of adults in the family
A = negative income tax allowances per adult
m = number of children in the family
C = negative income tax allowances per child
t = the rate at which negative income tax payments are reduced in consideration of family income from other sources
Y = family income from other sources

One of the first things we can observe from the formula is that more negative income tax allowances are allowed for additional members in a family and allowances are differentiated as between adults and children. This is not an esssential feature of a negative income tax, but most possess it and this permits the scheme to account for the needs of families of different size and composition.

A second feature of a negative income tax can be seen if we consider what happens when a family's income from other sources is equal to zero. That is, we suppose the family does not have any income from wages, bank interest, stock dividends and so on. In this case, letting $Y = 0$, our negative income tax formula gives,

$$N = (n \cdot A + m \cdot C) - t \cdot 0$$
$$= n \cdot A + m \cdot C$$

In words, the family's negative income tax payment equals its negative income tax allowances. The family is assured at least this much total income (income from other sources plus negative income tax payments) in any event. This feature is usually referred to as a guaranteed minimum income. In fact, negative income taxes are sometimes referred to as "the guaranteed minimum income." The larger are the negative income tax allowances, the larger is the guaranteed minimum income.

When a family's income from other sources, say from wages, rises above zero the amount of the negative income tax payment is reduced at the rate t. Suppose for example that $t = \frac{1}{4}$ and that a family earns income from wages equal to twice the amount of its guaranteed income. That is, suppose $Y = 2(n \cdot A + m \cdot C)$. In this case the negative income tax payment would be computed as follows,

$$N = (n \cdot A + m \cdot C) - \tfrac{1}{4}Y$$

or
$$N = (n \cdot A + m \cdot C) - \tfrac{1}{4}[2n \cdot A + 2m \cdot C]$$
$$= \tfrac{1}{2}n \cdot A + \tfrac{1}{2}m \cdot C$$

And, the family would enjoy a total income, negative income tax payment plus wages, equal to 2½ times the amount of its guaranteed income. If our hypothetical family's income from wages were higher, say three times the level of its guaranteed income, the negative income tax payment would be lower, but the family's total income would still be higher. This can be checked by substituting $3(n \cdot A + m \cdot C)$ for Y in the example above, calculating the negative income tax payment and then adding this amount to Y in order to determine the family's total income from wages and negative income tax payments. It is always possible for a family, under a negative income tax plan where t is less than one, to increase its total income by working or saving more.

As a family's income from other sources increases, a point is finally reached when negative income tax payments are reduced to zero. Call this income level, for a family of given size and composition, Y^*. Letting $Y = Y^*$ our negative income tax formula gives,

$$N = (n \cdot A + m \cdot C) - t \cdot Y^* = 0$$

We can now solve for Y^*, sometimes called the breakeven income level, in terms of the negative income tax allowances $(n \cdot A + m \cdot C)$, and the negative tax payment reduction rate, (t). This gives,

$$Y^* = \frac{(n \cdot A + m \cdot C)}{t}$$

Now it is clear from this formulation that for a given level of negative income tax allowances or guaranteed minimum income $(n \cdot A + m \cdot C)$, the breakeven income level, Y^*, will be higher, the smaller is the negative tax payment reduction rate, (t). For example, when $t = \tfrac{1}{2}$, $Y^* = 2(n \cdot A + m \cdot C)$ and when $t = 1/3$, $Y^* = 3(n \cdot A + m \cdot C)$. Larger values of Y^* mean that families at higher income levels will receive negative income tax payments. If there are only limited funds available to make negative income tax payments we are faced with a choice. For a given level of Y^*, it is possible either to encourage negative income tax recipients to earn more income from wages, interest, etc., by lowering the level of t and making the minimum income guarantee smaller or t can be increased and the level of the guaranteed income raised. It is not possible, however, to both lower t and raise the level of the guaranteed minimum income — unless of course Y^* is increased, in which case more funds would be required. It is clear that a trade-off is involved between having a more generous income guarantee and raising the incentive or rewards for working and saving. This comes down to a choice between helping the very poorest persons more or giving the rest of the poor a meaningful opportunity to earn income.

Table 1

**Illustration of the Operation of an Hypothetical
Canadian Negative Income Tax***

(all amounts in dollars per annum)

Income Before Personal Income Taxes or Negative Income Tax Payments	Negative Tax Payments (+) and Personal Taxes (-)†	Income After Personal Income Taxes or Negative Income Tax Payments
0	2000	2000
500	1750	2250
1500	1250	2750
2000	1000	3000
2500	750	3250
3000	500	3500
3500	250	3750
4000	0	4000
4500	(-55)	4444
5000	(-169)	4831
5500	(-289)	5210
6000	(-412)	5587
6500	(-539)	5960

*Family consists of head, spouse, one dependent child aged sixteen years and two dependent children under sixteen years of age. All income is assumed to be wages earned by the head. Employment expense deduction of $150 and standard deduction of $100 are taken.
†Includes provincial taxes at 30 percent of federal taxes.

Source: Data on personal income taxes adapted from *Summary of 1971 Tax Reform Legislation,* Honourable E.J. Benson, Minister of Finance, 1971, p. 17.

Table 1 illustrates the operation of both a hypothetical Canadian negative income tax and the personal income tax (as revised by the recent budget) for the case of a family consisting of head, spouse and three children aged seventeen, fourteen, and ten years respectively. Negative income tax allowances, in this hypothetical plan, are established at $712.50 per annum for adults, $275.00 per annum for children over fifteen years of age and at $150.00 per annum for children under fifteen years of age. This means the guaranteed income for this family is $2,000 per year. The rate of negative income tax payment reduction is established at ½ or 50 percent. Accordingly, our example family's breakeven income level is $4,000, that is

$$Y^* = \frac{\$2,000}{\frac{1}{2}}$$
$$= \$4,000$$

We chose the breakeven point in this example so that negative income tax payments would not overlap with the requirement to pay personal income taxes. If we accept this breakeven point as being fixed, say because of a budgetary restraint, we can see that the guaranteed income of $2,000 (for a family of this size) can only be increased if one is also prepared to raise the negative tax payment reduction rate, for example to ¾ or 75 percent. In that case the guaranteed income could be raised to $3,000 and the breakeven point would still be $4,000. That is

$$Y* = \frac{\$3,000}{\frac{3}{4}}$$
$$= \$4,000$$

If, on the other hand, the negative income tax allowances or guaranteed minimum income had been raised to $3,000 and the negative income tax payment reduction rate left at ½ the breakeven income level would rise to $6,000, as shown below:

$$Y* = \frac{\$3,000}{\frac{1}{2}}$$
$$= \$6,000$$

Negative Income Taxes in Canada

Although they are called by other names, Canada has one negative income tax plan in operation at the moment and another in prospect. The first mentioned is the Guaranteed Income Supplement for persons aged sixty-five years or more and the second is the proposed Family Income Security Plan for families with children aged fifteen years or less. Table 2 shows the operation of the Guaranteed Income Supplement and Table 3 illustrates the proposed Family Income Security Plan.

The rate at which Guaranteed Income Supplement allowances are reduced is approximately 50 percent. The guaranteed annual income established by the GIS plan alone, not including old age security payments, is $660 for a single aged person. The breakeven income level, then, is about $1,320. It should be noted that since all GIS recipients receive old age security payments of $900 the two schemes combined provide a guaranteed

Table 2

The Guaranteed Income Supplement*

(dollars per annum)

Income Before† GIS Payments	GIS Payments(+)	Income After† GIS Payments
0	660	660
500	410	910
750	285	1035
1000	160	1160
1250	35	1285
1320	0	1320

*The payments shown are for a single aged person.
†Does not include old age security payments.

Source: Adapted from, *Guaranteed Income Supplement*. Ottawa: Department of National Health and Welfare, 1971, p. 6.

Table 3

The Proposed Family Income Security Plan*

Income Before† FISP Payments	FISP Payments(+)	Income After† FISP Payments
0	192	192
1000	192	1192
2000	192	2192
3000	192	3192
4000	192	4192
4500	192	4692
5000	180	5180
6000	156	6156
7000	132	7132
8000	108	8108
9000	84	9084
10000	60	10060
11000	0	11000

*Payments shown are for one child only.
†The rate at which allowances are reduced is approximately 2.64% per child.

Source: Adapted from *Income Security for Canadians.* Ottawa: Department of National Health and Welfare, 1970, p. 45.

annual income of $1,560. The GIS negative income tax formula for one aged person can be written as follows:

$$N(\text{GIS}) = 660 - \tfrac{1}{2}{\cdot}Y \geqslant 0$$

The proposed Family Income Security Plan, on the other hand, has a guaranteed income or negative income tax allowance of $192 per child. There are a number of special features in FISP that are worth noting. These are a $4,500 exemption before allowances are reduced, similar to the personal exemptions in the income tax, and a reduction rate which depends on the number of children who qualify for allowances. For families of all sizes the breakdown income level is about $10,000. The FISP negative income tax formula can be written as shown below:

$$N(\text{FISP}) = m{\cdot}192 - m{\cdot}(1/28.6) \cdot (Y - 4500) \geqslant 0$$

It is interesting to compare the way each of these two negative income tax plans has settled the trade-off between high income guarantees and high incentives to earn income. In the case of GIS we could say that relatively more emphasis has been placed on securing a higher guaranteed income. Both the GIS income guarantee and the payment reduction rate are fairly high. This results in these transfers being confined to the very lowest income groups. In the case of FISP relatively more emphasis appears to have been placed on ensuring that the incentive to earn income is not impaired. Both the FISP income guarantee and payment reduction rate are low in relation to those of GIS. In fact, the FISP payment reduction rate is low enough to permit these transfers being made to middle income groups.

A common feature of both GIS and FISP is that they are partial negative income tax plans. That is, only part of the population is covered under either scheme. Families without children and where adult members are less than age sixty-five years are not included. Most often when the negative income tax is discussed, people do not have partial plans like these in mind. Rather, it is the universal negative income tax that is considered. In fact the term negative income tax has come to be almost exclusively associated with the universal version of the plan. The universal negative income tax would apply to all persons whose incomes are low enough to permit them to qualify for payments. No segment of the population would be excluded on the basis of age or any other criterion.

Summary and Final Comments

The reason for making transfer payments is to reduce poverty. In a sense transfer payments are palliatives rather than a cure for poverty but they are necessary because other means of attacking the problem take longer periods of time and because other methods will not necessarily work for everyone. A universal negative income tax plan might be preferable to other kinds of transfers because it would be more equitable and could involve fewer adverse behavioural changes. Canada already has some experience with partial negative income tax plans and is about to gain more. It is conceivable that these might one day form the basis for a Canadian universal negative income tax. Careful thought will be needed, however. We have noted some of the hard choices between incentives and income guarantees that will have to be made.

Part C
Inflation and Unemployment

The persistence of price inflation in Canada in the second half of the nine-teen-sixties led to a great deal of criticism of government policies and the "creation" of unemployment as a measure to cure inflation. The first selection presents the elementary theory underlying the so-called "trade-off" that is alleged to exist between unemployment and price inflation.

In 1971, a number of briefs concerning inflation were presented to the Senate Committee on National Finance. The second selection of Part C is composed of three such briefs which discussed the question of price and wage controls as a means of controlling inflation. The first brief presents the case for wage and price control or "incomes" policies while the second and third briefs raise questions about serious difficulties in executing such a policy.

Chapter 7
The Trade-Off Between
Prices and Unemployment*

R.G. Bodkin
E.P. Bond
G.L. Reuber
T.R. Robinson

The Concept of a "Trade-Off"

In everyday life, individuals frequently face the difficulty of choosing among several goals, all of which are highly desirable in themselves but each of which is inconsistent with some of the others to some degree, thus making it impossible fully to achieve all of them. Among the many examples which could be cited are the following: the desire for income (requiring effort) vs. the desire for leisure; the desire for speed in transportation vs. the desire for safety; the desire to consume current income vs. the desire to accumulate assets. Few, if any, individuals opt for all work or all leisure, maximum speed without any concessions to safety, or starvation in order to save all of their income. Most individuals elect a compromise between these extremes: some income and some leisure; a "safe" speed; some consumption and some saving. In this sense we can say that individuals are willing to "trade off" income against leisure, speed against safety, and consumption against saving.

Nations frequently face similar difficulties in choosing among the objectives of economic policy. In the modern world, policy-makers in most, if not all, countries aspire to a wide range of economic objectives: full employment, a stable price level, rapid and sustained economic growth, balance-of-payments equilibrium, wide regional dispersion of economic development, and greater equality (of income, wealth, and opportunity) is an illustrative list. If it were merely a matter of compiling a list of desirable goals, questions of economic policy would be comparatively simple. However, if the various goals considered important by society conflict with each other to some extent, the compilation of such a list is merely the beginning, not the end, of the process of formulating satisfactory economic policies. If all goals cannot be attained simultaneously, a hard choice must then be made as to how far to pursue one objective at the expense of the others. Under these circumstances, most societies, analogously to most individuals, can be expected to elect a compromise, trading off some portion of one objective in order not to fall further short on some other. It is true that the decision may not be a

*Chapter 1, "Introduction," (pp. 3 – 8) of *Price Stability and High Employment*, Special Study Number 5, for the Economic Council of Canada, September, 1966. Reproduced with the permission of Information Canada.

conscious one: the policy-makers may not view the matter in these terms or even if they take such a view, the "objective" trade-offs may differ from those considered most probable by the decision-makers. Consequently, past actions by the policy-makers may be an imperfect guide to their preferences, given the uncertainties pervading most "real world" policy actions. Nevertheless, if a conflict between goals is present, some form of compromise is usually reached in practice; in this sense at least, the policy-makers may be said to have traded off one goal against one or more other goals.

How much of one objective must be traded off in order to gain a particular amount of another depends, of course, on the degree to which the objectives are in conflict. Conceivably, objective A might not conflict at all with objective B: in this case, A can be fully attained without impairing in any way the country's ability to achieve B as well and hence no choice between A and B is required. At the other extreme, it is conceivable that A and B are mutually exclusive. Here the choice is between all of A and none of B, or none of A and all of B—one can choose either A or B, but no combination of the two. It is, however, the view of the writers of the present study that many objectives of public policy (including the two on which this study focuses, high employment and price level stability) are neither completely independent of other objectives nor mutually exclusive of these other objectives, but lie between these two limits.[1] Under these circumstances, a decision must inevitably be made, implicitly or explicitly, as to how far to pursue each objective. (In this context, an objective may be defined as the ideal that would be sought in the absence of conflicts.) Hence, in order to evaluate public policies a key question to be considered is how much of one objective must be foregone in order to move a step closer towards some other objective. In other words, what are the quantitative terms of the "trade-off" between goals A and B?

Trade-Offs between Price Level Stability and High Employment

In this study, we attempt to examine, primarily in the Canadian context, the issues of whether a conflict exists between the objectives of price level stability and high employment and if so, what are the trade-offs, at various levels of unemployment, between these goals. The approach underlying this investigation can be made explicit with the aid of the "trade-off" curve[2] of

[1] It is of course conceivable that two goals, considered as an isolated pair, may be mutually reinforcing or complementary, rather than conflicting or of the nature of substitutes. For example, the goal of rapid economic growth and that of a high level of employment may be such a pair, as one of us (R.G. Bodkin) has argued in a previous publication. See "An Analysis of the Trade-Offs Between Full Employment, Price Stability, and Other Goals," pp. 47–77 of S.F. Kaliski, ed., *Canadian Economic Policy Since the War* (no city given: Canadian Trade Committee, 1966).

[2] This trade-off curve is a derived relationship with "other things remaining equal," much like the partial equilibrium demand curve of economic theory. The theoretical relationships underlying this trade-off curve are discussed in Chapter 2 below [not presented here]; this theoretical discussion enables one to sort out some of the variables which may induce a shift in the trade-off curve, generally in a longer-term context. The nontechnical reader should be forewarned that there are a number of statistical (or econometric) problems connected with the estimation of the underlying relationships from empirical data. One of the most important qualifications relates to the probabilistic nature of the trade-off curve: points on the curve are of the nature of expected values or arithmetic averages, rather than iron-clad values of a mathematical function from which there is no escape. Thus, with "good luck", it is possible to end up below the curve (closer to the origin), while, with bad fortune, the economy will experience more than the expected amount of inflation for a given rate of unemployment (and a given environment). For simplicity of exposition, these qualifications are not mentioned explicitly again in this section.

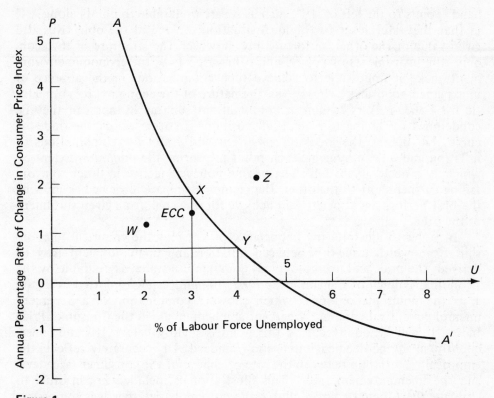

Figure 1

A Price-Change-Unemployment Trade-Off Curve*

*The points plotted are based on G.L. Reuber, "The Objectives of Canadian Monetary Policy, 1949–61: Empirical Trade-Offs and the Reaction Function of the Authorities," *Journal of Political Economy,* LXXII, No. 2 (April 1964), pp. 109–132. The trade-off curve is drawn on the assumptions that foreign prices remain constant and that the effects of the estimated lags have been fully worked out.

Figure 1. In this Figure, the level of unemployment as a percentage of the labour force is measured along the horizontal axis with the hypothetical zero rate of unemployment corresponding to the origin. The annual percentage rate of change of the Consumer Price Index is measured along the vertical axis, with (as is customary) points above the origin representing price level increases and points below it, price decreases.

As the trade-off curve *AA'* is drawn, when the unemployment rate is 3 percent, the rate of increase in the Canadian consumer price level which can be expected is 1¾ percent per year; if the rate of unemployment were raised to 4 percent, the consumer price level could be expected to increase by three quarters of a percent annually. Hence, between these two positions, one can "trade off" a one percentage point decrease in the rate of domestic inflation for a one percentage point increase in the unemployment rate. Similar trade-offs can likewise be derived for other pairs of points along this curve.

Before considering the factors determining the shape and position of this curve, it is useful to consider the significance of points such as *W* and *Z*, which lie on either side of the trade-off curve. Points to the right of *AA'*, such as *Z* are unsatisfactory in the sense that they can be improved upon in terms of both objectives by moving towards the curve *AA'*. On the other hand, points to the left of *AA'*, such as *W*, are preferable to points along *AA'* in that they are closer to the ideal situation for one of the objectives at a given value of the other; unfortunately, however, the structure of the economy, the instruments of policy, and other aspects of the economic environment make it impossible to achieve such combinations in the absence of unexpected good luck. Thus, given the nature of the economy, it is unrealistic for policy-makers to aim at combinations such as *W*, nor can they be condemned for failing to reach such positions. In other words, the trade-off curve *AA'* defines the locus of *consistent* and *attainable* combinations of inflation and unemployment, each point measuring the *minimum* extent by which it is necessary to fall short of one policy objective in order to avoid falling further short of the other. Hence the curve may be viewed as showing the best performance society can achieve for one goal, for a given fulfilment of the other goal.

In order to illustrate the importance of knowing the empirical relationship from which trade-offs between inflation and unemployment may be derived, the price and unemployment combination stated as desirable by the Economic Council of Canada in its *First Annual Review* is plotted in Figure 1 as the point marked *ECC* which shows a combination of a 3 percent unemployment rate and a 1.4 percent annual increase in the Consumer Price Index. It will be observed that this point is slightly below *AA'* and consequently might be deemed unrealistic *if* indeed *AA'* accurately reflects the empirical relationship between the rate of change of the consumer price level and the unemployment rate.[3] This illustration is included not in order to evaluate the Council's target, but rather to emphasize that it is impossible either to set or to evaluate satisfactorily any target combination of rates of inflation and unemployment unless one estimates, in some fashion, the "real world" trade-off relationship between these two policy objectives. Failure to do so means that one is assuming some sort of trade-off relationship in any event but doing so implicitly on the basis of intuition rather than analysis.

The general shape of the trade-off curve is that of being convex to the origin: the relationship is asymptotic to the price change axis and flattens out along the unemployment axis. This means that the expected rate of inflation rises increasingly rapidly as the rate of unemployment is reduced; the expected trade-off (slope of the *AA'* curve) is not constant over the usual range of unemployment. This is what one might expect from the nature of the economy; as unemployment is reduced due to an increasing demand for labour, it will gradually approach a frictional minimum level, at which wage increases will accelerate rapidly. Moreover, other stresses may be encountered in a high-pressure, low-unemployment economy; some industries will reach full capacity before others and attempts to expand output still further

---

[3] This point is reinforced when it is emphasized that *AA'* is constructed on the assumption of a zero rate of change in the price level of imports. By contrast, the Economic Council appeared to incorporate an estimate of the probable rate of foreign inflation equal to 1 percent annually. The effect of any positive rate of foreign inflation is to shift the trade-off curve upwards and to the right, as discussed in Chapter 2 below. The estimated relationship from Reuber's earlier study, on which Figure 1 is based, implies that, with the assumption of a 1 percent per year rate of foreign inflation, a 3 percent unemployment rate might then be expected to be associated with a 2.4 percent annual increase in the Consumer Price Index. This, in turn, is a full percentage point greater than the target rate of change of the consumer price level suggested by the Economic Council. As pointed out in Chapter 2, the Council based its implicit estimate of the combination of unemployment and price stability which might be regarded as an appropriate policy goal for 1970 on the assumption that a comprehensive manpower policy would be in operation.

will induce rapid rises in prices, at least in the short run in which it is very difficult to alleviate such bottlenecks. On the other hand, as unemployment is increased and the pressure of demand is reduced still further in an already slack economy, the gain in further price level stability might be expected to be rather small. Some of the unemployed labour force might be expected to lose touch with the labour market and so to exert very little downward influence on money wages (and hence on product prices); moreover, considerable excess capacity may have only a minor impact on the rate of change of final prices. For a variety of institutional reasons, prices and wages might be expected to move in a downward direction less readily than upwards, which is reflected graphically in the curve's flattening out at higher rates of unemployment. These rough and ready assertions about the nature of the economy's labour and product markets have been presented without rigorous proof or documentation, but it seems likely that many of them would be widely accepted by professional economists.

Factors which determine the slope and position of the trade-off curve include the underlying structural elements of the economy—e.g., its resource base, its rate of technical change, the attitudes and short-term expectations of the public, its institutional arrangements (particularly its labour markets and its price-setting mechanisms), and its international relationships. Such structural elements may themselves change, and, if they do, the curve will shift. Thus it is quite possible for an economy to generate spontaneous shifts in its trade-off relationship. It seems likely, though not necessarily inevitable, that such shifts will take place only during some comparatively long period of time. In a closed economy, only the structural features of the domestic economy are relevant. In an open economy such as the Canadian, the structural features of other economies (particularly the U.S. economy, in the Canadian case) enter the picture as well. In particular, the linkages (trade, investment, and direct pricing and wage spillover effects) of the various participants in the international economy may give rise to price and demand linkages of several types. In addition, balance-of-payments considerations can be regarded as a constraint conditioning the attainability of policy goals, making only a certain portion of the hypothetical trade-off curve relevant to the policy decision.

The shape and position of the trade-off curve may also reflect the number of policy instruments available for use, their impact on the economic structure, and the interrelations among the various instruments of policy. One idealized case is that in which all instruments are independent of each other and all objectives are similarly independent of each other. Here, Professor Tinbergen has shown that it is possible to attain each objective fully, thus avoiding conflicts among objectives, provided one uses as many instruments as there are objectives.[4] However, the realism of this case may be questioned; if the above argument is valid, objectives are generally not independent of each other but may conflict to some degree. The principal lesson to be learned from Tinbergen's discussion is, however, that the conflict among objectives is influenced by the number of instruments. Since it is widely accepted that the number of instruments generally falls far short of the

---

[4] Jan Tinbergen, *Economic Policy: Principles and Design* (Amsterdam: North Holland Publishing Company, 1956).

number of objectives that society wishes to pursue, this suggests that complete achievement of all goals may not be feasible, even with "perfect" management of economic policy.[5]

Finally, some mention should be made of policies designed to shift the trade-off curve. Wartime price controls would be a striking illustration of such a policy; they attempt to suppress the price pressures associated with a very high level of utilization of the economy's resources during such an abnormal period. More recently, many governments in the Western democracies have instituted policies that have come to be termed "incomes policies"; while the stated purposes underlying such policies have varied somewhat, a common strand has been the attempt to reduce the conflict between the goals of high employment and stable prices or, in other words, to shift the trade-off curve in towards the axes (closer to the origin). Since the theory and practice of such policies is the subject of a companion study,[6] the details of this type of policy will not be explored here. It may be observed, however, that an incomes policy attempts to reduce the amount of spontaneous wage and/or profit push to which an economy would otherwise be subject, at any level of unemployment below the "full employment" value.

[5] Of course, to the extent that a given policy is capable of "killing more than one bird with one stone," the conflict between objectives is further reduced. Thus, labour market policy may conceivably reduce (structural) unemployment, promote the efficiency of resource allocation in a static sense, enhance the growth of labour productivity, and lessen the conflict between high employment and price level stability, all at the same time.

[6] David C. Smith, *Incomes Policies: Some Foreign Experiences and Their Relevance for Canada*, Economic Council of Canada, Special Study No. 4 (Ottawa: Queen's Printer, 1966).

Chapter 8
Inflation, Unemployment, and Incomes Policies*

John Young
H.G. Johnson
Richard G. Lipsey

I. Brief Submitted by John Young

In the future as in the past, the management of demand in the Canadian economy through the application of fiscal, monetary and exchange rate policies will continue to be of central importance in efforts to keep the economy operating at or close to minimum sustainable levels of unemployment. This raises the question which has faced the Commission since it was established: What scope — if any — is there for the effective application of some form of prices and incomes policy as a means of supplementing demand management and longer-run structural policies in the pursuit of sustained high employment with reasonable price stability?

What is meant by a prices and incomes policy? In the context of this paper such a policy is taken to mean an attempt to use some form of direct public pressure to influence decisions about prices and incomes so that these will conform more closely with national economic objectives. The term is sometimes used in a much looser sense to embrace as well many of the structural, competition, and other long-run policies referred to above, which in recent years have been the administrative responsibility of particular government departments and also, in many cases, the subject of continuing study by the Economic Council of Canada. For purposes of convenience in this discussion of prices and incomes policy, the term is used in its more restricted sense.

A prices and incomes policy is intended to help limit the rise in the average level of domestic prices and costs over the economy as a whole. Price and income criteria of general application, perhaps with some exceptions, must be spelled out for the guidance of those involved in the determination of particular prices and incomes. So far as possible, this should be done on the basis of consultation and consensus involving the principal groups in the economy. Whether reliance is placed mainly on persuasion, mainly on compulsion, or on some combination of both, effective means must be employed for obtaining general compliance with these norms.

*Three briefs presented to the Senate Standing Committee on National Finance in Ottawa, 1971. Printed in this volume with the permission of the authors.

Under what circumstances might a reasonable case be made for temporary resort to some form of prices and incomes policy?

A good illustration is provided by the situation facing the Canadian authorities since the outbreak of severe inflation in the mid-sixties. The problem has been how to restore reasonable price stability with as little interruption as possible in the growth of output and employment, and with the aim of getting the economy back without delay on to a path of sustained expansion at high levels of activity.

Now if the size of price and income increases responded at all quickly and sensitively to restraints on expenditure such as tax increases and a tightening of credit, there is no reason why their moderation should involve severe or prolonged effects on the growth of production and employment. The fact of the matter is, however, that in a country like Canada decisions to raise prices and rates of pay are made by innumerable private groups and public bodies acting on the basis of expectations drawn largely from recent experience. Most of these groups are insulated in varying degrees from the immediate pressure of changing economic conditions and are strongly influenced by the views they have come to hold regarding the probable future trend of prices, the fairness of their share of income, and the increases they expect others to get.

Thus, long after the authorities have acted to reduce spending pressures in an economy in which excess demand has led to severe inflation, jockeying for larger income shares on the assumption that inflation will persist is likely to continue to push up costs and prices to levels well beyond those which market demand can support. The resulting sluggishness of sales, output, and employment then leads to demands that the attempt to control inflation be abandoned as cruel and misguided.

Could some effective form of direct pressure be devised to help moderate the size of price and cost increases in such circumstances? If so, inflation could be checked with less reliance on expenditure restraints, which hold the risk of temporary economic disruption and higher unemployment. And to the extent that price and cost increases could be moderated with greater speed and certainty, the authorities could act to stimulate renewed expansion of economic activity more promptly and with greater confidence of avoiding a recurrence of inflation.

That is the hope which encouraged the Commission in its search for some practical and effective form of prices and incomes policy in Canada over the last two years. It is also the hope that has encouraged similar efforts in many other countries in the last decade.

There are a few general observations arising out of our experience so far which may be of interest.

Important issues arise in deciding what forms of pressure, in addition to persuasion, should be invoked in order to obtain general compliance with the norms of a prices and incomes policy.

It is highly desirable, of course, that the central objectives of such a policy should be widely understood and accepted throughout the community. In a country whose last experience with an incomes policy dates back to the mandatory price and income controls of the Second World War, it is not surprising that we encountered a great deal of misunderstanding about what we were trying to achieve. To the business community, interference with the pricing decisions of management looks suspiciously like a political-ly-inspired raid on company profits. To professional groups, interference with their fee-setting activities raises the clear possibility that professional standards of service are about to be undermined by ignorant laymen. To organized labour, proposals that the settlement of wage and salary demands through collective bargaining conform with certain broad criteria suggest an anti-union bias. And to some observers, any strong concern with controlling inflation is seen as an irrational phobia which stands in the way of the all-out stimulation of economic activity and employment.

It is not immediately obvious to the public that, for any given rate of productivity change, price increases cannot be reduced unless income in-creases are also reduced. The price realized from the sale of a product or service is, after all, the source of the incomes received by those who jointly produce and market it. Thus if the price of a product is to rise less rapidly, somebody's money income will also have to rise less rapidly — either that of the employees, that of the management, stockholders and bondholders, or the incomes of all the groups involved.

The public must also be brought to realize that smaller increases in money incomes need not leave people worse off than before in any real sense so long as they are matched by correspondingly smaller increases in the price level. Thus a 5 percent increase in annual pay when the cost-of-living is rising by only 2 percent a year should be worth every bit as much to an employee as an 8 percent pay raise would be if prices were rising by 5 percent a year.

Trying to get the public to understand and accept the broad aims of a prices and incomes policy is only one part of the task, however. Many people were critical of the approach followed by the Commission last year on the grounds that it was naive to expect that voluntary restraints would be obser-ved. This was a mis-reading of what the Commission had in mind. We sought to obtain broad agreement on the part of those most directly affected not only on what standards of restraint should apply, but also on the need for effective surveillance and review procedures to determine whether these stan-dards were being observed in practice. Indeed, we also sought acceptance of the need for governments to bring pressure to bear in order to deal with serious cases of noncompliance.

At the National Conference on Price Stability in February of last year, the Commission was able to obtain broad agreement on these matters so far as the 1970 price restraint program was concerned. Our subsequent experi-ence with this program convinced us that in certain circumstances it was possible to operate a rather informal temporary price restraint program in this country on a reasonably effective basis. On the other hand, not much could be achieved in restraining increases in wages, salaries, rents, or other forms of income without adequate recognition of the need for such restraint on the part of those affected and without the strong support of governments to encourage compliance.

The kinds of pressure which have been suggested or tried in order to make a prices and incomes policy effective range all the way from lectures to unfavourable publicity, to tax deterrents, to fines or other forms of legal compulsion directed at those who refuse to comply. It is not surprising that mandatory controls should be regarded as a distasteful last resort in free societies, to be considered only when all avenues of persuasion and appeals for voluntary co-operation have been exhausted. But however voluntary or mandatory, any incomes policy which aims at exerting some degree of direct control over price and income decisions must find solutions for a number of difficult problems.

For example, if the norms of an incomes policy are to be readily understood, they must be spelled out in very simple terms which are bound to appear rather crude when viewed against the complexities of economic reality and the public's sense of what is fair and equitable. One way of trying to meet this problem might be to permit those administering the program considerable flexibility in the detailed application of these norms to particular situations. On the other hand, there would, of course, be strong objection to allowing too much latitude for administrative discretion. In general, the standards of behaviour which are put forward should do as little violence as possible to economic realities and to established institutional procedures for determining prices and incomes.

It has been suggested that these norms might be applied on a selective basis to the more strategic prices and pay structures in the economy rather than across the board. While such an approach has the obvious attraction of administrative simplicity, it raises awkward questions both of economics and of equity. It is by no means the case that the more spectacular price and income increases originate only in the activities of large firms and large employee groups. Thus, if the control system were limited to these groups they would justifiably regard as inequitable the exemption of the rest of the community from similar obligations.

A major source of difficulty arises from the fact that particular price and income levels are adjusted from time to time as part of an on-going process, and the changes are often substantial. An incomes policy must necessarily intervene in this process at a particular point in time, when certain prices and incomes are bound to be lagging temporarily and others are temporarily ahead of the game. Should these discrepancies be accepted as unavoidable, or should an effort be made to sort them out in applying the newly established norms of incomes policy? A related question is whether the general design of the policy should aim merely at freezing the existing pattern of income distribution for a limited period, or whether it should aim deliberately at effecting certain changes which are regarded as socially desirable.

From what has been said so far, it will be evident that reliance on any form of incomes policy is subject to a variety of limitations.

A fundamental limitation arises from the fact that changes in relative prices and relative rates of pay perform important economic functions, notably those of rationing excess demand out of particular markets and of shifting additional labour and other productive resources to such markets from areas of weaker demand. An incomes policy which seeks to contain increases in the general price level is bound to interfere to a greater or lesser extent with changes in particular prices and incomes and thus with the efficient allocation of productive resources.

These problems may not be unduly serious, however, if the period of intervention is as short as a year or two and if the degree of control imposed is not excessively detailed and inflexible. Certain types of incomes policy which have been suggested, such as the use of tax disincentives to try to discourage the granting of large income increases, are intended to permit enough flexibility so that their use over a longer period of time might be contemplated, although it seems unlikely that major problems of this kind could be entirely avoided.

The extent to which reliance can be placed on some form of incomes policy to contain price and income increases and thereby permit higher employment is also limited by the associated degree of demand pressure to which the economy is exposed. If market demand pressures are allowed to become generally excessive, the effectiveness of the control system will deteriorate rapidly and its termination will invite an upsurge of suppressed price and cost increases.

This is not to say, however, that temporary intervention to hold down cost and price increases need become ineffective or end in a price and income explosion if applied over a period in which demand pressures are not excessive in any general sense. Under such conditions, an incomes policy may perform the useful service of getting people's expectations and behaviour attuned once again to relatively low and stable rates of increase in prices and money incomes.

A third limitation on the use of incomes policy is that by no means all prices and incomes are determined in a way which lends itself to some form of direct control. Obvious examples are the prices of goods sold mainly on world markets, prices established by auction or tender, and the incomes of certain types of self-employed professionals.

In such cases, considerations of equity may lead to the conclusion that the introduction of a prices and incomes policy should be supplemented by appropriate use of governmental fiscal or regulatory powers to ensure a fair sharing of the burden of restraint.

Given the intractability of the high employment-price stability dilemma and the limited scope for resolving it quickly or easily by other means, the Commission is of the view that an effective and acceptable form of prices and incomes policy in Canada, though by no means costless in economic terms, could serve as a useful supplement to other policies, that it should not be impossible to devise such a policy, and that further effort and innovation in this direction would be justified.

II. Testimony of H.G. Johnson

With respect to my views regarding inflation, I have considered it primarily from a world point of view. I have become concerned in this problem in the past year or so because in the United Kingdom, the United States, Canada and the European countries there has been a great deal of concern regarding inflation. Therefore, this committee, in a sense, is conducting hearings which are paralleled in other countries.

There are two views on the temporary world inflation: one is that it is a series of accidents in a number of different countries, each to be explained by special sociological, economic factors. That view is espoused by the OECD, but I completely disagree with it. I think that we are facing a world inflation, or at least a western world inflation which has common causes. The main common cause is the inflation in the United States, which has been going on since 1965. This inflation communicates itself to the world because in the modern world the only real force putting pressure on governments to control inflation is the balance of payments. The United States does not have to worry about its balance of payments and, as long as it runs a deficit, no one else has to worry about theirs. In a world system of fixed exchange rates every country must endure, sooner or later, the U.S. inflation.

I remark in my paper on various arguments relating to that proposition. I think that is necessarily true, though the OECD and other commentators seem to think it is not. I would in this connection point out that it is very important for Canadian thinking on these matters to distinguish between what happened up to the beginning of June last year, when Canada was on a fixed rate, and the circumstances now with Canada on a floating rate. I will argue that the maintenance of a floating exchange rate is the only underpinning Canada has if it wants to pursue an anti-inflationary policy.

One of the things that you undoubtedly have been told, and I know you have from reading the testimony of Sir Roy Harrod,[1] is that somehow we face a new sociological situation, in which somehow unions have become more grasping, employers weaker, and so on. Therefore, all of a sudden, we have a collapse of a system. I think that is not true. I think that we can explain the upsurge of inflation in the last two years in the various countries with which we are concerned by lagged expectations, plus special factors which one can list for the various countries.

As I review the world system to the mid-sixties, it was stablized by price stability in the United States. That meant that other countries could have a certain amount of inflation, but it was limited by their ability to compete with the United States in world markets. Since 1965 the United States has had an accelerating inflation, which has meant that everyone else must also have that inflation. As I view it, it is not possible for a small country, and I would include the United Kingdom in that — being a Canadian, I look at the United States as my example of a big country — to fight inflation by the traditional tools of monetary and fiscal policy. As long as we have a fixed exchange rate we will have the world inflation. All we can accomplish by monetary and fiscal policy is to have more unemployment. That is perhaps exaggerating; you can, within limits, contain your inflation relative to world inflation, but you must have the world trend.

In particular, monetary restraint is likely to attract an inflow of capital, which will pose an insuperable problem for the central bank of a small country. In fact, the floating rate in Canada is exactly the result of that problem. If you want to have the benefits of relatively liberal trade and capital movement with the rest of the world, without inflation, you must have a floating exchange rate. That problem cannot be solved simply by revaluing from time to time, because that injects an element of disturbance; it is a transitory benefit, but it will not last.

If you have a floating exchange rate, and only then, you have a possibility of divorcing your price trend from the world price trend. I would emphasize it is viewed in the context of a closed economy, so it is either a policy for the world as a whole or for a country on a floating exchange rate.

The question is how to operate monetary and fiscal policy. I would agree with most Canadian economists, and those elsewhere, that the monetary and

---

[1] [This testimony may be obtained by writing to the Standing Senate Committee on National Finance, Ottawa.]

fiscal policy has been operated so far on far too much of a stop-go basis, which injects a lot of disturbances. It is probably bad for long-run economic growth and it would be better to have what I would think of as a framework policy, a framework for stable, economic growth. This involves not switching the budget from deficit to surplus year by year and not changing the rate of growth of the money supply rapidly year by year. Instead, it provides a long-run framework within which the business community can make projections of where the system is likely to go.

One proposal which you have heard already is for a stable rate of growth of the money supply geared to the economy's potential growth of output. The only point I make with reference to that is that you must recognize that only a flexible exchange rate will permit that policy to be pursued. It is no good recommending a stable monetary growth in an open economy; the monetary growth will be determined by your policy, plus your balance of payments. If other countries' policies are more or less inflationary, you just do not have control of domestic money supply.

One of the questions is: Why is price stability desirable? I would argue that, aside from the balance of payments, the only argument for it concerns the stability in the value of money and the redistributions of income that go with inflation or deflation of an unexpected kind.

To take up the first point, the balance of payments argument is not an argument for price stability; it is an argument for having the same rate of inflation, or deflation, as everyone else. In Canadian history, for most of the interwar period we had a floating rate. We went back to a floating rate for the 'thirties, the reason being that we could not stand the world inflation which we would otherwise have had to face. We went back to a floating rate again in 1950 and again in 1970, because we could not stand the inflation that the world system was imposing on us.

If we are to have a fixed rate of exchange, we must accept the world rate of inflation. That, I think, makes nonsense of any proposal for incomes policy. It is one thing to say we should have an incomes policy to stabilize prices. If there is a fixed exchange rate there cannot be stabilized prices; you have to accept whatever price trend the world imposes on you, which means that you might have to have a very severely inflationary incomes policy. In the modern world you would have to have it. The Germans tried it and they had to take a floating rate instead.

It might possibly be argued that it is possible to have an incomes policy which governs wage increases by the rate of productivity increase. However, to say there must be an incomes policy which makes wage increases equal to productivity increases, plus a guess at how much inflation we should have to fit world circumstances, is something quite different. I cannot see any administrative mechanism that could give that kind of policy.

Supposing there is a floating exchange rate so that you do not have that problem of having to inflate or deflate with the rest of the world, what are the arguments for avoiding inflation? One is to maintain stability in the value of money; the other is to avoid arbitrary redistributions of income and wealth.

With regard to the stability of money, all the evidence we have from any number of inflations is that any inflation within the bounds of possibility is something the public can digest pretty well. The market system will enable them to avoid it. As far as redistributions are concerned, the major redistributions that must be worried about are essentially redistributions of income between people on fixed, government-determined social security benefits, pensions or salaries and other people. It would be a lot easier and more efficient to make adjustments in those benefits, pensions and salaries than to try to stop inflation by deflationary policies.

I come to the argument for an incomes policy. This argument, I have no hesitation in telling you, seems to me to be absolute nonsense. It is the kind of argument people who are unable to face economic reality like to propose as a means of transferring responsibility from the elected representatives of the people to the people themselves, and therefore it seems to me to make no democratic sense whatsoever.

There are two kinds of argument of this kind, one of which is popular in North America and the other in England. I would remark that I have spent, off and on, 25 years of my life in England, and every year somebody wants an incomes policy. They have tried it about four times, and each time it has failed. But it is the old "Maginot line" mentality: find out where the enemy is strongest and then try to overwhelm him by superior numbers. Every time the incomes policy has failed a new generation comes along and says it has failed, not because it is a nonsense idea, but because the last bunch of guys did not have the guts and determination to push it through. If you see something fail four times you may perhaps start to think it was not a good idea to begin with, but that is not the way people react.

One of the arguments is that inflation is caused by the graspingness of trade unions, monopolies and so forth. That idea makes no sense at all to me. Monopoly is a bad thing; trade unionism is a bad thing from the economic point of view, because it raises the wages of some small group of workers by excluding others from the opportunity to have the jobs. But that is a problem society has to cope with; it may decide trade unionism is a good thing and monopoly is a bad thing, or vice versa. Different societies come down on different sides of that question.

Whatever it is, it is a question that is there all the time; it is not a question that comes up only when there is inflation. If I have monopoly power I want to grab the most I can, and I want to grab that every minute; I do not wait for an inflation to decide, "Now is the time to grab." Instead, when an inflation starts I realize it is eroding my monopoly power and I have to restore it by raising the money price of my product. So rises in prices by businesses and trade unions are not a cause of inflation, they are a reaction to inflation by people who have monopoly power and see it being undermined by the inflation. You cannot blame inflation or unions or big businesses; they are reacting to the environment created by whatever is producing the inflation.

The other argument for an incomes policy is that, on the average, people can only get increases in real incomes to the extent that productivity is increasing. If they ask for wage increases or price increases higher than productivity increases, they are fooling themselves. Why don't we just tell them, "Look, boys, for the good of the country don't ask for more than you can really have, and keep wage increases in line with productivity increases, keep prices constant," and so on. After 25 years in England that seems to me to be a misapplication of the public school spirit. The headmaster can call the boys into chapel on Monday and tell them, "Boys, for the good of the school you must eat less tuck; you must satisfy yourselves with shepherd's pie instead of steak," and so on and so forth. He can enforce it because he has the moral authority to do so.

However, that is not the way a capitalist system works. We do not have a headmaster in a capitalist system; we have competitors, and they are out for their own benefit and they are reacting to their own market situation. What we are trying to ask them to do is to ignore the evidence coming to them through the markets which says, "You can have a 20 percent wage increase this year, and if you do not ask for it you are being foolish because that is what you can have." It says to the employer, "You can afford a 20 percent increase this year because there is lots of demand, you need the labour. If you don't give them the increase you are going to have a strike on your hands and then you won't sell the goods," and that is the information they have; it is their own market situation.

What an incomes policy tries to do is tell them, "Forget about the 20 percent, regardless of the evidence of your own eyes " – on both sides, because it takes both sides to make a bargain – "Three percent or five percent is what we tell you from Ottawa you can have." What Ottawa will be trying to do in that circumstance is to persuade these guys to ignore the evidence of their own eyes and to take the words of a bureaucrat that this is the way to do it. I do not think our system works that way. Maybe in Europe they can do it, although all the evidence is that everytime they have tried they have failed. I do not see that our system works the way that system might work.

I had an argument, at the end of March in Paris, with people from the OECD. Their view is, I think, completely uneconomic. The sign of an economic scoundrel is that he resorts to sociology to explain something he does not understand. The idea of an incomes policy is a very simple idea, but it applies entirely to a closed economy. The idea is, if you have wages rising faster than productivity, prices have to rise. Nobody is better off. It is a lot of waste motion. Why not stop it? We will all agree to keep wage increases equal to productivity increases. Prices will be stable. Everybody will get the same thing out of it as he would have otherwise, and we do not have inflation. That is true for a closed economy in which you do not have any foreign trade or foreign capital movements, but if you have foreign trade and foreign capital movements, then many of the prices you are dealing with are determined in foreign markets, and, if the foreign markets are suffering inflation, those prices are going up, and your producers find that they can sell their exports at rising prices. They can afford to pay higher wages over and above the productivity increase. Your industries competing with imports can afford to charge higher prices. They do not have to keep wage increases down to productivity increases. So you find yourself with an inflation.

If you were to try an incomes policy in that period, the incomes policy would have to be productivity increase plus the rate of inflation that would keep us in line with foreign markets. That is, in modern times, but suppose you had thought about it in the 1930s, then we would have had to reduce wages by the world deflation minus the rate of productivity increase.

Well, I can see a target of price stability as something you might possibly be able to administer, although my friend John Young is much more sanguine about that than I am. But I cannot see a government saying, "Well, this year, chaps, you can have productivity increase plus 5 percent." And then next year turning around and saying, "Well, you have to have productivity increase minus 2 percent." I just cannot see any way you could administer that. If you tried to maintain prices as stable as the Germans have been doing, when everybody else is inflating, you would find yourself with a balance-of-payments surplus, capital inflow and foreign reserves coming in that you could not handle. Eventually, either you have to arrange to cope with those surpluses in capital account and current account, or else you have to revalue the currency, or else you have to do what the German did, which is to float up — up. Canada had that problem last year and Canada wisely decided to let it float, because we could not hold Canadian prices down when the Americans and everybody else were inflating.

III. Notes On Incomes Policies by Richard G. Lipsey

An incomes policy represents an attempt on the part of the Government to influence wages and prices using means that can vary from exhortation, through Review Boards to a full paraphenalia of controls with full legal sanction.

Incomes policies have been employed with many objectives in mind, but the most common one is the control of the rate of inflation. In some cases the objective has been to influence the long-term behaviour of the price level; in other cases, the objective has been to hold back inflation temporarily in order to deal with some temporary crisis possibly concerned with the balance of payments.

Incomes policy has been tried in various forms by many countries. It is very difficult to assess their effectiveness because (among other things) we need to have some way of knowing what would have happened under the same set of economic conditions but without an incomes policy. Empirical work has been done and it has greatly narrowed the range of our ignorance but has not produced a result agreed with certainty. Because of this it is quite natural that economists will come to differing conclusions on the usefulness and desirability of such policies.

The efficiency of an incomes policy depends partly on the causes of the inflation for which it is meant to be the cure. Economists distinguish broadly between demand-pull and cost-push inflation. The former are associated with conditions of excess total demand in the economy and often accompany a government deficit financed by inflation — creating increases in the money supply. The latter are associated with a rise in cost (most usually wage costs) but occur *independently of the state of demand*: if unions demand and obtain arbitrarily large increases in money wages whose size is independent of the state of demand; if these wage increases spread to other nonunionized sectors; and if these increases are passed on in terms of higher prices then we have a cost inflation. To be sustained, a cost inflation must be accompanied by a rise in the money supply (or the increased use of money substitutes).

The evidence is that it is very hard to contain a demand inflation for long by means of incomes policies. If for example a budget deficit or an undervalued exchange rate is maintained through increase in the money supply and prices are held down by the control, the gap between demand and supply widens progressively and sooner or later the "lid blows off." When it does "blow off" the price level rises to a level consistent with the state of total demand in the money supply and there is very little evidence to suggest that the controls did anything other than influence the timing of the inflation, leaving its magnitude to be influenced by such economic factors as the size of the increase in the money supply.

Demand inflation is controlled by fiscal and monetary measures, removing excess demand—although in an economy with severe sectorial imbalances, the overall rate of unemployment at which the demand pressure is eliminated may be undesirably high. To the extent that cost-push inflation exists, incomes policies have more to offer. Reducing aggregate demand in place of the cost-push inflation merely lowers output and raises unemployment without doing much to slow down the inflation.

One of the unsettled issues in economics is the extent to which recent inflations have been of the cost-push variety. It was generally agreed that up to the mid 1950's inflations were mainly demand-pull phenomena. In the late 1950's continued mild inflation in the face of slack economic conditions lead to the belief that cost-push elements were important. It is, however, extraordinarily difficult to settle this matter (although I intend to have a try for the Canadian economy in a study to begin in the fall). The matter is critical since the appropriate cure does depend greatly on the correct diagnosis of the causes of inflation.

If inflation is to be contained by an incomes policy the evidence (quoted by Professor David Smith in his study for the Economic Council of Canada) is that the *best* one can hope for is a modest slowing of the rate. Even this is uncertain for reasons explained below.

The key problem is the method of control. In an economy in which wage and price formation is decentralized it is possible that very little can be obtained without a comprehensive apparatus of direct control and sanction. These are costly and presumably would not be accepted unless the gains were thought to be substantial. Also, European experience shows that it is much easier on the cost side to control agreed *rates of pay* than to control *earnings* − although it is the latter that influences costs and hence prices. Where *rates of pay* are controlled in a tight labour market the phenomena of *wage drift* occur. Employers compete for labour by offering bonuses, guaranteed overtime, etc. and this raises costs in spite of a control over agreed rates. Supporters of incomes policy tend to accept what may be called the *key wage and price theory:* there are a few key wage bargains and *key* prices in the economy, and if these can be held down restraint elsewhere will follow more or less automatically. This is as yet an untested theory. If it is right, an incomes policy might be a low-cost operation; if it is wrong a full set of controls may be needed. There seems, however, little support for it in the European experience.

A serious problem with a policy to control wage increases is how to set the agreed or target increases. Smith concludes from his study of European experience that it is easier to enforce a crude policy such as "all wages will go up by the trend rate of productivity increase," but that by freezing the structure of relative wages serious distortions are introduced into the labour market. Further, wage controls policies that are effective in some sectors, for example the public sector, and not the private ones can influence relative wages and seriously affect the movement of labour between the controlled and the uncontrolled sectors. This has been a serious problem in the United Kingdom. A policy that is partly but haphazardly effective could be worse than no policy at all. One of the things on which we still have far too little knowledge is the extent to which relative wages really do affect the allocation of labour.

Canada's heavy dependence on trade with the U.S. makes it difficult for our prices to take a substantially different course from those in the U.S. With a fixed rate of exchange, there is therefore little room for an independent Canadian price level policy. Such a price level policy, with or without the help of an incomes policy, would require either a flexible rate of exchange or a fixed rate that was adjusted quite frequently.

A further problem is that a wage policy that sets a norm for money wage increase equal to the average rate of productivity increase can actually be inflationary. The norm may become a floor, and in rapidly expanding sectors it becomes necessary to allow wage increases in excess of the floor. This tends to build into the system inflationary wage increases that, in the short run at least, are not easily damped by normal policies that reduced total demand. In an empirical study of U.K. incomes policies made by Professor Parkin and myself and published last year, we estimated that during the latter part of the 1960's, U.K. incomes policy may actually have accelerated the rate of inflation by 1 to 2 percent.

Conclusion

If an incomes policy is to be used as a long-term cure for inflation it *must* be operated in a situation in which heavy excess demand pressures are absent. It must then be used to mitigate any cost-push pressures that may be present (and economists are as yet uncertain about how strong these are as long-run phenomena). If this is to work then it is probable — but still a matter of debate — that an extensive apparatus of control will be necessary. The policy is not without risk; a partially effective one can so easily distort the pattern of relative wages and prices and could have important effects on the internal functioning of the economy; even a fully effective policy faces the serious long-term difficulty of finding the right standard for adjusting relative wages and prices; a further risk is that if the norm becomes a floor the policy can actually encourage the inflation that it is meant to contain. The evidence of other countries, although still subject to debate, suggests that an incomes policy cannot halt inflation and the *best* that can be hoped from it is a moderation of inflation in the order of one or two percent.

The possible gains are small enough and the risk large enough to make it appear to me that serious consideration should be given to an alternative policy; (1) remove serious excess demand pressures by traditional fiscal and monetary measures; (2) build into the system inflationary hedges that remove the worst harms done by mild inflation, thus reducing the cost of mild inflation — which after all, most economies have lived with since the war — to a socially acceptable level.

A final problem raised by this alternative policy is whether a mild inflation can persist indefinitely or whether it will inevitably accelerate into a higher inflation. This is currently a subject of debate amongst economists but the postwar evidence of continued mild inflation suggests that, if there is such a tendency to accelerate, it is a very gradual one and we will have a great deal of warning before — if it ever happens — it gets out of hand.

Part D
Urban Economics

In 1971, a report on urban problems was prepared for the Federal Government. An introductory portion of this report is the first selection of this part. It outlines briefly the problems that exist in the city and suggests how policy formulation should proceed to deal with these problems.

The author of the second selection was one of the forces behind the citizen action group to stop the Spadina expressway in Toronto. Although there are a number of urban problems, transportation is one that affects many people in a direct manner. Professor Nowlan presents a simple, conceptual framework for understanding the economics of transportation and illustrates his analysis with numerous Canadian examples. He clearly shows how transportation projects and policies affect individual welfare.

Chapter 9
An Introduction to the Problems
of Urban Canada*

N.H. Lithwick

A. The Problem With Urban Problems

(a) The Superficial Consensus

There can be little doubt that the locus of most of our social problems in the future will be the city. Already there is widespread concern over the forgotten urban poor, the alienated young urbanites, the frustrated middle class seeking shelter, the accelerating pollution of the air and water in and around urban communities, the pointless transformation of most of our central cities into mammoth parking lots, and the general unsightliness of the urban landscape.

What is most striking is the degree to which this concern has recently become a national one. This has both fostered, and been stimulated by, a number of major public events. The *Fourth Annual Review* of the Economic Council of Canada (September 1967) contained a sweeping introduction to urban problems and policies in Canada. Three months later, a Federal-Provincial Conference on Housing and Urban Development was held in Ottawa (December 11, 1967). In August 1968, the Federal Government set up a Task Force on Housing and Urban Development under Mr. Paul Hellyer, and its *Report* was presented on January 22, 1969. The Science Council of Canada, in its Report No. 4, *Towards a National Science Policy for Canada* (October 1968) picked up the same theme, and included as two of the four areas for immediate planning of major projects, urban development and transportation. On February 9-12, 1969 the First Canadian Urban Transportation Conference was held in Toronto, sponsored by the Canadian Federation of Mayors and Municipalities. Finally, urban poverty was examined more closely by the Economic Council in its *Fifth Annual Review* (September 1968).

There appears to be a general consensus arising from these activities, and it is that the problems of the urban unit have multiplied and intensified so greatly as to threaten the long-term viability of the city as we know it.

*Part I (pp. 13-40) of *Urban Canada: Problems and Prospects*, a report prepared by N.H. Lithwick for the Honourable R.K. Andras, Minister of State for Urban Affairs, 1970. Reproduced with the permission of the author.

Present methods for dealing with these problems have been judged to be inadequate, and comprehensive new approaches have been advocated.

All this interest and excitement is probably to the good. For too long there has been insufficient awareness that we are a highly urbanized society, and that the city as it has evolved may no longer be adequate as the environment in which an economically and technologically sophisticated society must operate.

Unfortunately, this conviction that we are faced with impending disaster in our cities is not based on adequate evidence. The data, when used, are often of questionable value and relevance. And even if this information reveals serious problems, it provides little basis for understanding their nature and thereby dealing effectively with them. Few of the above-mentioned inquiries conducted or even drew upon meaningful research. Much was borrowed uncritically from other countries, particularly from the United States with its special racial problems and its particularly large urban conglomerates whose problems are quite different from those in even the largest Canadian cities. Finally, few of the grand new designs have any analytical content. They represent a peculiar amalgam of pure fantasy and particular prejudices. Thus, to date the urban crisis is more an article of faith than a well-understood phenomenon. It is the intention of this Report to inquire rather deeper into the meaning, dimensions, and roots of this so-called crisis.

(b) What Is Urban about an Urban Problem?

If our first task is to investigate the substance of urban problems, it is necessary at the outset to understand what is meant by an "urban problem." To many, this may appear a ludicrous effort — to them the problems are so obvious that this nit-picking constitutes a diversionary tactic preventing us from getting on with the job. Yet it is precisely because we are not clear about this matter that we have been so unsuccessful in dealing with urban problems. How else can we explain how three levels of government and the vast resources of a wealthy society have failed to make any progress towards solving them? There have been major attempts to meet obvious needs: a substantial flow of resources has been poured into housing, schools, hospitals, transportation improvements, and more recently, into low-income housing and urban renewal. But these policies do not appear to have had any ameliorating effect, and the urban problems grow more serious.

It is useful to examine the two principal issues involved in defining urban problems. The first has to do with the *urban-ness* of the problem, and the second with the question of whose problem it is.

The chief difficulty in understanding the urban nature of these problems lies in the failure to distinguish those problems that happen to occur in cities from those that are part and parcel of the urban process. Most discussion focusses on the former, which we shall call *problems in the city*. From this perspective, stress is laid on urban units because the dominance of urbanites in the total population is now clearly established, and indeed their relative importance is increasing dramatically, particularly in the major metropolitan areas. But the problems are not necessarily urban in nature. Urban poverty in backward regions is a reflection of regional underdevelopment, rather than some unique urban phenomenon. Pollution in a one-industry town is essentially an industrial problem, rather than an urban one. Unemployment and inflation, although obvious in urban areas, are not genuine urban problems; their roots lie primarily in the degree to which the nation's overall resources are fully utilized, rather than in the nature of the urban system.

This is not to deny the existence of genuinely urban problems — indeed there are many. There are important areas where solutions must come from other levels of public policy than urban policy, however, and this point must not be lost sight of.

Turning to those problems that are genuinely urban in nature — that are central to the urban process — we find that even here there are serious misunderstandings as to their sources and their very nature. As we shall show in Section C of this Part, and more fully in our research monographs, these problems share a unique characteristic: they are highly interdependent.[1] Housing is related to transportation and land use; these affect the urban poor, the quality of the environment, and the fiscal resources of local governments; and these in turn have severe consequences for housing.

This fundamental interdependence has serious implications for a policy approach that deals with each problem in isolation. Housing policy has added to the stock of urban accommodations, but has led to urban sprawl and fiscal squeeze for the municipalities. Transport policies have moved people faster initially, but have led to further sprawl, downtown congestion, pollution, and rapid core deterioration. Despite these interdependencies, we find, in Part III of this Report, [not presented here] that to date there is no serious attempt within levels of government or between them to coordinate policies. The available interdepartmental committees, with the possible exception of the research-oriented ones, are floundering because the complexity of the problem is overwhelming. No department has been found that seriously considers the impact of its policies on the urban system, despite a widespread awareness of the importance of that impact.

Our research in Part II of this Report [not presented here] offers an explanation for this failure to deal effectively with urban problems. We have found that their interdependence results largely from the fact that they are generated by the process of urbanization itself. The growth of large cities leads to competing demands for the one common feature of all cities, scarce urban space, driving core prices upward and households outward. Transportation, pollution, and poverty problems flow from this. Contained within the process of urbanization, then, are the seeds of the majority of the problems found in the city. From this perspective these problems do not just happen to occur within cities — they are fundamental aspects of the growing city. As such, we might call them *problems OF the city* to distinguish them from the simpler *IN the city* problems.

This view of urban problems demands a radically different approach in public policy. Long-term solutions require intervention in the urbanization process itself. This may appear to pose a severe policy problem. Specific urban problems must now be viewed as symptoms and removing them by traditional methods will not constitute a cure; therefore, our whole policy

[1] Eric Trist refers to this new type of social problem, which emerges from the increasing interconnectedness of the environment clustering formerly isolable problems, as "problem domains." See his paper *Social Aspects of Science Policy*, Paper prepared for the Roundtable on Science and Society (University of Toronto, March 1969).

framework must be reassessed. On the other hand, the key variables required to control the urbanization process may be both easier to manipulate because of their distance from particular individuals and interests, and more effective because of their enormous leverage and scope. The analogy to monetary and fiscal policy readily comes to mind.

If the analysis is correct, policy to deal with urban problems might become substantially more efficient (we explore alternatives in Part III). But this in itself would not constitute "urban policy." By urban policy we mean the pursuit of a carefully defined set of goals. The overriding goals of a society are contained in its national objectives. Traditionally, these include at least freedom, social justice, progress, and national unity and these are ranked in order of importance in different societies according to the desires of their respective members as filtered through the political system.

The urban system in advanced countries evolved largely in response to the pursuit of one of these goals, economic development, which is one dimension of the objective of progress . . . The urban context for development is made necessary by the demands of modern technology, particularly the requirements of large-scale production and hence mass markets, industrial specialization and hence close inter-industrial linkages, and large and specialized labour and capital resources. Because all these can occur only in large dense centres, cities are the *sine qua non* for industrialization and economic development. There can be little doubt that this goal of material progress has been more or less successfully achieved. In the course of achieving it, however, a number of other social goals appear to have been subverted. Thus, the requirements of modern technology appear to have substantially reduced certain individual freedoms, particularly in terms of work, political action, and fundamental consumption choices, while expanding the capacity to choose within the rules of the game established by our economic system. Specialization has improved the lot of those trained and motivated in the appropriate direction. Others have been less successful, and economic segregation has emerged which has made the achievement of community much more difficult.[2] Similarly, progress has provided enormous economic improvement for the majority of urbanites, but has locked a minority into a situation of relatively hard-core poverty, frustrating our goal of social justice.[3] Even the goal of progress contains contradictory elements. Economic progress has occurred, but the consequential destruction of our environment and the other familiar costs of economic growth — waste, built-in obsolescence, human redundancy, and so forth — must be deducted in measuring overall progress.

We have already stressed that these problem areas are natural outcomes of the urbanization process. In other words, the serious imbalance in achieving our national goals, involving sacrifices of most others for the sake of economic progress, is inherently linked to the evolution of our urban system. This is the central aspect of *problems OF the city* and may well be referred to as *the urban problem*.

[2] See Robert Dorfman, "The Functions of the City," in Anthony H. Pascal, (ed.), *Contributions to the Analysis of Urban Problems*, Rand Workshop on Urban Problems, December 18, 1967 — January 12, 1968 (August, 1968).

[3] For the inherent conflict between economic and general social objectives, see Mancur Olson, Jr., "Economics, Sociology and the Best of all Possible Worlds," *The Public Interest*, No. 12 (Summer 1968).

The implication is that equilibrium in achieving our national objectives cannot be restored without intervention in the urban system. This imposes upon us the need for an urban policy. The objective of that policy is the active management of our urban environment to better achieve our fundamental national objectives. We must be very clear on these national objectives and the priorities among them. We must learn much more about the urban process, and we must design strategies for using that process to our advantage. The challenge will be to continue to achieve economic progress while moving towards the attainment of other objectives. This means that the momentum of urbanization will have to be sustained, but carefully controlled.

Controlled urbanization is a particularly tall order, for there is little evidence that such effective meta-policy making[4] can be produced. Indeed, it is one of the anomalies of the modern urban-industrial system that in its expansion technological progress is cumulative. Every innovation builds on preceding ones. But there is little progress in the technology of public policy development. Changes do not constitute a process of steady improvement.[5] Rather, each change cancels out much of what preceded it, so that our current policy mechanisms are not much more advanced than those at Confederation! The growing gap between the technology of problem creation and the technology of problem solution is perhaps the best explanation of the failure of public policy for the cities, and it constitutes what we shall refer to as *the urban policy problem.*

(c) Whose Problems Are They?

The second set of questions that must be raised concerns the incidence of urban problems. Who are the people that really face these problems, and how representative are they of the majority of urbanites?

In a thoughtful essay, Raymond Vernon examines the question of the decaying inner city. He finds that pressure for revitalization comes not from the poor who seek to escape from it, nor from the middle classes who already have escaped, but from

> ... those persons who look upon the central business district as a place where they have to work ... they are leading businessmen, leading bankers, ... those who look on the central business district as an intellectual gathering point ... our intellectuals, our musicians, our principal architects. This is a pretty formidable group that represents the leadership of the community by and large ... they have formulated the problems to meet their own needs — without any intention in the world of disregarding others' needs, but without regard to the fact that their own needs do not constitute the growing problems of the urban area, if you count problems by counting noses.[6]

Although this was written a decade ago, and by a scholar deeply involved in the problems of New York City, the relevance for metropolitan Canada is

4 Y. Dror, *Public Policy Making Re-Examined,* Chandler (1968).
5 Robert Heilbroner, "Socialism and the Future," *Commentary* (December 1969)
6 Raymond Vernon, *The Myth and Reality of Our Urban Problems,* Joint Center for Urban Studies, MIT-Harvard-Stafford Little Lectures of 1961 (1962) pp. 63-64.

not diminished. Consider the kinds of activities that have been occurring in inner cities in Canada. Urban renewal has attempted to improve the core area, largely by displacing the poor and substituting commercial and artistic establishments in the place of unsightly housing. The massive Centennial subsidies were largely for cultural centres for the urban elite. Even the stress on open space in the core and the periphery, and the great pollution debate have been urged essentially for aesthetic purposes, and largely at the instigation of the elite, as are our high new housing standards and zoning laws.

For this elite, then, the problem of the city is the increasing threat to the environment in which they typically work and play. But this is not the problem of the majority. Indeed, while the middle classes no doubt face urban problems, by and large they have substantially benefitted from urban development. The majority have their bungalows with green space, their cars, and their durables — stereos, televisions, snowmobiles. Their problems are essentially social rather than environmental — decent schools, safe neighbourhoods, better jobs.

For the urban poor, the problems are even more social in nature. The problems of decent housing, of improved employment and educational opportunities, of adequate resources for the unemployable — these are their major concerns.

Because the elite as defined above are the articulate members of society, their problems have dominated the debate on the urban crisis. Thus, urban policies have been oriented to improving the urban environment, rather than improving the lot of urban residents.[7] As a result, there has probably been a substantial redistribution of resources in favour of the elite, aggravating the problem of urban inequity.

In our analysis of urban problems, we shall insist on preserving this dichotomy between environmental and social policies[8] and their distributional implications, largely because, as we have found in Research Monograph No. 1, the distributional problem is probably the most severe of all urban problems.

B. Problems IN the City

(a) A Catalogue of Problems

A careful reading of the literature suggests that the following are most often cited as the major urban problems:

> Poverty
> Housing costs
> Transportation congestion
> Environmental decay
> Social unrest
> Fiscal squeeze

---

[7] Some still argue that social improvement derives from environmental improvement. See Norman Pearson, "The Modern City and Society," *Queen's Quarterly* (1961).

[8] For a similar view on this dichotomy, see James Q. Wilson, "Urban Problems in Perspective," in James Q. Wilson, (ed.), *The Metropolitan Enigma* (Cambridge: Harvard University Press, Revised Edition, 1969), Ch. 12.

Others are often cited, but they are essentially constituents of the above-mentioned. Thus, urban sprawl is decried by many, but it is really because it supposedly leads to blight or expensive servicing, rather than because it is a problem in itself, that it raises concern. Rotting cores of cities are seen as a crucial problem, but again they represent a mix of blight, poverty, and housing problems. Pollution is the current major concern, but it is usefully seen as one aspect of the destruction of the environment.

No doubt there are others that do not fit neatly into our classification scheme. The reason for excluding them is to allow us to deal with the most significant ones. Hopefully, some of our findings will be relevant for these other less pervasive problems as well.

(b) Symptoms vs. Causes

In most analyses of urban problems, there has been a tendency to deal with them as if they were obvious ills for which direct solutions might easily be found. The presence of blight compels us to remove it; the presence of high housing costs urges upon us the need to reduce the most conspicuous elements of cost, land prices; the presence of congestion on our roads leads us to build more roads.

It should hardly surprise us that these problems have not been solved. In most cases the solutions have aggravated the problems. The removal of blight via urban renewal has led to its spread; the subsidization of land acquisition in the suburbs has led to costly sprawl and further land-cost increments; the building of roads has spread the population further and induced it to drive more cars for more miles.

The greatest difficulty here is that there has never been an adequate diagnosis of urban problems. There is little understanding of their extent, their impact, and primarily, their causes. As a result, policy has amounted to dealing with symptoms, not causes, and the underlying forces continue to generate the problems with increasing severity as the urbanization process accelerates.

(c) Myth and Reality

In an attempt to substantiate this claim and to trace out several implications, we review the two currently most stressed problem areas, housing and poverty. In both we find that there has been an inadequate comprehension of the problem. This stems partly from the complexity of the problems themselves, but more important is the failure to realize that the problems are in fact central to the urban process. As a result, they are functionally interdependent components of a highly complex evolving urban system. Attempts to deal with them piecemeal are likely to be ineffective and perverse.

(i) Housing

Increased concern has been voiced over the failure of the housing market. Rapid increases in the prices of new homes, in rents, and in costs of running older homes have been documented. Some evidence on this is presented in Table 1.

Table 1

**Elements in the Increase in Cost of Accommodations
in Canada, 1949-1968**

	1960	1964	1965	1966	1967	1968	Percent Change 1964-68
(a) Prices (1949=100)							
Rent Index	142.8	145.0	146.0	148.5	153.5	160.3	10.6
Home Ownership							
Index	145.0	162.8	169.5	177.0	187.0	200.6	23.2
Property Taxes	143.4	163.1	169.1	176.8	184.0	196.2	20.3
Mortgage							
Interest	109.3	121.3	125.5	130.8	137.2	149.3	23.1
New Bungalows							
Index	182.0	204.3	214.1	233.8	239.2	242.8	18.8
Land Cost	359.2	428.2	428.6	457.5	480.2	511.0	19.3
Construction							
Cost	159.2	173.4	183.5	200.7	205.0	207.4	19.6
Cost per Sq. Ft.	151.0	161.1	168.2	181.5	188.8	198.7	23.3
Consumer Price							
Index	128.0	135.4	138.7	143.9	149.0	155.2	14.6
(b) Apt. Vacancy Rates							
*Large Units**							
Halifax		3.4	3.9	3.4	2.5		
Montreal		6.6	5.9	4.4	1.2		
Ottawa-Hull		8.2	8.8	7.1·	1.9		
Quebec		6.6	6.4	5.1	2.2		
Toronto		2.6	1.5	0.9	1.1		
Vancouver		4.4	4.0	1.3	1.0		
Winnipeg		5.6	4.9	4.1	1.5		
All Metropolitan							
areas†		n/a	n/a	4.3	3.7		

*More than six units.
†All dwellings regardless of size.

Sources: (a) DBS, *Prices and Price Indexes,* and CMHC, *Canadian Housing Statistics, 1968,* pp. 53 and 76-80, and DBS, *National Accounts.*
    (b) CMHC, *Background Papers for the Federal-Provincial Conference on Housing and Urban Development,* December, 1967, Attachment No. 1.

Accepting for the moment the assumption that aggregative indexes are relevant, one is tempted to concur in the view that relative prices have turned sharply against housing. The conventional aggregative explanations of this phenomenon are less than satisfactory, however, and require some critical analysis. If price increases were due to excess demand, we would expect to find evidence of growing shortages concurrent with the rise in prices. The data on apartment vacancies are typically referred to and these do indeed show growing tightness in the major urban centres. But the rent index, which is the most relevant measure of price for this category, shows the lowest rate of increase — lower even than the rise in the Consumer Price Index.

As for housing, it is difficult to get a direct measure of changes in excess demand. One useful indicator is the degree of crowding. With shortages, we would expect an increase in crowding as one aspect of the adjustment process. The number of families per dwelling fell during the period, however, from .95 in 1951 to .85 in 1964 and to .84 by 1967.[9] It should be noted that this family measure may not be a wholly appropriate test, because almost all of the increase in demand for new housing has come from the subdivision of family units and the emergence of non-family households, resulting largely from the pattern of household choice by young adults.

An alternative measure that is concerned with all households does not change this conclusion. The percentage of crowded households, defined as ones in which there are more than one person per room in the dwelling, fell steadily from 15.4 percent in 1961 to 11.9 percent in 1968.[10] Even this measure might not capture one important adjustment to scarcity, which entails the increased use of lower quality space. Once again, the relevant data do not support the hypothesis of great shortage. Measures ranging from hot and cold water to flush toilets and baths show steady and substantial improvement.[11] Indeed, by the 1961 census, only 5.6 percent of all occupied dwellings were found to be in need of major repair, and in metropolitan areas, the proportion was even lower, 3.4 percent.[12]

These additional pieces of evidence do not negate the presence of housing problems, but they do suggest that the problems might have been grossly exaggerated. One particular dimension that is not captured by these aggregative measures is the distributional problem, a subject we shall return to following our discussion on poverty.

Attempts to explain the presumed housing crisis have been notoriously one-sided. Invariably the blame is laid on the supply function: the increasing concentration in the house-building industry, the scarcity of land, the backwardness of housing technology, high interest rates and taxes. Indeed, there exists much evidence on all these aspects in Canada. For example, 34 large firms, constituting less than 2 percent of this regionally segregated industry, built just under one-third of all the new dwelling units financed under National Housing Act loans to builders in 1968.[13] As for land, most indexes show substantial price increases relative to most other commodities.[14] Compared to best practices elsewhere, including modular and industrialized construction, we appear to lag significantly. Finally, the current trend to higher world interest rates and the 11 percent sales tax on building materials,[15] combined with a rapidly growing demand for publicly supplied urban services,[16] largely financed through the real property tax, have added substan-

[9] Calculated from M. C. Urquhart and K. Buckley, *Historical Statistics of Canada* (Cambridge University Press, 1965) p. 510; and CMHC, *Canadian Housing Statistics, 1968*. Table 98, p. 70, and internal CMHC stock of dwelling estimates.
[10] Calculated from DBS, *Household Facilities and Equipment, 1961-68*, Table 1.
[11] CMHC, *Canadian Housing Statistics 1968*, Table 92, p. 64.
[12] *Ibid.*, Table 93, p. 65.
[13] Large builders are those constructing more than 100 units per year. From CMHC, *Canadian Housing Statistics, 1968*, Table 92, p. 64.
[14] With one major qualification, and that is the fact that the indexes typically include serviced and unserviced land. Preliminary inquiry suggests that changes in the mix towards serviced land – usually through new municipal requirements – do bias the index upward substantially.
[15] Implemented by the Federal Government in three stages: June 1963 (4%), April 1964 (4%), and January 1965 (3%). Economic Council of Canada, *Third Annual Review* (November 1966) Chart 4-13, p. 111.
[16] These are Baumol goods typically, since the majority of them are not subject to productivity increase and hence face rapidly rising prices. W. J. Baumol, "Macroeconomics of Unbalanced Growth: The Anatomy of Urban Crisis," *American Economic Review*, LVII, No. 3 (June 1967) pp. 415 ff.

tially to the cost of home provision. Not surprisingly, the bulk of the report of the Hellyer task force was devoted to correcting the supply side.

Unfortunately, such moves are not costless; otherwise the approach would be unexceptionable, a pure efficiency gain. The moment resources must be used to influence supply, we must begin to talk about benefits, and this gets us into the whole question of demand — so conveniently ignored in much of the current discussion.

There are two ways to ignore demand: to assume that it is inelastic with respect to price; or to claim that it should be. Either way, all price changes can be blamed on the supply side and the conclusions already outlined can be drawn. The Economic Council and CMHC have employed the first assumption. Their forecasts of housing demand are completely price free. The demand for houses is determined by calculating the number of households, with some minor adjustments for vacancies and replacements. Table 2 presents the important elements in this approach.

Table 2

Sources of Demands for New Housing, 1951-1966 and Estimates to 1981

(Annual Averages, in thousands)

Period	Net Family Formation	Net Undoubling	Non-Family Household Formation	Total Net Household Formation	Demand for New Housing*
		Actual			
1951-56	84.6	7.1	12.4	104.1	99.2
1956-61	87.0	10.0	28.6	125.6	132.6
1961-66	77.7	10.3	41.0	129.0	140.6
		Estimates			
1966-71	113.0	10.0	50.0	173.0	195.6
1971-76	130.1	10.0	56.0	196.1	225.6
1976-81	146.9	10.0	60.0	216.9	255.5

*Includes replacement demands and vacancy requirements.

Source: CMHC, *Background Papers, op. cit.*

Such an approach to demand is highly questionable. It derives not from consumer preferences and their articulation in the face of a set of relative prices, but from a technocrat's perception of what they ought to have — their *needs*. If prices of houses were to go up, it is hardly reasonable to assume that the same number of units would be demanded — there would necessarily be some elasticity to the demand curve. Thus, to be useful, these forecasts require a projection of different quantities for each set of housing prices, a forecast of supply, and then an equilibrium price-quantity configuration. Independent of price, these measures of "demand" are quite meaningless and possibly misleading.

The alternative concept of demand is that it should be inelastic because of the belief that housing is a right — the view of the Hellyer task force.[17]

[17] "Every Canadian should be entitled to clean, warm shelter as a matter of basic human right." Task Force on Housing and Urban Development, *Report* (January 1969) p. 22.

This concept is essentially a philosophical one; the economic sources of such basic rights are impossible to determine. The economic *consequences*, however, are less difficult to deal with. Once again the question of supply comes to the fore, and the role of the marketplace is to supply these basic requirements as cheaply as possible. Market failures are necessarily blamed on supply and its determinants, and policies are hence supply-oriented: reduce speculation in land, promote technological progress in construction, reduce high taxes and financing costs. And it is just such recommendations that occupy the entire report of the task force.

When the two issues — inelasticity and housing as a right — are built into public policy, some serious consequences follow. But first, let us consider the evidence on elasticity. Chung has found that over time the price elasticity of demand for the housing stock is about − 1.0.[18] His estimating procedures create some difficulties in the acceptability of this figure because of an adjustment for bias; his initial estimate was − 0.35 which, though less, gives little grounds for accepting the zero elasticity assumption.

With some further information, a related point emerges. Oksanen has found that for roughly the same period the income elasticity of demand (stock) is 0.5.[19] Winnick's analysis shows that it is possible to conclude that there has been a shift of preferences by consumers away from housing if the income elasticity is greater than that for price. He finds that for the United States, such was the case over a long period of time.[20] The Canadian estimates are not sophisticated enough to draw such a conclusion, but the debate is highly suggestive.

It may well be that there has been a change in the tastes of Canadians away from houses and towards other goods and services. For example, between 1961 and 1966, despite similar trends in unit prices, the volume of new cars sold increased by 55 percent as compared to 40 percent for housing, so that by 1966 the total outlay on new cars was absolutely greater than that for new dwellings.[21] To the extent that these data are indicative of a change in tastes, failure to deal adequately with the demand side is bound to lead to serious policy errors. Related to this question is the changing nature of the commodity being sought, and this is explained largely by demographic and social factors. Thus, the growing number of elderly people and of independent young people no doubt contributes to the shift in demand away from houses as such to multiple-unit dwellings. From constituting one-seventh of all new dwelling units built in 1949, multiple-unit dwellings are now more than half.[22] This increase can be explained partly by the relatively greater increase in price of single units,[23] although the sharp divergence in price trends has been apparent only recently. When we realize that this shift took place in the face of concerted efforts by the public sector, and particularly CMHC, to promote the purchase and construction of single detached

---

[18] J. Chung, "L'analyse de la demande de logements-propriétaires: l'expérience canadienne," *Actualité Economique* (Avril-Juin, 1967).

[19] E. H. Oksanen, "Housing Demand in Canada, 1947 to 1962: Some Preliminary Experimentation," *Canadian Journal of Economics and Political Science*, XXXII, No. 3 (August 1966).

[20] L. Winnick, "Housing: Has There Been a Downward Shift in Consumers' Preferences," in W.L.C. Wheaton, G. Milgram, and M.E. Meyerson, *Urban Housing* (New York: The Free Press, 1966) pp. 154 ff. and subsequent criticism by Jack Guttentag, pp. 162 ff.

[21] DBS, *Canadian Statistical Review*, and CMHC, *Canadian Housing Statistics, 1967*, Tables 1 and 15.

[22] CMHC, *Canadian Housing Statistics, 1968*, Table 7, p. 7.

[23] See Table 1, page 94.

homes almost exclusively, the sources of the housing problem become rather clearer.[24] Rather than being faced with a clearly demonstrated taste for detached housing, the public sector promoted that taste and probably induced thereby an increase in the total demand for accommodation. Furthermore, that specific form of accommodation is extremely costly in social terms, raising very substantially the demand for scarce urban land, tying up larger quantities of capital per unit of dwelling, and compounding other urban problems. The housing crisis, then, is in large part a result of misguided public policy designed to cope with an issue that was only partially understood.

Thus far we have not come to grips with the question of *needs*, or housing as a "right." If society judges this to be a valid use of its collective resources in the light of full knowledge, then there is little one can do but indicate the costs and the possible allocational effects, including the impact of expanded social demand on price. There is certainly less than full knowledge on this issue, so the case remains tenuous. Furthermore, there is a tendency to confuse demand, and even need, with *wants*. It is judged that, because everyone wants a home, this constitutes a need. But this unanimity is neither surprising nor very useful. Wants differ from demands because they are unconstrained by income and price limitations. In addition, they are private, and hence provide no compelling reason to be accepted as needs. This three-fold confusion has plagued rational analysis of the housing market, and possibly it serves to explain the strong preference for neglecting the demand side altogether, although at great cost in terms of useful policy making.

(ii) Urban Poverty

The second important area over which great concern have been voiced, particularly by the Economic Council of Canada, is the whole question of poverty. The ECC found that three-fifths of all low-income non-farm families lived in urban areas in 1961, and 60 percent of these were in metropolitan areas. But the incidence of poverty was lowest in the largest cities, and indeed this group of urban poor amounted to less than 9 percent of all non-farm families in Canada.[25]

This evidence suggests that the magnitude of the problem of urban poverty is less than has been commonly believed — large cities tend to be middle class. And more recent survey findings suggest that there has been a steady decline in the proportion of non-farm families classified as poor, from 26 percent in 1961 to under 20 percent in 1965.[26]

But the finding that poverty is declining, and is relatively less prevalent in major urban areas, does not alleviate the problems of the poor. Unfortunately, the ECC made no systematic attempt to cross-classify the data collected on the poor, with the exception of educational attainment, so that it is

---

[24] CMHC, *Canadian Housing Statistics, 1968*, Table 14, p. 14. In 1960, publicly financed housing was 4:1 for single detached units, compared to 4:3 for privately financed. Only in 1968 was the emphasis on such units reversed.

[25] Economic Council of Canada, *Fifth Annual Review*, 1968, Table 6-3, p. 111. Data are from Jenny R. Podoluk, *Incomes of Canadians*, 1961 Census Monograph, DBS (Ottawa, 1968).

[26] Gail Oja, "Problems of Defining Low Economic Status for Poverty Studies," *Canadian Statistical Review* (September 1968) p. iii. The poverty line has been adjusted to account for price changes.

impossible even to describe the situation of the poor located in large urban centres.[27] As a result, most of the Council's generalizations about the characteristics of the poor are not very relevant for our purposes.

Our own findings (see Research Monograph No. 1) suggest that the prevalent view of the urban poor is excessively narrow and has led to misguided policy recommendations. We find that the urban poor are generally elderly individuals and persons who are otherwise unemployable. The unemployed and the under-employed constitute a very small proportion of the urban poor. Thus, the stress on job-retraining and manpower policies as a cure for urban poverty is inappropriate. They will no doubt assist some of the urban poor, but they can do little for the overall poverty problem.

It is not necessary to present in detail the analyses contained in Research Monographs Nos. 1 and 2. The point is that, to date, we have understood very little of the problems for which we have proposed solutions. The images of the problems that have arisen are based largely on myth and presumption, and until these are destroyed, urban policy is destined to be irrelevant.

C. Problems OF The City

(a) The Interdependence of Urban Problems

In the preceding section, several key urban problems were examined largely from a public policy perspective. The failure of public policy in dealing with the problems of housing and poverty was shown to be in part due to an inadequate perception of the issues involved. Thus, the demand for housing has been neglected, and the sources of poverty and the needs of the poor are not really known. Consequently, policy has been based on a collection of myths, largely untested, and usually wrong when more carefully examined. Indeed, much public policy has tended to aggravate these problem areas: housing has been a major contracyclical activity with potentially great distributional effects; slums have been seen as a problem of ugliness, the elimination of which has been extremely costly for the urban poor.

These perception and policy failures are not restricted to the areas discussed. In the field of transportation, for example, the problem has always been viewed as one of moving the extant population more efficiently. Rarely have innovations proven to be successful, however, for their introduction has induced changes that are ultimately self-defeating. The public economy of the city has been almost entirely financed from a very weak tax base. Real estate is but one component of property, and property itself is a poor measure of ability to pay, and even of benefit from urban goods. Yet the property tax is the sole direct source of revenue of municipalities. Grants from provinces have kept these economies functioning, but the provinces do not have the most elastic revenue sources — the personal and corporate income taxes which are largely federal. Thus, a poor tax base and fiscal squeeze impose efficiency and distributional costs on the urban community that other levels of government have not adequately alleviated.

---

[27] The evidence on education is suggestive: while less well educated than the urban rich, the urban poor are substantially better educated than the rural non-farm. *Ibid.*, Chart 6-3, p. 118.

Even if each of these problems were dealt with correctly, however, it is not clear that they would be solved. They are so interdependent that the effect of each on the others is more important than the mechanisms internal to any one in isolation. It is useful to examine this interdependence between the two problems discussed above — poverty and housing — to illustrate this hypothesis. One important area where they converge is in the question of slums. Once again, the general explanation of the emergence of slums relies largely on supply factors. Slums emerge because of an inadequate supply of housing. In the face of scarcity, the poor are least capable of competing in the open marketplace and are thus forced to crowd into inferior dwellings, adding to their deterioration.

As we shall argue later, this supposition neglects the central urban process which is instrumental in creating slums downtown where the poor are typically housed (Chart 1). It also neglects the important question of demand. Given low incomes, the poor cannot afford other than inferior housing. Their problem may largely be one of inadequate income — i.e., poverty — rather than a housing problem *per se*.[28] Attempts to solve the more basic problem by dealing with its symptom may be highly inefficient and indeed inappropriate.

Consider the action taken previously to eliminate urban slums. It was felt that if enough houses were built, the better off would move into newer units leaving an adequate supply to "trickle down" to the poor. It is generally conceded that this scheme was ineffective. The richer merely used more space and nothing to note trickled down. It was then felt that all that was needed was a push at the bottom. If slums were removed, the poor would have to improve their accommodations. This artificially created scarcity made matters worse; slums merely spread, and the poor were exported where spreading was resisted.

The third solution, public housing, also is questionable, because it identifies the poor by a most obvious symbol. Not surprisingly, it is resisted by some poor and most wealthier surrounding neighbours. Not once has there been a concerted attempt to deal with the demand side, despite the evidence that supply policies have not solved this persistent problem.

The issues of housing and poverty converge also in the general inability of a growing segment of the population to afford accommodation.

> This housing market of relatively short supply and relatively high cost has made the quest for adequate accommodation a major problem for more than the lowest income groups. They have a problem, to be sure, but so do those in the next income brackets, the "average" wage earners of the $5,000 to $7,500 range . . . the home ownership dream of many Canadians is just that — a dream. Instead they are left to scramble in the rental market to obtain accommodation, *much of it ill-suited for family living* . . . This is the group who, in many urban centres are *[sic]* increasingly earning the designation of the "affluent" poor.[29]

[28] This is confirmed in a recent study by Richard F. Muth, *Cities and Housing* (U. of Chicago Press, 1969) esp. p. 362.
[29] Task Force on Housing and Urban Development, *Report, op. cit.* p. 15. (Emphasis mine, N.H.L).

Chart I

Location of the Poor   Less than $4,250

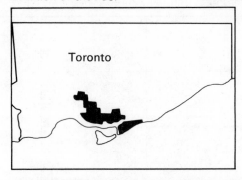
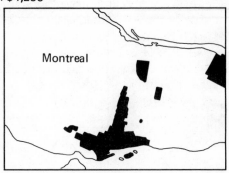

Sources: 1961 Census of Canada; DBS, *Population and Housing Characteristics by Census Tracts,* 1963. Montreal Catalogue No. 95-519. Toronto Catalogue No. 95-530.

It is not possible to trace accurately the relative movements of housing prices for various income groups. But for the period 1961-1965 some crude estimates can be derived.[30] For the lowest third of the income distribution,[31] family income rose by 25 percent over this period while the price of homes they typically purchased rose by 35 percent. The next 50 percent of the income distribution[32] had an income increase of 25 percent, with the price of homes they tended to buy rising by only 18 percent. It would appear that in this period, the poor were indeed made worse off by the trend in housing prices. In addition, although our crowding indexes suggest no increase in scarcity in the aggregate, the absolute position of the poor regarding housing might have deteriorated with improvements by the majority explaining the satisfactory national averages. Certainly the position of the "affluent poor" does not appear to have deteriorated in this brief period. Over a longer period, 1961-1968, again the increase in the cost of housing for the lowest end of the income distribution far exceeded that of the middle groups.[33] Thus, our admittedly weak evidence does not tend to support the theory of middle class immiserization regarding housing. Better longitudinal data would permit us to deal with this question more adequately, but in terms of overall priorities this problem appears to be less severe than claimed by the Hellyer task force.[34]

It would appear, on the basis of the above evidence, that the central feature of urban problems is indeed their interdependence. Because each problem is itself so complex, and the interdependencies are so variegated, it

---

[30] Income data supplied by Gail Oja, DBS. Housing costs from CMHC, *Canadian Housing Statistics, 1968*, Table 56, p. 44 and Table 66, p. 50.

[31] In 1961, they were found in the $0-4,000 income bracket, and in 1965, $0-5,000.

[32] In 1961, they covered the $4-8,000 bracket, and in 1965, $5-10,000. These are presumably the "affluent poor" in the quotation referred to.

[33] CMHC, *Canadian Housing Statistics, 1968.*

[34] It is true that all groups faced a very tight housing market after 1966, when housing starts fell to 134,000 from 167,000 the preceding year, and most of this decline was in urban centres. However, this is attributable to the tight monetary policy being pursued at the time. This shows up in the sharp rise in the interest rate on conventional mortgages from 6.9% in 1965 to 8.8% in 1968, and the increase in downpayments required. (*Ibid.*, Table 1, p. 1, and Table 53, p. 41.) This cyclical phenomenon is well known, yet the confusion over cyclical and secular patterns continues to plague much of the public discussions on housing. By 1968, housing starts were up to 197,000 and for 1969, the evidence suggests the 200,000 mark was easily surpassed.

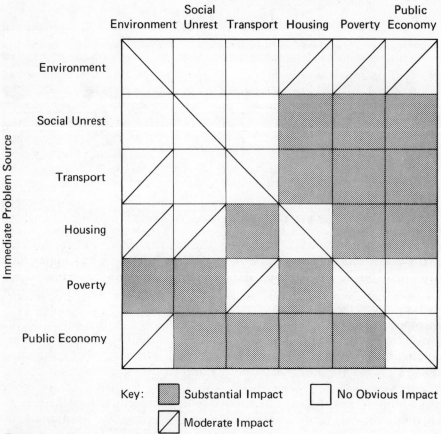

Figure 1
Hierarchy of Interdependence of Urban Problems

is difficult to measure the precise relationships between them. Despite this, it is useful to illustrate this interdependence and to assign some weights, based on our analysis, to the degree of that interdependence.

In Figure 1, we have triangulated this matrix, so as to indicate the hierarchy of interdependent problem areas on the basis of implicit weights.

It is of interest that there are only five zero cells in the thirty possible, and that there is major interdependence in seventeen of the thirty. The weakest problem area in terms of interdependence is environmental destruction; the greatest are the public economy problem and poverty, followed by housing.

It should be added that the system is recursive: a poverty problem aggravates the housing problem, which in turn augments the poverty problem, both directly and indirectly via transport and the public economy. This means that the links are highly complex and diverse, and that the ramifications of an urban problem are substantially wider than simple bilateral examination would tend to suggest.[35]

---

[35] This interdependence is used to indicate the possible perverse effects of simple-minded policy making in a study by Jay W. Forrester, *Urban Dynamics* (Cambridge: MIT Press, 1969).

(b) The Sources of Urban Problems

The evidence cited strongly suggests that urban problems are so intermeshed that they are indeed part and parcel of a total process that we have referred to as the urban process. This imposes upon us the need to understand that process more fully if we genuinely seek to deal effectively with these urban problems. Most useful in this connection is a dynamic approach based on the development of the urban system.

More than most systems, the urban network is dependent on its past development. The vast amounts of capital tied up in infra-structure in transit links and in private fixed investments dictate that changes are severely constrained. Thus the pattern as well as the location of most cities today is in large part a result of these historical developments. We intend to analyze only one dimension of these developments, the emergence of an urban economy. Because the analysis is limited to economic variables, the explanatory power must remain incomplete; geography, politics, social structure, and accident all contribute to the emergence and functioning of Canadian cities. Nevertheless, the model we intend to develop is able to provide additional insights into the process of urbanization and the emergence of urban problems. The full articulation of the model is presented in Part II of this Report [not presented here]. Here, we merely summarize the process.

Early Canadian towns emerged typically as Central Places,[36] providing the predominantly rural export-oriented economy with goods and services. As such, they were little more than collection depots, and a view of such urban units as essentially spaceless would be fairly accurate.

In the course of economic development in this country, the technical linkages established by our successive staple exports were increasingly located in certain key urban nodes.[37] This was due not only to location advantages, particularly in the case of port cities such as Montreal and later Vancouver, but also to the fact that important inter-industrial linkages could be established in these units. On the production side, the city provides a maximum degree of potential complementarity between industries. The role of final demand is also relevant here, for as incomes rose with successful staple exploitation, tastes shifted towards non-agricultural goods of the sort that — because of the aforementioned economies — are produced in cities. As a result, both supply mechanisms and demand pressures ensured the increasing relative importance of urban units, particularly as import replacement became feasible.

This process tended to become increasingly self-sustaining. As demands for urban goods grew, the compensation of labour in the urban unit grew apace, attracting labour and hence urban population. The expanded scope of production permitted increasing specialization and hence greater productivity, higher incomes, and so on.

The expansion of varieties as well as quantities of job opportunities together with an increasing spectrum of goods and services for consumption

[36] For a brief review of Central Place Theory, the gem of theoretical geography, see D. Michael Ray, "Urban Growth and the Concept of Functional Region," in N. H. Lithwick and G. Paquet, (eds.), *Urban Studies: A Canadian Perspective* (Toronto: Methuen, 1968) Ch. 3, pp. 46-54.

[37] See M. H. Watkins, "A Staple Theory of Economic Growth," in W. T. Easterbrook and M. H. Watkins, *Approaches to Canadian Economic History*, Carleton Library No. 31 (Toronto: McClelland and Stewart, 1967).

made the city irresistible to the rural population, more specifically to the young. Migration of the rural population to the city swelled the size of the urban labour force, kept wages relatively low, and induced further economic expansion in the city.[38]

Only a limited number of nodes could grow to become major urban units — economies of scale and transportation costs ensured that. Such factors as location, political vigour, and often good luck determined which ones would be favoured. Within these, increased functional differentiation laid the basis for self-sustaining growth.[39]

This view of the urban unit, as inextricably linked to the process of economic development, provides the first insight into the nature of modern cities as economically sophisticated production and consumption centres. Second, the particular mix of economic activity can be related to the spatial arrangements within the city. For an understanding of this combination of factors, a relatively simple but generally neglected aspect of urbanization must be taken into account. Early cities, as we have seen, were viewed as essentially spaceless. They were small units using small quantities of land relative to their hinterland. The large modern city cannot be so viewed. Increasing volumes of economic activity require increasing quantities of land as a direct input. Furthermore, the growing labour force requires land as part of its own housing input. This increasing demand for land conflicts with the limited supply that characterizes the urban unit.

Without transport costs, this problem would be non-existent — the supply of land would almost be infinitely elastic. But with present technology distance does impose costs, and each land user is compelled to trade off distance against the quantity of land desired to minimize costs.[40] Thus, we would expect that market-oriented activities, such as retail trade and services, will be found near the Central Business District, while manufacturing and wholesale trade would be more typically located towards the urban fringe. Evidence by Loewenstein for the United States confirms these hypotheses,[41] although no comparable Canadian evidence exists.

We thus have two mechanisms to explain the growth and pattern of cities: one is macro-dynamic, relating urbanization to economic development; the other is micro-static, allocating economic activities within the urban unit. The analytical device that can be used to relate them is the input-output table, where each activity is assigned locational and land using coefficients. No empirical work on this issue has as yet been produced, but the barriers are imposed largely by lack of data rather than by the theory. Thus, the analysis that follows is still in the form of hypotheses that remain to be proven, although casual observation suggests that they are valid.

How do these two mechanisms generate the urban problem? First, we have an economy that is undergoing rapid economic development. For reasons already cited, this takes place increasingly in an urban environment, and

[38] In this view, urbanization is the necessary institutional form for development based on cheap labour of the sort analyzed by W. Arthur Lewis "Economic Development with Unlimited Supplies of Labour," *The Manchester School* (May, 1954).

[39] In more technical terms, the off-diagonal elements in the urban input-output table became increasingly filled in. See W. Leontief, "The Structure of Development," *Scientific American*, 209, No. 3 (September, 1963) p. 148.

[40] This process is more fully developed in N. H. Lithwick and G. Paquet, *op. cit.* Ch. 5.

[41] L. K. Loewenstein, *The Location of Residences and Work Places in Urban Areas* (Scarecrow Press, 1965).

relatively more in large urban units. Evidence is available for the key economic and demographic variables, and some of the data are contained in the following table.

Table 3

Large City Population Growth in Canada, 1871-1961

	1871	1901	1921	1941	1951	1961
(a) Number of Urban Complexes						
100,000 and over	1	2	7	8	15	18
30,000 – 99,999	2	8	11	19	20	25
5,000 – 30,000	16	43	70	85	102	147
over 5,000	19	53	88	112	137	190
(b) Percent of Population						
Urban	18.3%	34.9%	47.4%	55.7%	62.4%	69.7%
Percent of Population in PRMD's[†]	n/a	26.0%	35.4%	40.2%	43.3%	48.3%
(c) Increase of population over previous decade						
100,000 and over	n/a	n/a	32.2%	9.8%	14.2%	28.2%
						MA* 45.4%
30,000 – 99,999	n/a	n/a	27.0%	12.2%	33.2%	33.3%
						MA* 37.4%
over 5,000	n/a	n/a	31.8%	12.0%	18.7%	28.5%
						MA* 30.9%

*Including Metropolitan Area Fringes.
†Principal Regions of Metropolitan Development.

Sources: L.O. Stone, *Urban Development in Canada,* DBS, 1961 Census Monograph, Ottawa, 1967.
  (a) Table 4.2, p. 72.
  (b) Table 2.2, p. 29.
  (c) Table 6.2, p. 132.

It can be seen that the largest centres, including their suburban fringes, underwent the most rapid increases in population in the past. This trend will continue so that by the end of this century, well over one-half of all Canadians will be living in the twelve largest metropolitan areas. The implications in growth terms are even more impressive. Of the sixteen million persons added to our population by that time, 11.5 million or three-quarters of this increment will be located in these twelve centres. The largest centres will be affected most: Montreal and Toronto alone will accommodate more than half (6.5 million) of all this metropolitan growth, together accounting for one-third of the entire Canadian population by the end of the century.[42]

The concentration of economic activity in these centres further accentuates their dominance. By 1966, Montreal and Toronto accounted for over one-third of all employment in Canadian manufacturing, wholesale trade, and finance.[43] In addition, 60 percent of all Canadian taxpayers resided in those cities in 1963.[44]

[42] See Part III of this Report [not presented here].
[43] W. G. Gray, M. Jalaluddin, and F. Charbonneau, *A Tale of Two Cities: Economic Growth and Change in Toronto and Montreal*, Economics Division, Policy and Planning Branch (ARDA) (August-December, 1968) p. 2.
[44] *Ibid.*, p. 3.

As for family incomes, in large centres they are more than 50 percent higher than in rural areas, and 30 percent higher than small urban centres,[45] so that the economic weight of the large cities is much greater than their simple demographic weight. Thus, the growth of Canadian cities in terms of ecomomic activity and population has been not only an important source of our rapid economic development,[46] but a major consequence as well.

This rapid growth leads to a rapidly expanding demand for urban space. Given the fixed supply of urban land, price is driven up as fast as these demands rise. This increase in price leads to the exclusion of certain users with lower demands, occasioned by lower incomes or acceptable alternatives, from particular sub-markets. As they move into other sub-markets, prices there are forced up and the process continues to rebound throughout the urban system. Thus, the urban unit is the locus of a continuing struggle to acquire increasingly scarce land, and it is this struggle that underlies many urban problems.

Consider first our housing problems. To the extent that urbanization makes sound/economic sense because of consumption and production gains, we will expect an increasing level of demand for urban space. If to this we add the taste, manufactured by public policy or not, for land-intensive single detached dwellings, the demand will increase even more, and in the face of scarce urban land, prices will soar, as we noted in Table 1. But this will induce the population to seek land more remote from the Central Business District, as distance is traded off against more land. This is the source of the pressure for suburbanization. But moving farther out imposes increased travel costs, directly through greater distances and indirectly through the opportunity cost of time spent not working. Given a fixed transit system, congestion also is increased, and as a result private and public pressures for more and faster systems increase. As new systems are installed, however, driving down travel costs, land farther out becomes more accessible and further suburbanization takes place, increasing demand on the system as more automobiles per family are required. This solution might not end the vicious circle but it could at least prevent deterioration, except for one difficulty: the inability to expand the transportation system at all points. The greatest demands occur in the core, both in flow requirements and in storage needs, yet it is there that land prices are highest, streets are narrowest, and alternative uses with large fixed investments already exist. This dramatically increases the cost of any transportation improvement in that area; yet without it, congestion is inevitable. With concentration and congestion come pollution, noise, and general environmental decay.

---

[45] Jenney Podoluk reports the following estimates of average family income in 1961 by urban type.

Metropolitan Areas	$6,422
Urban Centres: 30,000-99,999	5,848
10,000-29,999	5,477
1,000- 9,999	5,073
Rural	4,247

Op. cit., Table 7.18, p. 174.

[46] It is true that beyond some size cities may become dysfunctional and actually retard future growth; it is claimed that New York and Los Angeles are beyond that point. There is little accurate evidence for the claim, and even less grounds for believing that the major Canadian cities — Montreal and Toronto — have surpassed this level, although by 2001 they will be in the same size league.

Here the dilemma of problem interdependence is starkly revealed. "Curing" the transit problem without regard to the locational choice of households is self-defeating, and housing policy without an eye to transit systems is as unpromising. Yet housing policy is conducted to this day as if the transit problem were non-existent, and engineers design better transit systems, blissfully ignorant of the long-term impact on housing and urban structure. Both problems have their root in the growth and structure of cities, and are not amenable to partial solutions.

Most problematical, but strongly related to the central process of urbanization, is the question of urban poverty. The characteristics of the phenomenon are familiar: slum housing near the core, endemic unemployment, high crime rates, disadvantaged children, and so forth. The role of urbanization in this area is less clear and requires some elaboration. Families with low incomes have limited locational choices. Despite the high cost of land downtown, compensation can be made through crowding. The alternative of suburban living is just not possible, because for most low-income families the essential transit mode, the automobile, is inaccessible. Thus, in the absence of a low-cost rapid transit system, these persons are forced into the fringes of the downtown area. Crowding invariably leads to a deterioration in the quality of the housing stock, and slums emerge. Similarly, employment opportunities in the core are typically for semi-skilled and clerical workers. Indeed, perhaps the most drastic change in the economy of the downtown area in the past was occasioned by the move of manufacturing to the suburbs as technology introduced single-floor flow-operations that are land intensive; at the same time, concentration and specialization led to an increasing dependence upon national rather than local markets for the major firms. These developments weakened the locational advantages of the core and induced the migration of firms to the suburban fringe, where easier access to inter-metropolitan transportation routes is typical, where land costs are less, and where the increasing number of white collar, and semi-skilled and skilled workers required by modern technology are domiciled. These groups, to preserve property values, try to keep out unskilled, low-income families through zoning laws that prevent both doubling up in single units and the construction of high-rise, low-rent units.

Thus, the poor are locked into their slums, with prices and rents continually squeezing them as urbanization proceeds. Furthermore, the availability of urban services such as schools, hospitals, and the promise of a better life continue to attract immigrants and those Canadians being squeezed off the farms and out of small towns as national economic development proceeds. The slum population swells, increasing crowding and further driving up land values. This forces the slum to invade adjacent areas where possible, driving away further users of unskilled labour. Thus, the problem of urban poverty is not only serious; it necessarily deteriorates, creating a situation of hostility and violence in the downtown portions of most of our major cities that is the most alarming of all our urban problems.[47]

If our analysis is valid, and if a city must be seen as a highly complex, dynamic system with a multitude of problems inherent in its evolution, then

---

[47] In the United States, where the ghetto dwellers are typically black, the reaction has been more violent, reflecting the growing awareness of a clearly identifiable group.

policies that treat these as *problems IN the city* are doomed to be ineffective. As we shall indicate in Section D, such a perception persists to the present.

D. The Urban Policy Problem

(a) The Theory of Public Policy

The theory of public policy is essentially a theory of decision making. Society has a set of objectives such that movement towards them constitutes an increase in social welfare. Since the resources of any society are limited, hard choices must be made among objectives at any point in time. Rational policy making thus involves making those public decisions which maximizes social welfare in the light of scarce social resources.

Some basic needs must be met if the public sector is to perform its task effectively. First, there must be a clear notion of society's *objectives* and the relationship between them, so that priorities can be assigned. Second, the volume and composition of society's *resources* must be known so that the resource-costs of different policy mixes can be assessed. Finally, the technology of objective attainment, or policy *strategy*, must be understood, so that the objectives can in fact be attained.

Theoretically, this is simplistic. The questions of interpersonal and intergroup conflict, of the implications of time and uncertainty, are excluded. These all modify the formal results. Despite these qualifications, however, the basic requirements for a clear notion of objectives, resource limits, and policy technology remain intact. Without them, policy will necessarily be irrelevant, unrealistic, or unattainable. With them, there is no guarantee that policy will be optimal, but there is some assurance that, properly qualified, it will be moving in the appropriate direction.

This is not the place to engage in a debate about these elements. For our purposes it is sufficient to note that in Canada, little is known about these three elements. There appears to be no agreement anywhere on objectives, only vague and often one-sided views about resources, and little imaginative work on policy development. Thus, there is an enormous conceptual gap at the pinnacle of policy development that colours all derivative policies and frustrates any attempt to bring order into the overall policy system.

(b) The Urban Policy Vacuum

In no area has the absence of clear policy development been so detrimental as in the urban field. There has never been a clearly stated set of urban objectives that derive from and contribute to the nation's goals. It may be claimed that it is unfair to say that there has been a failure to perceive urban problems. Indeed, that is what cities and provinces are primarily concerned with. The difficulty, however, is that there is no framework for dealing with these problems. Solving problems is not policy making, except by default. The seriousness of a problem can be measured only against some standard of what is normal or acceptable. The seriousness of poverty, for example, depends on what our view of non-poverty is. The seriousness of housing costs depends on what cost configuration we judge to be acceptable. In other words, we require a set of objectives against which we can evaluate our performance. But even this is not enough, for it neglects the need to relate problems to each other. How serious our poverty problem is relative to our housing problem depends on how much we value equity as opposed to satisfactory housing conditions. Thus, we need in addition a set of priorities among our objectives. These must relate to our national goals. Until there has been a shift in focus from problems *per se* to problems in a full policy context, there will be little meaning to our efforts to achieve urban goals.

If there has been little appreciation of the essential requirement of agreed-upon urban objectives, the rest of the policy making apparatus is in even worse shape.

Extremely little is known about the structure and potential of the urban system, and there is literally no machinery for developing a rational set of urban policies. This is not to deny that there have been many policies that vitally affect the urban system. Indeed, . . . most public policy at all three levels of government in Canada has had a substantial impact on this system. But these impacts are random, often perverse, conflicting, and generally chaotic. That the urban system should therefore be in trouble is hardly surprising.

But if the lack of a national urban policy is debilitating, the actual conduct of urban policy in the small is totally inadequate. At the local level, there is a lack of overall policy formulation stemming from archaic jurisdictional divisions, a perverse revenue-raising system, and a strictly environmental concept of planning. No city appears to have any clear set of urban goals; most live from hand to mouth, trying to wrestle with particular problems as they become intolerable. In general, greater attention is paid to physical problems and the provision of physical services than to social problems and social services. This no doubt reflects the strong architectural-environmental bias in the planning departments of the major cities and the political power of the elite group concerned with environment. Some attempts to alleviate jurisdictional problems by creating a new tier of government — metropolitan or regional government — have been made. They appear, however, to be extremely limited in scope and orientation, and their overall effectiveness remains to be seen.

Turning to the provincial level, we again fail to discover a full blown notion of urban policy. Departments of municipal affairs do exist, but they are generally not innovative, serving rather as constraining bodies for city programs and as intermediaries between local and federal government bodies, particularly CMHC. The rigid tying of grants to the municipalities in conjunction with the unproductive property tax which is the sole independent source of municipal revenue is one feature of this relationship. The rigid criteria of municipal planning is another.

As for the Federal Government, there has never been any federal urban policy in name or in practice. The closest we have come is CMHC's housing, urban renewal, and public housing and land acquisition programs. A careful review of these, however, reveals that they stem from a number of conflicting motives; they do not derive from any concept of an urban system or even an urban unit as a total unit. Other agencies — National Harbour Board, CNR, and Public Works — also have substantial impacts on urban units, but these remain unplanned and uncoordinated.

(c) Towards an Urban Policy

Clearly any attempt to develop an urban policy not only must start from an overall policy vacuum, but must overcome the bottlenecks and the vested interests already built into the political system. The essential requirements are
1. An agreed-upon set of urban objectives;
2. A fuller understanding of the limits of public policy in the urban field;
3. A procedure for directing resources to achieving these objectives with these limits — in other words, strategy development.

(i) Urban Objectives

An attempt to specify urban objectives requires a procedure for collecting interests, aggregating them to eliminate conflicts, and rendering them consistent with overall national objectives.

The collection stage is possibly the most difficult both practically and conceptually. While urban goals must, in the large, be consistent with national goals, they must also, in the small, be based upon the wishes of the inhabitants of the various urban areas. Theoretically we would expect local government to be the vehicle for expressing these local wishes. In fact, there are grounds for raising questions about this presumption. In the increasingly contentious area of urban renewal, for example, it has become apparent that local government has tended to act more in the interest of articulate and powerful groups — the elite-developers, financiers, and businessmen — and against the interest of weaker, though usually larger, groups. Again, in highway planning and land zoning, this bias in local politics has arisen.

Part of the reason for its ineffectuality is the underdeveloped state of local government. The organizational forms and the short planning horizons are throwbacks to the town-meeting politics of the last century. Local government also lacks decision-making authority, as a result of its constitutional status.

Consequently, the priorities in urban decision making reflect those of rural-oriented provincial legislatures, jealous of their own political power and fearful of the large urban centres with their economic power and their cosmopolitan outlook. The individual urbanite has very little say in the decisions that affect him most. Had the urban system been managed better, this problem might be relatively remote. As we have stressed, policy in the urban area has been totally inadequate. The recognition that the public sector has been unable to manage this increasingly complex process has led to a crisis of confidence on the part of urbanites, involving those that are most severely penalized by that process as well as those that have a more remote but no less profound concern that the quality of their existence in the cities may fall far short of their aspirations.

Any attempt to reverse this trend, in which decisions are made increasingly by bureaucrats and politicians generally neither familiar with nor sensitive to local needs and wants, must involve an attempt to provide machinery for including urbanites at a very micro-cosmic level within the process of interest accumulation.

This goal is not impossible, although it requires an imaginative approach. Within the federal system, there are severe constraints on federal-municipal interaction. To the extent that municipal governments fail in any event to be accurate refractors of local needs, the fact that the Federal Government is a national government opens the possibility of direct community-federal contact. Some institutions for this already exist in embryonic form, such as urban renewal protest groups and tenant associations. Other more comprehensive groupings can be conceived, ranging from neighbourhood councils to local chapters of national parties. The point is that these interests do exist, they urgently require being plugged into the policy system, and they can be within our current constitution.

These, then, are several of the dimensions of interest collection. Following upon this is the process of interest aggregation. Aggregation requires a procedure for resolving conflicts that are bound to arise among the various interest groups. Preferably this should entail discussion, debate, analysis, further discussion, and hopefully, resolution. In cases of severe conflict, adjudication procedures must be developed.

Overall consistency with national objectives must be ensured by a federal presence in this procedure of setting objectives. Otherwise, national policy making itself becomes an *ad hoc* process of accumulating bits and pieces of interests generated from below. The rationale for a Federal Government quickly dissolves in such a situation.

(ii) Constraints

The chief constraints of the urban system are the limited national resources available for dealing with urban objectives, and the underlying rationale of that system — its form, structural interdependencies, and dynamic mechanisms and the means by which this system creates urban problems. These are matters to which much of this Report is directed.

(iii) Strategy Development

Directing resources towards achieving urban objectives is the purpose of urban strategy. On the basis of the agreed-upon objectives and fuller knowledge of the limitations, specific goals can be formulated and assigned priorities. The machinery to ensure that the goals are attained must then be developed. Much of this will exist, but will need to be redirected and rationalized before constituting a useful component of the strategy. Finally, the process must be given specificity by the designing of a set of feasible targets over time, the cumulative attainment of which will ensure ultimate goal achievement.

These, then, are the formal requirements for any rational approach to urban policy. Much of this study is an attempt to discover the evidence currently available on urban objectives, on the urban system, and on urban strategy. On the basis of our findings, limited policy innovations will be suggested. Much more stress will be laid on developing procedures for expanding our policy-making potential — for learning more about urban objectives, constraints, and strategy development.

One substantive finding does emerge from even this theoretical statement, however, and that is that the manpower required to operate this kind of machinery just does not exist in Canada at this time. The few competent persons available are diffused throughout the system — some in government, others in university, and still others in consulting. There is no concentration of effort, and no consequent advance in the technology of policy making in the urban area. In other words, the scarcest resource for the foreseeable future will be manpower.

Two implications follow. The first is that steps must be taken to conserve and rationalize the energy of those available. The second is that an intensive training program must be launched immediately. The two need not be independent; a large institute of advanced research could serve also as an effective training ground for graduate students. Without such moves, the gap between our urban problems and our capacity to deal with them will widen dramatically over the next few decades — a gap that may ultimately preclude any but the most drastic solutions. Closing this gap may well prove to be the greatest of our urban policy·challenges of the future.

E. Conclusion

In view of this analysis, defining the urban problem entails much more than a listing of problems found in urban areas. First, the reality of these problems must be assessed. Then there must be an understanding of the centrality of their relationship to the urban system, which imparts to them their essential urban nature. We have found that many urban problems are of this sort, and that it is therefore critical to approach them from a total urban perspective. Finally, that perspective ideally should reflect the ultimate desires or objectives of the Canadian people, particularly those who live in urban Canada.

Chapter 10
Project and Policy
in Transportation Planning*

David M. Nowlan

The provision of transportation and communication facilities is seldom beyond the pale of public interest or, increasingly, public controversy. We
appear to have emerged from an age of innocence in transportation planning,
when any project that moved people or things was automatically good — or,
if not good, at least worth a few votes — to find ourselves badly in need of
institutions and analytical tools that will provide a more comprehensive,
rational approach to the transportation sector of our economy. The need to
diversify the mixture of people-carrying transportation modes — which has
come to be dominated by aircraft and roads — is being increasingly commen-
ted upon; and the irony is being savoured of paving our way out of environ-
ments we are destroying, only to find the same destruction elsewhere when
we had hoped to escape.

It is true that the intensity, almost the insanity, of our urban areas has
been largely responsible for persuading use of the need to define more adequately transportation policy; but the policy re-definition itself is being
focused on more than just urban areas, and on more than just people-carrying facilities. A pipeline into the Arctic warrants as much scrutiny as an
urban expressway; and the impact of modern electronic communication
equipment, especially as it influences the technology of remote-control industrial activities in hinterland regions of Canada, needs enlightened policy
guidance.

Institutions that provide us with transportation are not under the direct
control of any one level of government; nor are they even wholly in the
public sector. This means that the transportation issues facing a government
go well beyond a simple scrutiny of the projects that particular government
is providing. Projects must be analysed, but also policy must be formulated
— policy that will influence the transportation decisions of other levels of
government and of the private sector. In this paper my purpose is to provide
a conceptual framework for understanding today's transportation issues, and
to discuss some of these issues in the light of this framework.

*Dr. Nowlan is no stranger to transportation economics. Along with his wife, he was author of *The
Bad Trip*, a book which dealt with one of the most contentious issues in Toronto, the Spadina
Expressway. Chapter 10 was especially written for this volume and the editor appreciates his contribu-
tion.

In dealing with another tangled economic's problem, the eminent British economist Joan Robinson once wrote: "In order to know anything it is necessary to know everything, but in order to talk about anything it is necessary to neglect a great deal." We may need to solace ourselves with this bit of philosophy as the complexities of transportation planning become apparent. The key to wisdom lies in knowing what to neglect, and when to neglect it.

A Conceptual Framework

Good planning requires that transportation issues be faced at two levels of understanding, a policy level and a project level. Much confused debate could be eliminated if the conceptual difference between policy and project were more widely recognized, and if the interplay between the two were made a more explicit part of transportation planning.

At the policy level, we must deal with the broad, background issues of transportation. Questions like these emerge: What proportion of our national (or of our urban) resources should we be spending on transportation in total? Should we be encouraging more dispersion of activities and more transportation facilities, or should we be encouraging more compactness with less spending on transportation? Should we be subsidizing interregional transportation? Should we be promoting more public transportation facilities, or providing for better private mobility? Should we be encouraging better air facilities, or more high-speed ground connections between cities? Policy on these questions is decided by comparing in broad terms the relative costs of choosing one alternative rather than another, by attempting to judge the future that each policy decision implies, and then picking the future that most suits the community, the nation or the particular individual who is setting policy.

At the project level, we deal with the actual dynamics of a transportation system, with the problem of going from what we have today to what we should add tommorrow and the next day. Should we widen a road, straighten some particular curve, double track a rail line, build a STOL airport at some particular location, increase bus fares, issue more taxi licences, and so on? At this project level we are looking at the irreversible elements of transportation planning. At the policy level we can reverse decisions and biases literally from day-to-day, as new policy-makers take over, or as policy is evaluated in the light of some new consideration or technical breakthrough or new analytical techniques. But we can't build a road and then decide not build it, or issue a taxi licence and then decide not to issue it.

However, there is, or if there isn't, there should be, a strong relationship between project analysis and policy formulation. The evaluation of and decision on a project needs to take place within the framework established at the policy level. The purpose of policy-level analysis is to establish the biases that should be brought to decisions at the project level. Whether or not to widen a highway viewed solely as a project decision is about the question of congestion versus costs of widening. Users and other taxpayers may prefer to accept congestion rather than pay for improvements. But the analysis of costs of construction and costs of congestion must be supplemented by policy considerations. Perhaps, rather than widening the road, better train service should be introduced; or perhaps air transportation should be provided; or a bus route initiated. This consideration of alternate types of service for a given transportation need is a second level in the hierarchy of alternatives that is part of the decision to widen or not to widen.

At an even higher range in the hierarchy of alternatives that should be brought to bear on the highway-widening decision is the question whether a re-location of the activities that give rise to the transportation use of this highway mightn't be better than simply providing a better facility. This is an important consideration even for a superficially simple road-widening problem, because transportation facilities often feed on themselves. Better transportation encourages greater separation and greater specialization of activities, two features that themselves add to the demand for transportation. To let congestion build up, rather than to widen the road, may be the simplest way to achieve a re-location of activities and to help encourage the self-sufficiency of a region. In some cases more self-sufficiency is too costly; in other cases adding to the transportation facilities is too costly.

This unfortunate complexity of a project decision, typical of decisions that our governments are faced with day in and day out, will not disappear just by declaring ourselves "men of affairs," who in the interests of getting the job done, are not willing to strip away the surface layers to see the various components of the problem. Instead we should try to conceptualize the issue, to abstract it into its important components and then to decide how to feed this understanding into an analysis of the initial question. It is worth becoming abstract theoreticians for a few pages before returning to the affairs of the world, so that we have some way of making intelligent comments about those affairs.

The considerations of alternatives that need to be applied to any transportation problem may be divided into a hierarchy of three ranges. Range I is the first and the narrowest of these considerations. At this level virtually the whole structure of the economy and of the transportation needs of that economy, are given. Where people live and where they work are given; where goods are made and where they are sold are given. The division of the transported goods and people among the different transportation modes — road, air, water, rail, bus, auto, etc. — is given. The Range I type of consideration is simply whether to add to the capacity of a particular transportation mode in a particular transportation corridor. The problem is simplified — indeed we have made it simple in our conceptual, abstract world — because the parameters of the problem (the given structure of the economy and the transportation modes) are so broad. But the solution cannot be vouchsafed solely on account of the relative simplicity of the issue at Range I. It requires an analysis of the existing degree of congestion on the route and mode in question, and a conclusion from this analysis whether the congestion is either too intense or, alternatively, preferable to the resource cost of adding capacity to the facility. Contrary to common and sometimes high-placed opinion, every single congestion on a road, every person turned away from a scheduled flight or every person bumped from a crowded subway train is not a signal that the facility is overtaxed and should be added to.

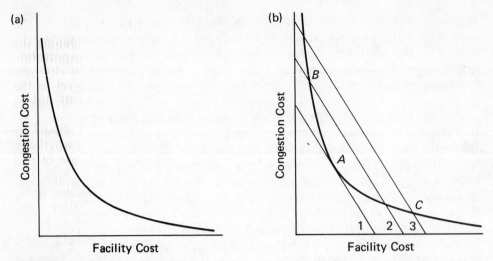

Figure 1

The Range I problem and its conceptual resolution are shown in the first diagram. The axes of Figures 1(a) and 1(b) show two kinds of costs: on the vertical axis is the cost of congestion, perhaps measured by the annual amount of money that users of a particular transportation facility would be willing to pay to eliminate the congestion on the route; on the horizontal axis is the annual cost of the facility, including interest charges on the capital cost and maintenance charges. The parameters of the economy are given right down to and including the total amount of traffic demand for this route and this facility. Given that demand, we can in Figure 1(a) draw a "requirements" curve that shows conceptually the trade-off in cost between adding more to the facility (e. g. widening a road or putting in more frequent air services) and so reducing the cost of congestion, or, moving the other direction to the north-west, providing less of the facility and handling the same traffic requirement but with more congestion. The hyperbolic con-cave-outward shape of the curve suggests that it is difficult if not impossible to eliminate completely congestion even with the provision of facilities ex-cessively far to the right along the horizontal axes. On the other hand, as we reduce expenses on the transportation facility itself, congestion costs mount at an increasingly rapid pace.

The trade-off curve in Figure 1(a) has been re-drawn in Figure 1(b), but this time some new information has been added to the diagram. The straight-line downward sloping curves labelled 1, 2, and 3 are what we call "indifference curves" of the particular communities or group of people who are interested in this transportation facility. Each "line" shows combinations of facility cost and congestion cost that give the same amount of dissatisfac-tion. Indifference curve 1 shows how the community is willing to trade-off congestion cost for facility cost. It costs money to provide more trolley buses or another road, so the community of taxpayers whose indifference curve is shown would clearly like to avoid this cost. But the more of it they avoid, the more congestion there is on the route — the more waiting for a bus, the longer the line-up at traffic lights. More of both kinds of costs is obviously less desirable than less of both, so indifference curve 2 shows less desirable positions for the community than indifference curve 1; and curve 3 would be worse than curve 2.

Remembering now that for this Range 1 problem the demand for the route and mode is given, we can see that the conceptual resolution of the problem is to meet this demand, within the technical possibilities shown by the concave requirements curve of Figure 1(a), by juggling facility cost and congestion cost until we are at the lowest or best indifference curve. If we moved along the requirements curve to point A in Figure 1(b), tangency with indifference curve 1 would be reached, and this is clearly as low an indifference curve as we could get to. If we decided to meet the demand at point B, we would be on indifference curve 2 and so in a less desired position with too little invested in the facilities and too much congestion. On the other hand, if we moved to point C, we would have over-built and put the community on the less desired indifference curve 3.

Conceptually, that all looks very simple, and it would be nice if it turned out to be an easy decision because we are after all only at Range I and haven't even begun to consider the other ranges of the problem. To go from the Range 1 conceptual analysis of Figure 1(b) to the reality of making a decision clearly requires some knowledge about the shape and position of the requirements curve and the indifference map. And that really is the transportation problem at this level. The technical requirements curve is hard enough to get at because it requires an evaluation in some usuable units (such as dollars) of the cost to the community of congestion — and that clearly is a cost that depends in part upon the acceptability of congestion on the part of individual communities or individual societies. If the British really do love a queue, that may be a sign that their society is more accepting of congestion than that of the impatient North America. The indifference map is hard to know for this same reason; but it comes with the additional complication that individuals in this community may have completely differently shaped indifference curves. Whose do we take? In part, the answer to this question comes through the political process where the resolution of conflicts between those who hate taxes and those who hate congestion may emerge. In our society, however, much of the answer comes in the form of a bureaucratic decision by civil servants at the various levels of government. Whose indifference curves are we then using?

After having analysed the Range 1 problem, we can move up the hierarchy of conceptual levels to the Range II type of problem. At Range II, certain of the given parameters of Range I are made variable. We retain the given location of economic activity. Where people live and where they work are still fixed, as are the location of production and the location of markets for goods. What is variable is the type of transportation system that can meet the demands of these fixed-location activities.

Several descriptive indexes of the different transportation modes to be analysed at Range II are possible, but the most general pair of characteristics of a mode is speed and storage. This pair will be used to describe the general Range II problem. The parameters of the problem are such that the number of ton miles that has to be moved per year, or the number of passenger-miles if we are dealing with passenger rather than goods transportation, is given. To move this given tonnage the required distance, the system can either move small amounts quickly or larger amounts more slowly. The amount of tonnage either in motion or waiting to be moved by the system is the storage capacity of the system. Thus the storage of the system (in tons or some

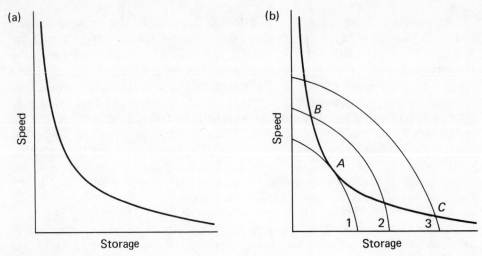

Figure 2

similar unit) times the average speed of the system (in miles per year) gives us the parametric quantity, ton-miles per year. Thus the requirements curve, shown in Figure 2(a), has a shape given by the equation: tons × miles per year = the given ton-mileage to be moved. In other words, storage times speed equals a constant. The curve is hyperbolic.

The goal of the Range II problem is to meet this transportation demand at the least cost. In Figure 2(b), I have redrawn the trade-off curve of Figure 2(a) and added to the diagram three constant-cost curves. These convex curves are the locus of equal-cost combinations of speed and storage characteristics of transportation systems. The combinations shown by curve 1 are cheaper than the combinations shown by curve 2, which in turn cost less than the combinations shown by curve 3. Each point on a given curve can represent a mixture of different modes such that the average speed and total storage are at the given point. Thus some point on curve 1 towards the northwest end might represent a relatively heavy investment in air transportation facilities (thus giving a high average speed to the system and a low storage capacity), while an emphasis on train or boat transportation might yield a point somewhere towards the south-east end of the curve.

Two things should be borne in mind about the equal-cost curves of Figure 2(b). First, the storage cost would include any spoilage or waiting cost that resulted from slower movement of the goods; and second, the facilities represented by each point on the curve are assumed to be provided in the best (or the efficient) amounts that emerge from the Range I analysis. In other words, in conceptualizing about the Range II problem, we are assuming that the right adjustments are being made at Range I.

To meet the transportation needs shown by the curve of given ton-miles per year at the lowest cost would mean providing facilities such that the speed and storage characteristics of the system were at point *A* in Figure 2(b). If you build too much speed into the system — too many air routes and not enough train lines, or too many automobile rights-of-way and not enough pedestrian paths — you end up at a point like *B* on Figure 2(b) with a higher expense than necessary to provide the service. If the system is too slow, you might be in a position like point *C* where the higher-than-necessary costs are shown on curve 3.

The problem of passenger or commuter movement at the Range II level introduces an additional complication into the attempt to determine the cost curves in Figure 2(b). Just as costs of storage include costs of spoilage when goods transportation is being analysed, so the costs of storage include the preference of passengers for being en route (i.e. in storage) for shorter rather than longer times. A good deal of the energy of transportation planners is devoted to analysing the reasons for people preferring one mode of transportation rather than another. A bushel of wheat probably doesn't care a lot whether it's shipped air freight from field to bakery, or takes a slow boat to China. But it's a fair presumption that people do care — although in what way they care is still very ambiguous.

Commuters generally prefer to travel faster rather than slower, other things equal. But a move to speed up the system by going from A to B say, in Figure 2(b), would, if nothing else, cost more per person travelling. A move from C to B would be desirable. How do you know whether you are starting from a point like A or one like C? Obviously, you must know the market-priced resource costs to begin with. An urban planner with fifty million dollars to spend on transportation facilities could begin by estimating the kind of speed storage combinations he could get for his money. Then he might try to make an estimate of the cost in time lost to commuters of having a slower rather than a faster system. This would cause his equal-cost curve to become somewhat steeper. If he was a good urban planner, he might then try to estimate some of the other costs unaccounted for in either the budgetary construction estimates or in the time-cost estimates. If one of his options is a faster, low-storage urban expressway system, he would be worried about the environmental problems of air pollution, noise, neighbourhood effects, and so on. These would make the slope of the cost frontier less steep. At this stage of the transportation decision we cannot take into account directly, the fact that some families in the urban area may not have an automobile. That these families would have to use public transportation is part of the analysis of the average speeds of different mixtures of transportation facilities. However, the fact that whatever we build will have implications for the distribution among people of the benefits, and of the costs through taxes or environmental effects, should at some point be recognized as part of the policy problem.

Finally, at Range III we are faced with the most general of the policy issues that can usefully be brought under the transportation planning umbrella. Now only the most basic economic characteristics of the country, the region, or the city are given. These parameters are the size of the population, the output and consumption characteristics of this population and the origin and destination requirements of goods and people that a transportation system would have to satisfy. The basic Range III problem for which policies need to be formulated is whether these origin and destination needs can best be met by separating activities and constructing transportation modes, or by having activities closer together and thus reducing the need for transportation facilities by making the whole system more compact.

Our abstract analytical tools can be brought to bear on this problem in order to help point in the direction of understanding and policy formation. In Figure 3(a) a requirements curve is drawn for a given number of "contacts" a year. A contact is a move from an origin to a destination, and the

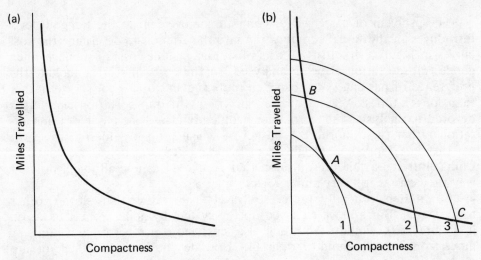

Figure 3

number of such moves is the basic parameter at Range III. If the vertical axis in Figures 3(a) and 3(b) is denominated in "miles travelled per year" and the horizontal axis is given in terms of the "compactness" of the system which is measured by the inverse of the average distance apart in miles of each origin and destination, then the requirements curve is again a hyperbola with each point on the curve representing the same, given number of contacts for the system. A less compact system requires more miles of movement each year to achieve the given amount of contact; and vice versa. Again, such a requirements curve is drawn on the assumption that at each point, the proper or least-cost adjustment has been made at the lower levels, Range I and Range II.

For a given cost, distance and compactness may be traded off as shown by the equal-cost curves of Figure 3(b). There are decreasing returns to increasing compactness as the economy has less opportunity to take advantage of the natural differences among geographic areas and as the problems of close-together living, producing and consuming activities become more intense. At the other, north-west end of the equal-cost curve, diminishing returns to transportation facilities set in as average distance apart of activities, increases and compactness is reduced.

The point of tangency of the requirements curve with the set of cost curves, point *A* in Figure 3(b), illustrates the cheapest way of solving the Range III problem. Conceptually, that is easily said; but once again the practical problem comes in working out and interpreting the actual shape and position of the cost curves. If the system is interpreted as being at a point like *B* in Figure 3(b), the analysis of individual projects should reflect the fact that relatively more compactness and less transportation was called for. At point *C*, the policy orientation should obviously be the reverse of this.

In spite of its crude appearance, this simple conceptual analysis at Range III can be subject to quite probing questions, and can handle quite subtle issues. For example, the slope of the cost curves needn't reflect simply the construction costs of transportation facilities traded off against the compactness costs of waste disposal, denser building and so on. The costs may, and generally should, include any costs unaccounted for by the market place

120

such as environmental costs of roads or railways, or the often-felt isolation of families in modern suburbs; and the similar costs associated with certain kinds of compactness — noisy neighbours, for example or the ugliness of high-rise boxes and the social decay that may accompany their appearance in a neighbourhood — may also be included.

Armed with this conceptual apparatus we can move into the real world of policy and project analysis with some bases by which to judge the actors and the action.

National Issues

The transportation system of the nation is built bit-by-bit, facility-by-facility. It is clear that the process of project selection and construction at Range I of the conceptual framework can go on quite independently of policy considerations at Range II or Range III. The construction of individual facilities is frequently a response to a narrow perception of local needs. Whether the sum of these individual parts adds up to a comprehensive and satisfactory transportation system depends on the existence of a well articulated transportation policy and an administrative or legal structure by which this higher-range policy can be brought to bear on project decisions.

As we move up to the administrative levels from local or municipal government to provincial and national governments the consideration of transportation policy, as opposed to project, becomes increasingly important. The national government does undertake some direct translation of policy into projects, especially in the development of northern transportation facilities, and the provincial governments are even more involved in direct project construction; but the more important role of these levels of government is the provision of an environment — through a system of subsidies or penalties, and through licencing and direct price controls — in which the transportation project decisions of lower levels of government, of the private sector and of crown agencies are biased in a way that is consistent with policy considerations.

In the absence of any explicit analysis, policy at Range III — the trade-off of distance for compactness — is generally biased towards the greater provision of transportation facilities. New transportation links are seen as signs of progress; harbingers of economic growth; or even, under some circumstances, a necessary part of the definition of a nation or other political entity.

At the national level in Canada, this policy bias is reflected in legislation such as that providing for subsidized grain movements from western Canada, the Crow's Nest Pass Rates,[1] and for subsidized freight movement westward from the Atlantic provinces, the Maritimes Freight Rates Act. It is reflected in the early and heavily subsidized provision of transportation facilities into the northern part of Canada and it is reflected in the policy of building and subsidizing trans-Canada highway facilities.

The linking together through transportation arteries of regions or provinces or suburbs does tend to permit economic specialization to occur by

---

[1] For a recent analysis of these grain rates see John Lorne McDougall, "The Relative Level of Crow's Nest Grain Rates in 1899 and 1965," *Canadian Journal of Economics and Political Science*, XXXII, No. 1 (February, 1966).

encouraging the exchange of goods or people. Regions can specialize in the products for which they have some economic advantage; areas within a city can divide themselves into dormitory sections, business sections, and industrial sections — all of which divisions are made easier by the greater provision of transportation facilities.

What is frequently ignored in our relentless pursuit for more transportation and communication links is that the development of regions or areas with homogeneous production, consumption, or living patterns can have serious negative side effects. This may be especially, and increasingly, apparent at the urban level, but it is an important consideration as well at the national and even the international level. Dominant economic and social centres in a country tend to build and feed upon transportation and communication facilities. An area that is isolated from a dominant centre has an opportunity to develop an autonomous economy and an independent society that it does not have when communication links to the centre are intense. In Canada, as in so many parts of the world, there is a tendency to use our hinterland provinces and our hinterland areas within provinces as resource suppliers and consumer areas for the more developed manufacturing centres of the country. In the absence of explicit policies to the contrary, it is difficult in a private-enterprise economy to encourage the independent and equal development of regions. It is clear that we have not yet had notable success in Canada in working towards this goal; and it is unlikely that we will have much more in the future if transportation linkages alone are to be our major national-development strategy.

The paradox of transportation is that interregional linkages are vital to efficient growth, but the provision of these linkages reinforces the tendency in our economy towards central control. Transportation routes build empires; they also build imperialism.

It will be especially important to remind ourselves of this paradox as transportation and communication policy towards the north is formulated. We obviously will want to develop strategies — Range II and Range III policies — for linking the north to the highly developed southern fringes of Canada. We must guard against having these northern-development policies become a form of modern-day, internal colonialism simply through ignorance of the impact of sophisticated communication links. Both traditional transportation facilities and modern electronic communication devices will create a tendency for the executive, the financier, the engineer, and the politician to live in the already dominant economic centres of Canada while controlling activities in the north. It may be that this is a desirable and useful pattern of development. But presumably it would only be acceptable if adequate measures are introduced to ensure the autonomy of northern populations and the absence of interregional social stratification that can too easily follow in the wake of economic specialization.

Until the 1960's the articulation of national or provincial transportation policy seldom moved down to the Range II level, where policy towards different modes of transportation could be formulated. This gap began to be filled, however, with the Macpherson Royal Commission on Transportation which reported in 1961. Basically, the Commission argued that the national-policy emphasis on railway subsidies to provide continuing transportation services between regions and centres of population distorted the use and availability of different types of transportation, a distortion measured in terms of higher-than-necessary transportation costs. To overcome the bias, it recommended that subsidies to unprofitable railway lines be greatly reduced, or at least subject to more severe scrutiny. Market prices and demand could then work towards rationalizing the transportation modes that could most cheaply meet the requirements given at the Range II level.

A similar theme of government-induced concentration on one transportation mode was repeated a few years later in the Atlantic Provinces Transportation Study of 1969. That study came to the recommendation that the 30 percent subsidy to west-bound traffic from the Maritimes to central Canada be extended to other forms of transportation, a recommendation that was adopted in the Atlantic Region Freight Rate Assistance Act of 1969. The following year the Atlantic Region Transportation Committee reported that the subsidy to rail movement within the Atlantic region had generally operated to hinder the development of truck traffic, and it recommended that a subsidy be extended to highway movements.

It is somewhat ironic that this relatively recent awareness of the need to develop more comprehensive Range II policies has come in the form of reports recommending against preferential treatment for rail freight shipments. For passenger movements, especially in the more densely populated parts of the country, there is a rapidly developing view that fixed-rail modes of transportation, which have been of declining importance for a number of decades, should be increasingly encouraged. This view has grown partly from the recognition that broad expanses of highways and an almost exclusive reliance on motor car transportation has serious environmental effects in crowded areas; but it has also grown from the newly acquired knowledge that our present emphasis on private-vehicle transportation cannot efficiently provide the needed degree of mobility in and around crowded metropolitan regions, or between major population centres. The recent successful attempt by commuters to the east of Toronto to keep adequate subsidized rail services into the downtown part of the city is an example of the type of pressure that is being brought to bear on government to re-examine its policy towards different modes of transportation.

The Canadian Transportation Commission, established by the National Transportation Act of 1967, has further contributed towards the articulation of Range II policy. One of its major research studies, for example, has been of inter-city passenger movement between Quebec City and Windsor, Ontario.[2] The prime purpose of the study was to calculate the most efficient ways of carrying passengers over the next several decades in the long corridor from Windsor to Quebec, especially the densely travelled section between Toronto and Montreal. To accomplish this it analysed the current travel behaviour of passengers in the corridor, and used this analysis to estimate the likely impact of future modes of transportation such as short take-off and landing aircraft (STOL) and tracked air-cushion vehicles (TACV). The general conclusion of the study is that near-future transportation needs can be most cheaply met by improvements in existing modes of transportation, including the increasing use of high-speed turbo-trains. For the longer range future, the development of TACV is favoured over STOL aircraft.

[2] Canadian Transportation Commission Research Branch, *Intercity Passenger Transport Study* (Ottawa: Information Canada, September, 1970).

Urban Problems

As we move from regional issues to more specifically urban problems we find the transportation situation in high political profile. Battles over transportation facilities are being waged in Montreal, Toronto, London, Winnipeg, Calgary, and Vancouver. Almost everywhere at issue is the extent to which reliance should be placed on the private automobile and downtown expressways to handle future urban transportation needs.

Concern in Canada is matched by a similar concern in major centres in other countries. In London, England, for example, the expressway proposals of the recently presented and now much-debated Greater London Development Plan were the subject of an important and highly critical book by a London School of Economics' economist, J. Michael Thomson.[3] One professional review of the book saw it as highlighting "the patent bias of the London Traffic Survey towards the demand pressures from private road traffic to the exclusion of almost all else." In the United States the situation was summarized in a *New York Times* article in February 1970. The headline read "Expressway Construction Lags Across the United States as Officials Heed Urban Outcry," and the article went on to say

> ... the faltering pace of construction of interstate 95 through metropolitan areas is matched by that of other expressways in city after city across the country as urban dwellers give voice to social and environmental objections with increasing effect ... some 133 miles of the interstate system alone are being held up in 16 cities ... in Philadelphia the expressway is stalled by apparently successful demands of residents that it be depressed and covered with a landscaped lid and by the insistence of conservationists that it not damage the wildlife refuge. For similar reasons interstate 95 has been delayed in Boston, Baltimore and Washington following many other cities such as San Francisco, New York, New Orleans and Milwaukee. Other highways considered essential by engineers and planners have been scuttled altogether in response to protest.

Two of the largest individual projects in Canada have recently been the objects of bitter debates — the Spadina Expressway in Toronto and the East-West Expressway which is part of the Trans-Canada Highway through Montreal.

The downtown part of the East-West Montreal route had been on the drawing boards for a number of years when, in 1970, Premier Bourassa and his cabinet picked it as one of their prime make-work projects in the face of our Ottawa-induced unemployment crisis. Unfortunately, the proposed highway is almost classic in the destruction it would bring to stable, low-income neighbourhoods of the inner city. Joseph Baker, a professor in McGill's School of Architecture, has written a full and poignant description of the impact of this expressway on the communities along its route. It is well worth the effort to look up and read his article in the *Montreal Star* of January 2, 1971.

[3] J. Michael Thomson, *Motorways in London* (London: Gerald Duckworth and Co., 1969).

124

Although debate will continue, the Spadina Expressway issue[4] in Toronto has now been resolved after a decade of argument that reached a climax in 1970 and the first half of 1971. In deciding not to proceed with the six-mile expressway from the northern suburbs to the city-centre (two miles of which had already been completed), Premier Davis and the Ontario cabinet appear to have set the stage for a more explicit consideration of urban-transportation policy in Ontario.

What have been the reasons for our abysmal performance in developing viable urban transportation systems? In part the answer must lie in the virtual absence of explicit transportation policies. While policy languished, the analysis of individual projects fared hardly better. Because of the widespread view that the paramount urban need was to provide facilities for private-automobile travel, transportation planners were seldom called upon to develop policy alternative or to defend project proposals. With the serious challenge to this view that has now arisen, it is important that we understand how to use the planning tools at our disposal, how to develop both policy and project analysis, and how to ensure that transportation alternatives are subject to the discipline of public debate.

Basically, any proposed urban transportation project can and should have a life of its own, whether an expressway, a subway line or any other proposal. An exclusive, bus-only lane might prove to be an excellent project even in an area that had opted for heavy reliance on private transportation; and an expressway might make sense even in a situation where greater use of public transportation was being promoted. The role of the policy – in these cases, for or against public transportation – is to bring to bear certain criteria in the evaluation of the individual project. An expressway proposal in an urban area that had decided to encourage the greater use of public transportation would have to pass more stringent project-evaluation standards than a similar proposal in a city with a policy of catering to private traffic.

The development of high-speed computing machines and their programme software has meant that better quantitative analysis can now be brought to bear on transportation planning at the policy level. Since the early 1960's, for example, Metropolitan Toronto has used a computerized systems approach in its analysis of various alternative transportation plans. Unfortunately, the results of this exercise have not been used to develop an understanding of the appropriate policies to adopt in Toronto; instead the analysis has been used for the much narrower purpose of justifying project decisions already taken. Much of the potential use of the technique was thereby lost.

The first report on the Toronto analysis was published in 1964 by the Metro Planning Board.[5] The aim of the study was to evaluate three alternative transportation plans for the Toronto area, all of which were long-range plans any one of which would cost well over a billion dollars to implement and would take forty or fifty years to construct. The basic parameters of the study were the distribution of people and of jobs that could be expected in

[4] For background to the issue and the state of the argument in January 1970 see David and Nadine Nowlan, *The Bad Trip: The Untold Story of the Spadina Expressway* (Toronto: New Press and House of Anansi, 1970).
[5] Metropolitan Toronto Planning Board, *Report on the Metropolitan Toronto Transportation Plan* (Toronto, December, 1964).

Metro Toronto by 1980. The analysis was focused on a pure Range II evaluation. Given where people lived and where they worked, what could be said about the most efficient way of providing rush-hour transportation?

Interviews and other studies were conducted to determine the travel behaviour of Toronto's population, and these characteristics were then used to determine how people would respond to the characteristics of the different plans: the costs of travel, the total time for a trip, the amount of waiting time, and the variation in these responses by different income groups. The programme using these characteristics was adjusted until it "predicted" reasonably well the travel patterns that were then being observed. Finally, the three alternative plans were analysed as if they were completed and operational in the forecast year, 1980.

Of the three plans, one emphasized the development of public, rapid-transit facilities; another concentrated development on limited-access expressways; and the third was intermediate in the use of private and public facilities, although much closer to the full expressway plan. On every criteria of efficiency, including that of cost (which was not analysed in the report), the rapid-transit plan performed best.[6] Yet, the report was used to defend the intermediate plan, which contained two politically committed although not built expressways, the Spadina Expressway and the Scarborough Expressway.

The reason for this strange interpretation of the results that the Metro Planning Board obviously felt strongly compelled to make, lay in a misinterpretation of the role of policy formulation, of Range II analysis. The fact that plans that could not be completed until well into the next century were analysed on assumed 1980 data is enough to suggest that the purpose of this type of systems study is not to arrive at decisions on specific plans or on specific projects. Rather, its point is to come to some quantitative understanding of the likely sensitivity of travel in the urban area to different approaches to facility development. On the basis of this study, expressway projects might have been required to pass more stringent project-evaluation criteria than otherwise and additional effort to prepare rapid-transit proposals might have been called for. Instead, the results of a very broad-scale policy-type analysis were used to evaluate and recommend on the specific facilities in the alternate plans.

The subsequent use in Toronto of basically the same systems programme has done very little to add to our understanding of urban transportation at the policy level. A re-run of the programme on forecast base data for 1995 did not even attempt to test alternative long-range plans,[7] but instead simply re-analysed the plan that had been recommended in 1964 — obtaining results that suggested disastrous traffic implications of that expressway dominated plan. However, there were two minor sensitivity tests run for the 1995 study, both of which produced interesting and useful information and serve to point the way towards the proper use of this analytical tool.

One of the sensitivity tests attempted to determine the effect on automobile traffic into the core of the city during the morning rush hour of

---

[6] See our analysis in *The Bad Trip, op. cit.*, pp. 39-47.

[7] The new study is contained in a report by the consulting firm Kates Peat Marwick to the Metro Toronto Planning Board. The report was introduced as evidence in the January 1971 hearings by the Ontario Municipal Board on the Spadina Expressway and is at least available to the public in the O.M.B. files if it hasn't yet been released by the Planning Board.

raising the daily parking charges. The result of the test was that an increase in the parking charge from $1.25 to $3.10 would reduce the number of cars coming into the core from 133,000 to 100,000 and correspondingly cause 39,000 drivers and passengers to switch from private automobiles to public transportation. The result is important because one of the issues in urban transportation planning is whether or not the use of private cars is responsive to price effects.

A second sensitivity test was run on the traffic implications of greater self-sufficiency in the core area. The basic assumption of the study was that of all the rush hour trips that were started from homes in the core of the city, 42 percent went to destinations in the core. If this degree of self-sufficiency could be raised to 67 percent, the sensitivity test suggested that there would be a reduction in travel by all modes into the core of 15 percent, and a reduction in outbound trips of 50 percent. These results help shed some light on the Range III policy issue of the cost of trading distance for compactness.

Except for this second sensitivity test, no quantitative work has been done on Range III policy for the Toronto region. However, the current public debate over Toronto's transportation facilities has served to highlight a growing awareness that the shape and form of a city are important factors in any workable solution to urban transportation problems. What quantitative results that do exist on this issue in a North American context are nicely summarized by Ron Rice in a paper he prepared for the first Canadian Urban Transportation Conference.[8] He considers three basic city forms: a single-centre city, a many-centred city, and a homogeneous density plan. For a given level of transportation service, his general conclusion is that

> considering capital costs only it can be concluded with some certainty that the central city concept gives the highest cost and the multi-centred plan the lowest . . . However, if both transportation investment costs and user costs are considered, it is the homogeneous density pattern which results in the greatest cost, with the many-centred plan still the lowest and the single centre plan intermediate between these two extremes. An important point to be noted here is that there is a substantial difference in mode utilization for each of these plans, with higher transit investment (and lower highway investment) being required progressively from the homogeneous, to the multi-centred, to the single centred concept.[9]

The results of current policy-level analysis all point the way towards the need for a strong bias against choosing automobile and expressway projects in large urban areas. And yet, even without this bias, a downtown commuter expressway is almost impossible to justify at a Range I evaluation. For construction and land-acquisition costs alone, thirty million dollars a mile is not a large sum for an inner-city, six-lane expressway in a large urban area. At the very most, an average of eighty thousand cars a day might pass in both directions a given point on the highway, say thirty million cars a year as an outside figure. If the annual value of the facility including maintenance is

[8] R. G. Rice, "Urban Form and the Cost of Transportation: The Policy Implications of Their Interaction," *Plan*, 10, No. 2 (August, 1969).

[9] *Ibid.*, p. 43. A detailed cost analysis of compactness versus distance in a Latin American urban setting is provided by Robert Jones, "Transport, Urban Design, and Housing," in Elwin T. Haefele, (ed.), *Transport and National Goals* (Washington: The Brookings Institution, 1969).

taken at 10 percent of the initial capital cost, these thirty million cars would have to pay ten cents a mile, as a minimum figure, to cover this cost. That is an almost prohibitively steep toll charge, but even so, it is a charge that does not take into account either the environmental impact of an expressway in an urban area or the congestion to other parts of the urban transportation network that an expressway brings.

It is not hard to reach the conclusion that many urban areas are at the point where ways alternative to the private automobile of moving large masses of people must be rapidly expanded. There must be a strong policy emphasis, through such devices as greater provincial subsidization of rapid transit and less of urban highways, on inducements to spend our transportation dollars on the greater provision of public transit facilities. It seems that only by this means will we be able to continue to enjoy, when the occasion warrants, the door-to-door convenience provided by the private automobile.

The downtown street system of many cities is at capacity for parts of the day. The surface area of the core is fixed and the size of the automobile is, for the moment at least, given. If we insist on bringing more cars into the city at the expense of other transportation facilities, we will congest our side roads and arterial streets to the extent that automobile movement becomes ludicrously slow, pedestrian traffic and residential life is unduly interfered with, and truck deliveries become intolerably difficult. At that point we decide to ban general purpose travel by automobile in the inner city.

Outside the central part of metropolitan areas, our continued emphasis on the automobile for commuter trips leads us to accept a very sprawling type of suburban development. As this kind of growth progresses, the automobile serves to defeat itself in the suburbs as well as in the core. The only kind of accessibility becomes accessibility by car: entertainment and shopping facilities must be driven to, and high-quality public transportation services become difficult to maintain. Moreover, as the sprawl expands, our accessibility to more rural park and recreation areas is reduced. Once again, by so heavily emphasizing the automobile as a means of transportation, we will contribute to its increasing inability to serve us; and we will have foregone the chance to give rational shape and form to our city through the provision of corridors of high-speed public transportation facilities.

How much more there is to be said about urban transportation problems will be apparent to anyone who has done even the most cursory reading on the topic.[10] Especially important is the analysis of the differential impact on different income groups of alternative types of transportation.[11] Important too is the need to experiment with new ways of providing the personal convenience and flexibility of the private automobile with fewer of the disadvantages — expanded taxi or jitney services, dial-a-bus schemes (perhaps using regular buses for this during off-peak hours) or the co-operative ownership or use of cars. My purpose, however, has not been to catalogue the problems but to provide at least one framework for a better understanding and analysis of the issues.

---

[10] For a recent survey see Tom E. Parkinson, *Passenger Transport in Canadian Urban Areas* (Ottawa: Canadian Transport Commission, 1970).

[11] See John F. Kain et. al. *Conference on Poverty and Transportation* (Brookline, Massachusetts: American Academy of Arts and Science, June, 1968); and a study by Toronto's Bureau of Municipal Research, "Transportation: Who Plans? Who Pays?" *Civic Affairs* (Autumn, 1970).

Part E
Pollution

Pollution and its control is one of the most widely discussed public issues today. In the last two or three years, we have witnessed the emergence of new government departments and agencies to deal with widespread demands for a better quality of life. In the first paper which follows, the author argues that the deterioration in the quality of the environment is basically an economic problem, resulting from the imperfections of our market economy. Pollution abatement can be achieved but there will likely be profound economic implications. The second paper is a critical evaluation of Canadian fiscal policies that have been legislated to discourage pollution. Since many new policies are likely to be introduced during the next few years, an understanding of the implications of the present legislation is essential.

Chapter 11
An Economic Analysis
of Environmental Pollution*

D.A.L. Auld

What has economics to do with problems of pollution? Pollution of water, air, and land occurs when foreign material is added to the natural environment in such quantities or at such a rate that the environment can no longer support this material without an appreciable alteration in nature itself. Is this a matter for economics, the study of how man satisfies his wants? For two reasons, the answer must surely be an emphatic "yes." First of all, economic activity has been, and is involved in, creating environmental pollution. The second is that economic thinking can be useful in analysing the problem, assisting in the preparation of abatement solutions, and curtailing possible future pollution.

Mankind, to a considerable extent, satisfies his wants or desires through material consumption. Most of this consumption is in the form of goods, which are produced in processes using air, water, or both as factors of production. It would appear from what has happened to air, water, and perhaps land, that these resources have been utilized in a rather careless manner. In fact, many would argue that air and water have been more seriously mismanaged than any other resource.

One of the major reasons for the disregard of these resources is that they have not been regarded as economic goods, goods which are relatively scarce. The use-value of both air and water has always, of course, been recognized, but the apparently "endless" supply made them "free." This, and the particular physical characteristics of water and air, made it difficult to accord them any property rights, either private or public. True, there is a substantial body of international law dealing with water as it pertains to a country's sovereignty. And within some countries, laws and regulations exist with respect to stream or river rights. However, the extent to which regulations cover the quality and use of air and water is limited. In areas where laws do exist, administration and prosecution has been weak and sporadic, although this may be due to an unwillingness on society's part to devote funds for this purpose.

*Chapter 9 (pp. 111 – 119) of *Environmental Change,* edited by D. Elrick, published by the Scientific Research Association, Toronto, 1970. Reproduced with the permission of the author.

Let us examine first the relationship between production and pollution (see Dales, 1968, for a more detailed analysis). The basic aim of any producer, whether an entrepreneur in a capitalistic economy or a plant manager in a command economy, is to maximize output or profit through efficient utilization of resources used in the production.[1] Regardless of the degree of efficiency, however, most production processes involve some amount of waste, and it is this waste which causes pollution of the air, water, or soil. Total use of all wastes to produce economic goods would be one method of arresting pollution, but this kind of production efficiency is some distance in the future. However, some success has been achieved recently in this direction, for example, the use of gaseous waste from smelter operations to produce fertilizers.

The disposal of waste products is an integral step in the production process. If the disposal of wastes becomes expensive for the firm or plant, solutions will be sought to reduce wastes or convert them into economic products. On the other hand, if disposal costs remain zero, no such incentive exists, unless, of course, the waste can be transformed into a profit-making product. Looking at costs to the firm or plant itself, we can illustrate this as follows:

If disposal costs (D_w) equal zero, then the firm or plant will convert its waste into economic products as long as:

$$W\, C_w < P_w W_t \qquad (D_w = 0) \qquad (1)$$

where

$W\ $ = waste products (quantity)
C_w = per unit cost of converting waste product
P_w = per unit selling price of converted waste
W_t = converted waste product

Even if the disposal costs are greater than zero, it would still be economical for the firm to convert the waste as long as:

$$(W\, C_w - P_w W_t) < D_w \qquad (D_w > 0) \qquad (2)$$

It must be remembered that (1) and (2) represent situations as seen by the firm in the light of profit maximization. If we were to add the social costs of pollution, E_w, the above relationship is modified such that from the social viewpoint, treatment of waste products or pollutants should be undertaken when:

$$(W\, C_w - P_w W_t) < D_w + E_w \qquad (3)$$

Suppose

$$
\begin{aligned}
D_w\ &= 31 \\
E_w\ &= 100 \\
W\, C_w &= 120 \\
P_w W_t &= 90
\end{aligned}
$$

[1] Our definition of capitalistic economy assumes that some degree of competition prevails.

From the firm's point of view [see (2)], and of course society's [see (3)], it is worthwhile to treat the pollutants. However, if $D_w = 29$, then it will not be worthwhile from the firm's point of view to convert waste, even though it remains worthwhile to do so from society's point of view.

Historically, disposal costs have been close to or equal to zero, and, because of this, there was little incentive to treat waste material. Air, water, and land — the convenient avenues of waste disposal — were zero-priced as far as the firm was concerned. In addition, there was little interest or immediate reason to be concerned about the external effects of waste disposal. After all, water and air were "free" goods, available in endless supply. Thus, the only situation in which waste was treated and sold as a different product was that described by (1) above.

The above discussion has been in terms of industrial pollution, but automobile pollution or municipal sewage-disposal can be used as examples with equal ease.

For the municipality, the objective is to dispose of waste in the cheapest possible manner. Provided there are no external effects on the area immediately about the waste-disposing municipality, E_w and D_w are close to or equal to zero. Automobile manufacturers have always been aware that the internal combustion engine produced a toxic, gaseous waste. But with disposal costs small and little awareness of external costs, there was no reason to develop and install exhaust afterburners. Without government regulation, firms would find it profitable to install such devices only if consumers demanded them. We are coming to realize, however, that the external costs are likely very high in terms of disease and health costs. Even if D_w and $P_w W_t$ are zero, there is increasing evidence to suggest that $E_w > W C_w$ indicating that from society's viewpoint afterburners on internal combustion engines are necessary.

In retrospect, one might argue that if more attention had been given to the legal and economic aspects (ownership, use, and costs of air and water), the pollution story would be quite different. Even recently published textbooks in economics consider this question only very briefly. Inman (1959, p. 113) *Economics in a Canadian Setting* notes that air is a free good, " so abundant that there is no necessity for economizing . . . " In discussing free goods, another author (Dorfman, 1964, p. 121) states that, "Air is the most obvious example." Apparently, a good may be considered "free" because of its abundance now, but it will be "economic" (scarce) in fifty years. The point should also be made that a good which appears to be "free" to an individual may be "scarce" to society. Establishing now that it is a "free" good makes it difficult to alter its legal status as it becomes scarce.

Even if air and water were free goods, are they not subject to ownership? I would argue that there exists a collective responsibility for these resources, and that one or more levels of government represent the ownership of them. If so, society has had the opportunity to do something about the "free" nature of air, water, and land. Unfortunately, through irrationality, ignorance, and the problem of "spill-overs," we have not taken this opportunity.[2]

---

[2] A "spillover" occurs when the activity of a person or firm creates a disutility for another person or firm in such a way that compensation cannot be made for the damage caused.

Water and air are resources used in production. But, because of their undefined nature with respect to ownership and the problems associated with measuring opportunity costs, these resources are not optimally priced.[3] In fact, they have been seriously under-priced, often even at zero. Thus, the cost of producing certain goods is below that which it would cost if all factors of production were priced to reflect their value to society. The result is that social costs exceed private costs. Consequently, there tends to be over-production of those commodities using the under-priced resources of water and air, with a corresponding misallocation of resources in general.

Another way of looking at this is to consider the physical nature of air. For example, air is what we would call a collective good — no one can be excluded from consuming it. Consequently, there can be no private market for air, where individuals express their preference for clean air by purchasing certain quantities at a price. Without a market for air, the individual is rather helpless in promoting efficient use of this resource.

It is worthwhile to consider what might have occurred if air and water had been treated as goods incorporating collective action. These resources may have been under the direction or trusteeship of government. Although this would not, of course, guarantee optimal resource-use, at least there would have been more collective decision-making. Even private ownership of such a scarce factor as clean air may not produce optimal resource-allocation. A greedy person could hold out in an attempt to get a high price for his share of "air." Since no production could commence until everyone (in an area) sold his air rights, a serious distortion could result. If the government charged users for the use of air, industries would have developed the technological means of reducing pollutants or else the prices of products would have reflected the cost of these resources. Another option, that of strict quality regulations, would have forced producers to eliminate pollutants or cease production.

Either of these courses would have resulted in products priced higher than they would be if air and water were free. It would appear that this is of no importance today, since society is faced with substantial costs if it wants to reclaim some of these resources. The health injury that air pollution has caused in some cities is a high price to pay for marginally lower-priced products.

The economic process has, in part, been responsible for pollution, but economics as a discipline or method of study can help to solve the problem. Welfare analysis, public finance, and price theory are tools that can be used to arrive at ways and means of reducing pollution. This must be carried out in conjunction with other areas of study, such as geography, political science, and biological science. The market, or price, system has not been very successful in dealing with pollution problems. But the market system was devised by man to serve certain purposes, and it can be altered to attain new objectives in a changing environment.

What alterations, then, in the market system are required to assist in solving pollution problems? The most important and most difficult is the

---

[3] Some attempts have been made to measure pollution costs. See R. G. Ridker, *Economic Costs of Air Pollution* (New York: Praeger Publishers, 1968) and references cited in A.F. Kneese, *The Economics of Regional Water Quality Management* (Baltimore: John Hopkins Press, 1964).

quantification of E_w, the social costs of pollution. This is what Professor Dales calls "pollution costs," or "the money value of the damages caused by wastes after they are released into the environment" (Dales, 1968, p. 13). These social costs are comprised of the expenditures required to render the polluted resource fit for use, the expenditure required to avoid pollution effects, plus the cost of the damages inflicted upon society by the wastes themselves. Sorting these costs out is not always easy.

The corrective part of pollution costs is not difficult to quantify, as it is equal simply to the expenditures made by an individual or public authorities to purify water or air. For example, how much does it cost industry X to purify polluted water in order to obtain the water it needs in its production process? Avoidance costs are also measurable in terms of such expenditures as air-conditioning equipment or movement away from the polluted area. Estimating the cost of the damages caused by pollution is the more difficult task. If we wish to place some value on air and water, however, an estimate of this cost is necessary. The following is a brief examination of these costs, how they can be measured, and the validity of such estimates.

In the case of water pollution, the damages created are largely in terms of disappearing fishing-industries and the slow destruction of present or future recreational areas. Losses to fishing-industries can be estimated by examining the statistics that reveal declining catches in a polluted area. But it involves more than just a lost source of income. In some areas, it means the loss of a way of life to people who have known no other. It means dependence on welfare payments, social upheaval, and other associated disutilities to which a cost in terms of money cannot be ascribed. Losses of recreation areas can in some cases be measured, but in many instances it means a personal loss when a lake or river is closed to fishing, swimming, or boating, and the value of this sort of loss cannot be readily ascertained.

Air pollution damages are many. Current scientific and medical evidence indicates that such diseases as emphysema, bronchitis, tuberculosis, and the common cold are precipitated or at least made more acute by the presence of pollutants in the atmosphere. How do we evaluate, in dollar terms, the premature deaths caused by diseases accelerated by polluted air? To what extent do hospital, medical, and drug expenditures in large cities depend on pollution-induced sicknesses? There are techniques for estimating such losses, and some progress has been made in this type of measurement. Together with increased health costs, polluted air often means greater expenditures on cleaning and painting. These are examples of the corrective or avoidance costs involved with pollution. An estimate of additional cleaning costs due to pollution in one large American city is as high as two hundred dollars per capita. Then there are the "immeasurable" costs, such as not being able to see clear blue sky because of smog.

A discussion of the precise methods used to estimate pollution damages is too great to be undertaken here. We shall concern ourselves, therefore, with a brief outline of the methodology used, highlighting some of the factors that must be evaluated before measurement can be attempted. Firstly, it is usually assumed that other factors having the same effect as pollution are constant. Secondly, in comparing polluted to non-polluted areas, differences in geography and climate must be noted, because both may affect the acuteness of pollution. Thirdly, the tools used to measure pollution must be reliable. Finally, shifts in the labour force and other factors likely to have occurred as a result of pollution must also be noted.

The next task is to establish a relationship between the amount of damage incurred by an object, the number of objects affected, and the level of pollution. The damage function is the responsibility of the combined efforts of the engineer and the economist or the biologist and the economist, so that physical or medical damages can be readily translated into monetary sums. Air pollution damages in the form of increased levels of bronchitis, for example, can be translated into medical bills, hospital expenses, drug costs, and income loss as a result of illness. Here, market prices are used to estimate costs. In another instance, the economist must make his own judgment about costs or resort to such tools as personal-survey analysis.

Finally, let us consider the actual abatement of environmental pollution. Having determined that there is a substantial social cost caused by environmental pollution, the question is what can society do about it. Regardless of the method used, it appears that the authority involved will be some level of government, or perhaps a government-appointed agency.

The most widespread method of control is regulation of the disposal of waste products by municipalities, firms, and individuals. This has not been very effective to date, because of incomplete legislation and the lack of enforcement of those laws that do exist. Regulation of waste disposal could be made effective very simply, by strengthening existing laws and by the introduction of new laws stringently enforced, with stiff fines for infractions. A second method is for the government to grant some form of tax credit. This applies mainly to firms and individuals. For example, a municipality could allow firms to deduct the value of anti-pollution equipment from their taxable real-estate assessment. A possible variation would be to permit companies to deduct the cost of such capital outlays from their tax base when computing corporation income-taxes. A third approach would be to allow firms to write off or depreciate this equipment at an accelerated rate. Other types of tax credits could be devised to assist corporations and individuals to install pollution-reducing equipment.

Another category of assistance involves loans or grants from governments. The Provincial government, for example, could make conditional grants or low-interest, long-term loans to firms as well as municipalities for the installation of pollution-free waste-disposal equipment. This method has an advantage over the tax-credit system, which cannot be used to handle the municipal sewage-waste problem.

Finally, the government can assume property ownership of air and water and charge polluters for the damages they cause. This approach presumes that the social costs of pollution are measurable. In place of this, the government can sell disposers of waste products the "right" to use water and air (Dales, 1968, Chapter VI).

All of these abatement measures are costly, but the distribution of the cost over society will depend on the method chosen. Assuming that abatement is required and desired, the economist must then determine the most economically-efficient method of achieving the objective. What, then, are some of the factors he must weigh? Strict regulation, enforced by prohibitively high fines, will bring about one of two immediate effects: the installation of anti-pollution equipment or the shut-down of the industry. Only the

136

former option is open to municipalities. In this case, such expenditure will be followed by higher taxes or reduced municipal expenditure in other areas. A firm installing such equipment may try to offset the cost by raising prices of its products, reducing its profits, or combining these alternatives. If it decides to shut down its operation, there may be unemployment in the area, if the labour force cannot be absorbed by other employers. Either of these results is likely to have further repercussions on the economy in the immediate area.

Tax-credit measures mean one thing: reduced government revenue. This would affect the government in the same manner that the enforced regulation would affect the municipality. Conditional grants would have a similar effect, as higher tax revenues would be required to finance the grants, or there would be reductions in other areas of government expenditure. Public charges for the use of air and water involve the government in the very complicated task of determining what to charge those who are causing pollution. To determine the final cost benefit of each of these measures is something which should be examined carefully in the future.

Regardless of the method used to combat pollution, society will have to pay the price. If it means higher taxes, the burden will be distributed according to the incidence pattern of the particular tax by which the money is raised. If it means higher prices for certain products, then those consuming the higher-priced products (including foreigners purchasing our exports) will assume the costs. Our task is to make people aware that pollution abatement will cost money. An awareness of both pollution costs and estimated costs of abatement will enable us to proceed more rapidly with solutions to the problem.

References

Dales, J.H., *Pollution, Property and Prices*. Toronto: University of Toronto Press, 1968.
Dorfman, R., *The Price System*. N.J.: Prentice Hall, 1964.
Inman, M.K., *Economics in a Canadian Setting*. Vancouver: Copp Clark, 1959.

Chapter 12
Fiscal Instruments and Pollution:
An Evaluation of Canadian Legislation*

Leonard Waverman †

The federal and provincial governments have introduced a multitude of fiscal policies – fines, subsidies, loans and tax incentives – to induce firms and individuals to limit their pollution. Economists consider such instruments to be both less effective and more costly than a system of prices for the environmental factors. The federal government, appearing to heed economists' advice, incorporated into the Canada Water Act an effluent charge system – which was loudly condemned by provincial governments and many civic anti-pollution groups as a scheme of "licences to pollute."

This paper is intended to clarify the confusion about the nature of effluent charges.[1] First I shall discuss the nature of pollution in order to derive criteria for judging measures designed to eliminate pollution. Next I shall describe some of the existing policies for the control of water pollution, and evaluate them in terms of those criteria. Many actual policies are found to be inferior, in terms of effectiveness and cost, to a scheme of effluent charges. Tax incentives are shown to be the worst alternative to a system of charges. Finally, I consider a tax scheme that would combat pollution by making taxes similar to prices. There appears to be little merit, however, in using such a scheme: it merely renames a price system, and it obscures tax policy.

Prices and the Environment

Much academic literature has discussed the benefits of instituting a pricing scheme for the environmental factors.[2] The major usefulness of such a

*"Fiscal Instruments and Pollution: An Evaluation of Canadian Legislation, "Canadian Tax Journal, 18, No. 6, 1971, pp. 505 – 513. Reproduced with the permission of the Canadian Tax Foundation and the author.
† Assistant Professor of Economics at the University of Toronto. My colleague Richard M. Bird was most helpful in formulating many of the thoughts presented here.
 1 This papers concentrates on the problem of restricting water pollution, although the discussion of policies can be generalized to include other pollution problems as well.
 2 See, for example, J. H. Dales, *Pollution, Property and Prices* (Toronto: University of Toronto Press, 1968); A. V. Kneese and B. T. Bower, *Managing Water Quality: Economics, Technology, Institutions* (Baltimore: Johns Hopkins Press, 1968, for Resources for the Future, Inc.); and L. Waverman, "Pollution: A Problem in Economics," in L. H. Officer and L. B. Smith, (eds.), *Canadian Economic Problems and Policies* (Toronto: McGraw-Hill of Canada Ltd., 1970).

scheme is that by allowing firms themselves to compare costs of reducing pollution in different ways, it ensures that an acceptable standard will be attained at the lowest possible resource cost, while at the same time guaranteeing that polluters alone, rather than the public at large, pay for clean-up costs.

The nature of pollution is that the polluter imposes some of his internal costs – namely, the cost of waste removal – on innocent third parties. The factory that pollutes the air is in essence forcing all the individuals in its locality rather than its customers to pay for its waste removal through higher cleaning costs and more respiratory illnesses. The factory itself (and those who buy its products) should bear the costs of waste removal either through installing devices that limit pollution or by paying for the right to use a public good – air – for waste removal. The solution is not so simple, however, as forcing a few factories to install abatement devices. If all pollution were the result of a readily identifiable waste product from a known source soiling clothes, remedies would be simple: insurance and the courts.[3] It is the impossibility of identifying the specific automobile (it may even be one's own) that deposits the lead on one's farm land that creates the need for public policies.[4]

The primary objective of public policy should therefore be to ensure that the amount of pollution is lowered to a socially desirable level while eliminating the imposition of costs by polluters on third parties. Fiscal instruments designed to limit pollution should therefore ensure that the polluter rather than the general public pays for clean-up costs.

If the government wanted to improve the quality of the environment, it could do so by ordering all polluters to diminish their discharge of waste by a certain percentage. While this policy would lead to the desired improvement, it would not do so at lowest possible cost. Take for example, two firms, one of which (A) discharges a highly toxic effluent, but whose cost of abatement is low, while the second firm (B) discharges an unsightly but non-toxic effluent whose costs of abatement are extremely high. Ordering both firms to reduce their pollution by the same percentage ($x\%$) is clearly not the best procedure, since it may be cheaper to remove most of the toxic waste of firm A than to remove $x\%$ of the harmless effuent of firm B. What is needed for this purpose is, first, a device to measure the costs and benefits of abatement for a single firm and, second, a comparison of the relative costs and benefits among all firms. One way of doing this might be to create a government agency to measure effluents and to suggest standards for different firms. Regulation of this sort would be very costly both in the amount of public funds needed for such a vast army of scientists and in the time it would take to arrive at a consistent policy.

Since a pricing system is used to ration other scarce resources, proposals have been made to use a pricing scheme for air and water.[5] The argument is

---

[3] In fact, the courts and insurance are used when the source of the pollution is identifiable. The Electric Reduction Company at Port Maitland, Ontario, has been sued by individuals in the area for flouride pollution. Oil tankers carry insurance for third-party liability in case of break-up and resulting pollution.

[4] In economists' terminology, air and water are to a large extent collective goods subject to technological external diseconomies.

[5] Dales, *Pollution, Property and Prices*; and Kneese and Bower, *Managing Water Quality*. There are differences in the proposals of spokesmen such as Dales and Kneese. Dales suggests that the government establish the desirable level of pollution and auction off pollution rights to the highest bidder. Kneese's schemes are more conventional and are described below.

simple: establishing a price for water would induce those firms whose per-unit clean-up costs are less than the per-unit price to install abatement devices, while firms with relatively high abatement costs would continue to dump their wastes and pay the price. The desired standard would thus be achieved in the most efficient manner.

There is no ground whatsoever for characterizing a pricing scheme for water as a licence to pollute. The price is the implicit value to society of the resource – a unit of clean water. If a firm chooses to buy this resource and use it for waste removal, to say it has acquired a licence to pollute makes no more sense than to say that purchasing a raw material input constitutes a licence to destroy.[6]

Most arguments against pricing schemes appear to reduce to arguments concerning not the *nature* of the scheme but either the expected level of the price of the federal intervention in local or provincial matters. The concern of civic anti-pollution groups over the scheme proposed in the Canada Water Act is probably justified given the ineffectual impact of government anti-pollution policies in the 1950s and 1960s (especially on industry). However, it can be quickly pointed out to these groups that effluent charges are not pollution licences, since the price for the environmental factors could be set so high that no firm would pay the price and all would install abatement devices. Therefore, much fear over the establishment of the system set forth in the Canada Water Act is not fear of the price scheme per se but fears – perhaps justifiable – that the price will be set too low.[7]

Fiscal Instruments Presently in Force

Present federal regulation utilizes all forms of controls and inducements to promote a desirable quality of water: standards establishment (Fisheries Act, National Health Act, etc.), loans and grants (National Housing Act), tax incentives (Income Tax Act, Excise Tax Act), fines and effluent charges (Canada Water Act).[8]

6 The information package accompanying the Canada Water Act attempts to falsely legitimize effluent charges by suggesting that the funds acquired will be used to install governmental clean-up projects. The proper price should be set so as to produce the socially desirable use of water; earmarking of the funds from selling water is immaterial, except as a political selling point.
7 The price very likely will be too low in the short run. The method of choosing the proper price is to set a rate, determine firms' reactions and the resulting level of pollution, then adjust the price up or down, to more closely approach the desired pollution level. Given the facts of political life, it is probable that an initial price will be too low.
    There is a great similarity between a pricing scheme and a system of fines. A fine creates a uniform price to be paid no matter how grossly a firm over-pollutes, and a zero price if the firm meets the standard. Fines are clearly inferior to per-unit prices if the fine is for the mere offence of polluting (as it is today) rather than for the volume of pollution (a price). If fines are graduated in accordance with the amount by which a standard is exceeded, then they will amount to prices.
8 A concise summary of existing legislation is given in The Canadian Council of Resource Ministers, *A Digest of Environmental Pollution Legislation in Canada (Air, Water and Soil)*, September 1967; and Systems Research Group, *Canadian Legislation Pertaining to Environmental Quality Management*, Working Paper No. 3 (Toronto, 1970). A complete analysis of the legislation affecting the Great Lakes Basin is given in H. Landis, "Legal Controls of Pollution in the Great Lakes Basin," *Canadian Bar Review*, (March, 1970).
    Other federal instruments have been the Winter Works program (Ontario, for example, received $3,900,000 between 1961 and 1965 under this program) and Special Orders in Council specifying payment for victims of pollution.

Tax Incentives

Under section 1100(1)(t) of the Income Tax Regulations, assets acquired after 26 April 1965 and before the end of 1973[9] "primarily for the purpose of preventing, reducing, or eliminating pollution"[10] can be amortized at the accelerated rate of 50 percent per annum. Note that the word "primarily" suggests that new plants incorporating pollution controls as part of general production equipment would not be able to write off these pollution abatement devices at the accelerated rate.[11] Furthermore, pollution-reducing equipment that leads to the recovery of materials or by-products can utilize this provision only if these materials or by-products after 26 April 1965 "were being discarded as waste by the taxpayer, or were commonly being discarded as waste by other taxpayers who carried on operations of a type similar to the operations carried on by the taxpayer."

Under the Excise Tax Act equipment specifically used in pollution reduction, sewage disposal and water purification systems is exempt from federal sales tax.[12]

Loans and Subsidies

Under the National Housing Act, the Central Mortgage and Housing Corporation has since 1960 advanced two-thirds of the cost of construction of sewage treatment plants and main sanitary sewers (but not storm sewers[13]), for approved municipal projects. If the project was completed by an agreed date, 25 percent of the loan was forgiven. Between 1960 and 1968, $272 million was lent for 1,381 projects in 905 municipalities.[14] The increased public awareness of pollution in recent years has increased the demand for these loans to the point where C.M.H.C.'s loan budget of $50 million for fiscal 1969-70 was fully committed by September 1969.

Fines and Effluent Charges – The Canada Water Act

On 26 June 1970 Bill C-144 was enacted, "to provide for the management of water resources of Canada . . . ." The basic provisions of this Act are as follows. With respect to water either where there is a "national interest" (s. 4) or, in the case of interjurisdictional waters, where water quality has become a matter of "urgent national concern" and where the province has refused to upgrade this quality of water (s. 11(1)), the Minister may with the approval of the Governor in Council establish with the province (or on federal initiative alone) agencies to control the quality of specific water

---

[9] Extended from 1 January 1971 in the 1970 Budget.

[10] Income Tax Regulations, Schedule B, Class 24.

[11] At least, this is an economist's interpretation of the Act.

[12] For example, Schedule III, Part XII(i)(e) of the Act exempts "goods for use as part of sewerage and drainage systems".

[13] This omission is questionable. Studies in the United States (e.g., American Chemical Society, *Cleaning Our Environment: The Chemical Basis for Action*, Washington, D.C., 1969, p. 120) have shown the runoffs from combined and separate storm sewers to have significant pollution effects. It appears this is a problem in Toronto, which otherwise has one of the best municipal systems.

[14] The average project was therefore just under $200,000 and the average loan to a municipality was approximately $300,000. Assuming all projects to have finished on time, the total grant by C.M.H.C. was $68,000,000 or roughly $50,000 per project and $750,000 per municipality.

basins. In any federal waters, the government may also unilaterally establish such management agencies. These agencies may establish local quality standards, design and operate sewage treatment facilities, and prosecute offenders (who would be liable, on summary conviction, to fines of up to $5,000 per day). The senior governments would advise and coordinate research, while the Governor in Council may establish procedures and criteria to be followed by each agency in setting quality levels, fees, etc.

While economists cannot pronounce judgments on the constitutionality of the Canada Water Act, they can offer opinions on the need for federal supervision.[15] As Richard Bird and I have argued elsewhere,[16] water pollution is essentially of a local or provincial nature (since water basins are essentially local or provincial); the sole reason for federal involvement is the competition between municipalities and provinces for the fiscal dollar. The imposition of necessary standards or taxes to control pollution reduces the desirability of any one municipality or region for industrial location as compared to municipalities or regions that have no such pollution control. Thus, few areas will on their own initiative introduce strong anti-pollution laws unless other areas do so first. Hence the need for federal legislation, to ensure that while pollution controls vary somewhat among areas to reflect local needs and desires, no one area becomes a pollution haven to the detriment of the tax base in all other areas. This need is answered by the Canada Water Act.

Effluent charges are mentioned in a few sections of the Canada Water Act. "Except in quantities and under conditions prescribed . . . including the payment of any effluent discharge fee prescribed therefor, no person shall deposit . . . waste of any type in any waters comprising a water quality management area . . ." (s. 8). Later sections authorize the agency to recommend such effluent fees (13(1)(iv)) and collect effluent charges (13(3)(c)), and authorize the Governor in Council to prescribe effluent charges (16(2)(d)). Nowhere in the Act is there any mention of *how* these charges are to be set.

Provincial Fiscal Instruments

Every province has some agency that is responsible for water quality in that province. Few provinces have, however, established significant fiscal programs for the elimination of water pollution.

Present Measures in Ontario

As an example of advanced provincial assistance, the schemes of the Province of Ontario will be briefly outlined.

Tax Relief. The federal provision of accelerated depreciation has been approved and is duplicated under Ontario income tax jurisdiction.

---

[15] Landis, in "Legal Controls of Pollution," presents exceptionally well-argued views both on the unconstitutionality of the Act and on the existence of federal waters. In addition he shows how conflicts may arise if both provincial and federal laws are enacted.

[16] R. M. Bird and L. Waverman, "Some Fiscal Aspects of Controlling Industrial Water Pollution," Institute for the Quantitative Analysis of Social and Economic Policy, Working Paper #7005. Also to be published in D. Auld, (ed.), *Pollution Dollars and Sense* (Toronto: University of Toronto Press, Fall, 1971).

Grants and Subsidies. (a) In 1967 the Province instituted a system of tax expenditure grants equal to the Ontario sales tax on approved abatement equipment installed by industries and municipalities. (Expected cost for fiscal 1970-71 is $2 million.)

(b) In 1969, the Ontario Water Resources Commission began a program of subsidizing the costs of sewage or water treatment plants for an area where the per-capita costs of such a project were greater than the provincial average of $120.00 per capita for sewage plants and $100.00 per capita for water systems. The subsidy is up to 50 percent of per-capita costs in excess of these averages.

(c) Also in 1969, the O.W.R.C. began to subsidize 15 percent of the cost of projects whose capacity was greater than the present needs of the area.

Loans. The major agency concerned with water pollution in Ontario is the Ontario Water Resources Commission, established in 1956 to improve water quality. Besides setting standards and approving all sewage gathering and treatment and water treatment systems in the province, the agency has promoted water quality by borrowing funds on provincial credit and allocating these funds to municipalities. By 1969, $1.2 billion had been lent to municipalities.[17] In addition, the agency has constructed 333 water and sewage projects under provincial ownership and operation. Municipalities are charged the cost of such projects according to their use.[18]

Water Use Charges. Effluent charges relate to the reduction *in quality* of the water resulting from the waste flow. Many provinces presently have in force charges relating to the *quantity* of water used by the firm.[19] While these charges are uncoordinated among provinces, and probably do not reflect the true value of water to society (few charges have for example, been increased in the last decade), their existence provides a base on which to build a full effluent charge system.

Four provinces — Alberta, British Columbia, Nova Scotia and Saskatchewan — levy a single non-recurring charge when they license the right to use water. Eight provinces (all except Prince Edward Island and New Brunswick) and the federal government (Yukon and the Northwest Territories) levy an annual fee for the use of water in the production of hydro-electric energy. These annual fees vary among provinces but are related to the installed capacity of the hydro plant. While five provinces — Nova Scotia, Quebec, Newfoundland, Saskatchewan and British Columbia — also charge an annual fee for water usage, only the charges of the last two provinces[20] are designed to reflect the quality and quantity of water used.[21] Charges for the use of a public resource — water — are therefore not something new to Canada (in fact, British Columbia first assessed water fees in 1859).

---

[17] From data for 1956-1964, one-third of O.W.R.C. loans were earmarked for water supply and purification projects rather than for sewage treatment and disposal (J. A. Vance *et al.* "The Diverse Effects of Water Pollution on the Economy of Domestic and Municipal Water Users," Background Paper A 4-1-5, Canadian Council of Resource Ministers, 1966). Therefore, $800,000,000 was lent for pollution control purposes.

[18] For example, the Lake Huron Water Supply System, begun in 1964, controls, operates and sells water to customers (mainly the City of London) at cost.

[19] Canadian Council of Resource Ministers, *Environmental Pollution Legislation in Canada.*

[20] Saskatchewan's fees were first introduced in 1968.

[21] This does not imply that other provinces do not control effluents. They establish standards but do not use effluent charges.

The Impact of Fiscal Instruments — in Theory

The nature of pollution is that costs are imposed on those who desire neither the pollution nor the concomitant good produced. Any scheme is therefore to be condemned that either continues to allow third parties to bear the producer's internal costs or merely transfers these costs to the public purse, rather than forcing the absorption of real costs by the polluter. As will be shown below, tax incentives and subsidies are not adequate answers to the pollution problem since they do not force the producer to pay all his relevant costs.[22]

Tax Incentives

Tax incentives are in many ways the worst alternative to pricing schemes since their true cost is hidden and they distort firms' investment decisions.

The usual incentive policy, accelerated depreciation, has often been labelled by members of the business establishment merely an interest-free loan. This label is misleading, since accelerated depreciation provisions can have five substantial misallocative effects. First, if the resulting loss in tax revenue is compensated for by increasing taxes on those who do not pollute, then accelerated depreciation involves subsidization of polluters by non-polluters. Second, accelerated depreciation is available to all (at least to all those with profits) regardless of credit rating and regardless of the value to society of the project being undertaken. Third, the true costs to society of this policy are never made public.[23] In addition to these faults, accelerated depreciation provisions are applicable to capital assets in place and thus create incentives to invest in capital-intensive abatement techniques that qualify for tax treatment although less capital-intensive techniques may be less costly.[24] Finally, the effect of accelerated depreciation provisions and therefore their incentive depends on the tax rate of the firm — that is, on its profits. The provision is of no use to firms making losses and it is therefore useful (in the short run) to those who can best afford abatement investment without the program.

The remission of sales and excise taxes is really only a token measure.[25] These remissions, however, have this much to be said for them: the imposition of such taxes on intermediate goods is inefficient, and the effect of the provision is not dependent on the firm's profits.[26] However, the remission of taxes on equipment but not building materials again may bias the firm's choice of pollution abatement method.

An investment credit (not used in Canada) avoids some of the undesirable features of tax incentives since the amount of aid is not related to the

---

[22] Bird and Waverman, "Some Fiscal Aspects of Controlling Pollution"; R. W. Judy, "Economic Incentives and Environmental Control," Paper presented to the International Symposium on Environmental Disruption in the Modern World, Tokyo (March, 1970); and M. J. Roberts, "River Basin Authorities: A National Solution to Water Pollution," *Harvard Law Review*, 83 (1970).

[23] Ontario estimated the costs of accelerated depreciation at $2-$3 million for fiscal 1970-71 (Budget Speech). The costs to the federal authorities are probably $25-$40 million (assuming Ontario has one-third of polluting industry and federal tax revenue is four times provincial revenue).

[24] For example, land-intensive techniques such as treatment lagoons may be dropped in favour of capital-intensive schemes.

[25] Again, probably in the order of $2 million for Ontario, and $10 million federally.

[26] Taxing capital goods confuses incidence unnecessarily.

level of profits of the firm. However, an investment credit is related to initial investment expenditures and thus creates the incentive to substitute original capital in place for operating costs (substitution of capital for labour). Moreover, the general public still foots the bill. No tax incentive scheme or subsidy forces the polluter to directly pay for the damages he is causing.

Subsidies and Grants

Direct federal public grants to cover investment or operating costs for either municipal or industrial pollution control are unwarranted: there is no reason why the resident of some mountain resort should subsidize those living or producing in our smog-shrouded metropolises. Those responsible for polluting the air and water, be they residents of some urban megalopolis or owners of a mine in Alberta, should not expect the public at large to help clean up local pollution.

The argument mentioned above that municipalities and even provinces have little incentive to introduce strong pollution laws unilaterally (especially for industry) is not an argument for federal aid but only for the federal establishment of fairly uniform laws.[27]

Loans

While no good reason can be found for the provision of subsidies to municipalities or industries to reduce their pollution, there may be very good reasons for providing temporary loan assistance on the introduction of anti-pollution laws. The capital requirements of many firms and local governments will be greatly increased with the establishment of strict standards. If imperfections in the capital market make it difficult for firms or municipalities to get funds, then there may be good reason for the provincial or federal government to float or guarantee bond issues for pollution control purposes. Such federal provision will reduce the cost to the smaller borrowers both through the reduction of risk yielded by the federal signature and through reductions in the transaction costs of one large issue as compared to floating a large number of smaller bond issues. Loans from federal or provincial sources thus alleviate the short-run dislocations of new strict pollution laws without removing the necessity of the polluter's bearing the full costs of its operations in the long run. Furthermore, loan programs can be run at little cost (other than accounting) to the federal authorities. If some subsidy is thought politically expedient, then either the interest or some portion of the principal can be forgiven in special cases. At least with this type of subsidy the exact costs to the granting authority are known.

Evaluation of Existing Policies

Present policies are a mixture of loans, loans with grant provisions, tax incentives, simple standard establishment, and, under the Canada Water Act,

---

[27] Bird and Waverman, "Some Fiscal Aspects of Controlling Pollution."
  There may be firms that prefer to shut down rather than meet the standard. This is no reason to subsidize those firms that threaten to go under. For example, monetary policy increasing the cost of capital forces some firms into bankruptcy. Should these firms be able to receive federal assistance when federal monetary policy leads to higher interest rates? This would negate one purpose of the policy.

effluent charges (of which no example exists at the moment). The loan provisions of federal agencies such as the Central Mortgage and Housing Corporation, which administers the provisions of the National Housing Act, and provincial agencies such as the Ontario Water Resources Board are for the most part excellent, for they attempt to minimize the cost of funds to municipalities. However, certain policies of each of these agencies are inequitable. Under N.H.A. rules, if the sewer or the treatment plant is completed by a given date then 25 percent of the loan is forgiven. This is inequitable to municipalities that cannot meet N.H.A. requirements for a loan. The O.W.R.C. in 1969 decided to subsidize the costs of sewage treatment for municipalities where the expected per-capita cost of constructing and operating treatment plants is above the provincial average of $120.00 per capita. The program will be used to subsidize the resort areas of Port Carling ($135.00 per capita) and Haliburton ($150.00 per capita); it is estimated that by 1976, $89 million will be spent in this way.[28] That the residents of Sudbury or Niagara Falls should have to subsidize vacationers in resort areas seems a better example of perverse distributive effects than of equity.

The reliance on accelerated depreciation provisions in the federal, Ontario and Quebec income tax statutes must be condemned for the reasons discussed above: the provisions are inefficient, costly and misallocative of resources. They create an incentive to invest in capital-intensive abatement techniques. Furthermore, Regulation 1100(1)(t) as presently written allows the accelerated depreciation of structures built *primarily* for reducing pollution. It is often cheaper to change the production process itself than to add on capital-intensive controls at the end of the process.[29] Under present legislation, firms are induced to add on such features rather than change the production machinery.

The effluent charge scheme proposed in the Canada Water Act is good in principle, and it is difficult to argue against such good principles. But there is no information on how the price is set, how it will be changed and how it will vary among various water basins. Judgment on the impact of the charge system must therefore be reserved until more information is available on the mechanism that will be used to establish the specific prices.

A Tax Scheme to Limit Pollution

While the use of tax incentives is an inefficient means of combating pollution, tax policy can be useful if it can be altered so as to be more like a price system. A tax based on the toxic content of effluence would have the same effect on the producer as a price for using the resource, if the tax varied with the reduction in quality of the environment resulting from the discharge.[30] It may even be politically advantageous to utilize such a tax scheme rather than a price system since it is highly unlikely that anyone will call a tax a licence to pollute.[31] Furthermore, the tax could probably be administered by existing bureaucracies and machinery rather than requiring a new set of branches to administer effluent charges.

[28] Ontario Budget, 1970.
[29] Roberts, "River Basin Authorities."
[30] Of course, such a tax scheme would be most difficult to design.
[31] Which of course points up the inherent irrationality of labelling effluent charges licences to pollute.

A form of pollution not discussed in this paper is the waste content of final consumption rather than the toxic element in producer's waste discharge. Charging for air or water will of course not limit the plastic containers, aluminum cans and non-returnable bottles used by consumers. This solid waste could be limited by introducing a tax on the waste content of production at either the producer's or the consumer's level.[32] Raising the price of these materials will limit their use.[33]

There are a number of important reasons, however, why I feel that the problem of pollution control should be left entirely out of the tax sphere, even though, as was suggested above, tax policy could be a powerful tool. Primarily, tax policy is designed to transfer purchasing power from the private sector to the public sector. Introducing these types of corrective tax measures confuses tax policy needlessly. Furthermore, if effluent charges are disguised as taxes, then businessmen may get the idea that with the return of prosperity, taxes, including air and water taxes, should be reduced. Also, the government could start to think of the tax as primarily for revenue-producing purposes and attempt to adjust it for that purpose rather than for pollution control. Air and water are truly scarce resources and should be priced. To disguise these necessary prices in tax schedules defeats one of the purposes of the price – informing everyone that clean air and clean water are not available for the taking.

We are all concerned about reducing pollution. Let us not, in our haste to improve the quality of our lives, however, impose unnecessarily harsh standards on firms (for example, reduce all effluence by 80 percent) or subsidize polluters out of the public purse. To establish realistic standards and force those who use the public's air and water to pay for that right can most easily and efficiently be done by the government's establishing effluent charges. Rather than criticizing such a scheme, the public should ensure that the prices for the environmental factors are set high enough and that the subsidization of pollution abatement is stopped.

---

[32] Senator William Proxmire, as reported in the *New York Times* (May 8, 1970). (See "Wanton Waste Makes Woeful Expense," in the last issue of the *Journal*, p. 441. – Ed.)

[33] If society feels that some specific form of solid waste is clearly undesirable, then society can ban that product.

Part F
Foreign Investment

The debate concerning the advantages and disadvantages of foreign investment in Canada is far from over. Arguments and debates on the issue often contain more emotion than fact and therefore make it difficult to evaluate the policies put forward by various political parties and other groups. The author of the first paper in this section is an economist who has been concerned with the undesirable effects of American foreign investment in Canada, and his paper stresses this point. The second paper carefully outlines the benefits that Canada has derived from foreign investment and questions certain proposals to restrict such investment.

Chapter 13
Development and Dependence:
The Canadian Problem*

Abraham Rotstein

Dependence is generally thought to be the condition of a poor and under-developed country.[1] Canada however, is an illustration of the fact that this is also a condition that is possible among rich countries — indeed in the second richest country in the world where a developed and diversified economy has emerged in the postwar period.

While this paper is designed largely to set out the empirical features of Canadian economic dependency, some brief theoretical comments may be in order, particularly in regard to some of the terms used in this paper.

Our main concept, *dependence,* is in essence a political term even when the condition described refers to certain structural elements of an economic relationship. Its main reference is to the element of power in the economy and its connotes an asymmetrical distribution of power. This requires explicit theoretical recognition.

The problem of dependency is virtually ruled out, or given at best only a marginal and uneasy recognition within the confines of traditional economic theory. This theory tends to view the economic process as articulated essentially through market institutions, whether perfect or imperfect. A view of the economic process which is confined to the functioning of markets builds in its own implicit political framework. Other political features of the real world are thereby screened out. It may be important to pause for a moment and examine what is involved in the politics of a market perspective.

The individuals or firms operating on a free market enter into transactions on a totally voluntary basis. They deal at arm's length and without coercion for the sake of their mutual advantage. Admittedly there is a latent antagonism in the market relationship insofar as each party tries to accrue a greater benefit to himself at the expense of the other. But insofar as both enter into the market of their own free will, and there are alternative buyers and sellers, there is deemed to be an even-handed relationship between the partners. Within such a free market therefore, the problem of dependency is inherently ruled out and receives no theoretical recognition.

---

*A paper presented to the Conference on the Pacific, Institute of International Studies, University of Chile, September 29, 1969. Printed in this volume with the permission of the author.

[1] Portions of this paper touching on the analysis and proposals of the Watkins Report draw on my previous paper, "Foreign Ownership of Industry, A New Canadian Approach," *The Round Table* (July, 1968).

Since we are so often inclined to view the economic process (at least in English-speaking countries) as the proliferation of a system of market institutions — even when the realities have changed so dramatically — it is revealing to see, at least in the Canadian case, how a dependent relationship comes about in practice and what it consists of. I turn therefore to both a political and economic discussion of the Canadian situation, and am indeed tempted to refer to this as an exercise in political economy.

No more dramatic case exists than in Canada of the trained and cultivated incapacity to perceive the dilemma of national dependence. The dilemma emerged unwittingly as we proceeded, in an aura of goodwill and good intentions, to hobble and frustrate our own powers of economic self-determination. In the course of our economic development we became the architects (in Mr. Harold Wilson's phrase) of our own twentieth century helotry. The future of an independent Canada is in the gravest doubt and only now are the theoretical and institutional elements of our misperceptions becoming clear.

Some international importance attaches to the recent experience of the Canadian economy. Canada has been in the front line of a new global phenomenon — the expansion of the multinational corporation abroad. It is estimated that the total production of these corporations outside of their home countries already exceeded $300 billion in 1968, a figure considerably larger than the whole of noncommunist world trade in that year. The foreign production of these corporations alone, now forms in aggregate, the third largest economy in the world, following only the domestic economies of the United States and the Soviet Union. Precise figures on their present rate of expansion are not available, but it is conceded to be phenomenal. Multinational corporations alone are expected to control one-third of the output of the noncommunist world by 1987. Since the majority of these are American multinational corporations, at least one authority, Professor Jack Behrman estimates that the total share of noncommunist world production under American control is expected to rise from the 55 percent of the mid-sixties, to 64 percent by 1980 and 80 percent by 1990.[2]

The political implications of this phenomenon are enormous and are only now coming to be realized and clearly understood. In the light of these developments Canada stands as a DEW line, a distant early warning system for many countries facing the increasing economic penetration by the multinational corporation.

In a review of the strong links which have been forged in the creation of a Canadian dependency on the United States, we begin with foreign trade.

By far the largest source of imports for Canada is the United States and this proportion has been rising. In 1948, 69 percent of Canadian imports came from the United States. By 1968 the figure rose to 73 percent. Exports to the United States increased in turn from one-half of total exports in 1948 to two-thirds in 1968.[3] Over this period imports exceeded exports by a total of $12.5 billion (Canadian).

---

[2] Kari Levitt, *Silent Surrender, The Multinational Corporation in Canada* (Toronto: Macmillan of Canada, 1970) p. 92.
[3] *The Canadian Statistical Review,* Dominion Bureau of Statistics, (Ottawa: Queen's Printer, May, 1970).

The content of these imports and exports also varied considerably over the period. In 1948, 64 percent of Canadian imports consisted of raw and semi-processed materials and 36 percent were finished products. In 1968 the situation was virtually reversed. Imports of raw and semi-processed materials dropped to 35 percent and finished products rose to 65 percent.

On the export side, raw and semi-processed materials accounted for 80 percent of the total in 1948 falling to 64 percent in 1968. Finished goods rose accordingly from 20 percent to 36 percent. Thus while some diversification has occurred in Canada's export pattern, raw and semi-processed materials continue to predominate while we have become increasingly dependent on American finished products.[4] These general trade patterns have led Professor Bruce Wilkinson to observe that, "Canada's position resembles more closely that of a less developed nation than that of other developed countries."[5]

The sizeable trade deficit Canada has incurred with the United States, has been financed in part by a trade surplus with other countries and in part by large capital imports from the United States. Approximately 85 percent of Canada's foreign capital requirements have come from the United States in the period 1948-68. This has led to a situation where 57 percent of our manufacturing and 60 percent of our mining industries are foreign controlled, approximately 80 percent of this portion by American companies. Specific industries may be cited where American control is particularly high: 96 percent in motor vehicles and parts, 90 percent in industrial electrical equipment, 82 percent in small electrical appliances, 83 percent of rubber products, 72 percent of synthetic textiles.[6]

At the end of 1969, foreign investment in Canada is estimated at book value by the Dominion Bureau of Statistics to be $46 billion, up from $40.2 billion a year earlier. Long-term investment (at book value) equals $41 billion of which about 80 percent is American-owned. This exceeds the total of U.S. direct investment in Europe and also the total U.S. investment in Central and South America.

The conventional wisdom in Canada has always been that we were short of capital for economic development. Whatever truth there is in this view, it now becomes apparent that long-term foreign investment drains away capital in the long run. While in the 1950's in Canada, U.S. direct investment inflows exceeded remitted profits by $1.2 billion, in the period 1960-67, remitted profits ($5.9 billion) exceeded new capital inflows ($4.1 billion) by $1.8 billion.

Viewed on a global scale, this reverse flow of funds to the U.S. was the typical pattern. In the eight years 1960-67, U.S. foreign direct investment abroad equalled $19.4 billion while the inflow to the U.S. of dividends and royalties amounted to $33.3 billion. For Latin America alone in this period, U.S. subsidiaries sent home $8.8 billion while investing only $1.7 billion.[7]

[4] *Eleventh Report of the Standing Committee on External Affairs and National Defence Respecting Canada-U.S. Relations*, Ian Wahn, Chairman, (Ottawa: Queen's Printer, 1970) p. 14. (Known hereafter as The Wahn Report).
[5] B.W. Wilkinson, *Canada's International Trade: An Analysis of Recent Trends and Patterns* (Canadian Trade Committee, 1968) p. 17.
[6] The Wahn Report, *op. cit.*, p. 22. The data refer to the year 1967.
[7] Kari Levitt, *op. cit.*, p. 94.

One other relevant feature of the financial situation in regard to American subsidiaries should be noted. This forms a corollary to the previous figures which have been cited. In recent years an increasing amount of the funds required to finance the expansion of these subsidiaries in Canada has been drawn from Canadian sources. In 1967, 64 percent of this expansion or $374 million was provided to U.S. subsidiaries from Canadian sources. It was one consequence of the United States foreign direct investment guidelines, which are discussed below.[8] Thus Canadians are beginning to realize that in addition to the capital drain on their economy that results from American subsidiaries, further growth of these subsidiaries is being financed largely from Canadian sources.

Benefits of foreign investment can be identified as well. The obvious contribution consists of new jobs, tax revenues, new technology, and management techniques. An approximate measurement of the net economic benefits of foreign investment in Canada in the 1950's reveals that it has been responsible for about one-fifth of the *increase* in *per capita* income. These benefits might have been considerably higher but for the fact that American subsidiaries have higher unit production costs than their parent company. They often attempt to reproduce most of the products of the parent firm while remaining much smaller in size. Short production runs, lack of competition, and the effects of both the Canadian and American tariff have created a relatively inefficient industrial structure in Canada. This has, in turn, reduced considerably the economic benefits from foreign investment.

We must also identify briefly certain additional economic costs even though these are less easily measured. The dependence on imported technology and entrepreneurship becomes cumulative and eventually inhibits or stifles indigenous technological innovation.[9] Government assistance in Canada to stimulate Research and Development has, in turn, gone to a substantial degree to foreign-owned firms.[10] It has also become clear that distortions in the balance of payments occur in various ways through the presence of American subsidiaries in Canada. The latter tend to purchase more from their affiliates in the United States than do Canadian companies[11] thus increasing the adverse trade balance in Canada. The prices at which parts and materials are valued moreover, remain a subject for further study. With the total discretion available to multinational corporations for setting prices on parts and semi-finished products to their subsidiaries abroad, it is likely that the terms of trade between such closely integrated economies as Canada and the United States have been substantially affected. Restrictions are also placed on subsidiaries in Canada in regard to marketing of exports and licensing provisions in accordance with the global interests of the multinational corporation.

We turn at this point to the political features of the Canadian-U.S. relationship, particularly the consequences of these developments for Canadian independence and sovereignty. A succinct and realistic prognosis is provided

---

[8] The Wahn Report, p. 24
[9] Kari Levitt, *op. cit.*, p. 104ff.
[10] The Wahn Report, pp. 30-31.
[11] Department of Industry, Trade, and Commerce, *Foreign-Owned Subsidiaries in Canada, 1964-67* (Ottawa: Queen's Printer, 1970) p. 9.

by Mr. George Ball formerly of the U.S. State Department, in his book *The Discipline of Power:*

> Sooner or later, commercial imperatives will bring about free movement of all goods back and forth across our long border. When that occurs, or even before it does, it will become unmistakably clear that countries with economies so inextricably intertwined must also have free movement of the other vital factors of production – capital, services, labour. The result will inevitably be substantial economic integration, which will require for its full realization a progressively expanding area of common political decision.

I need hardly underline the significance of the last phrase – "a progressively expanding area of common political decision." How has this very process been developing in Canada till now?

The scope of the legal and administrative directives that may be issued by the United States to its "multinational" corporations is revealing. A review of the present areas of control by the American Government over its subsidiaries abroad illustrates the underlying principle involved – namely, that the American Government operates on the assumption that these subsidiaries are a proper area of its own jurisdiction. It is not prepared to relinquish this jurisdiction in any way; it defers to the interests of the host country through particular administrative concessions only. Specific policies are created in an *ad hoc* fashion to meet new American objectives and crises as they arise, although the present scope of controlling legislation is still limited.

American laws and directives in regard to subsidiaries fall into three main areas: control of exports, control of mergers, and balance-of-payments policy. (Other areas such as securities and exchange regulations will be ignored here.)

Under the Export Control Act of 1949, the Office of Export Control of the United States Department of Commerce controls the export from the United States of all commodities and all technical data. These regulations also apply to the re-export from third countries of all goods containing American components or goods manufactured through the use of American technical data. Communist destinations, of course, face the severest controls. While Canada enjoys a special position under these regulations through an "open border" arrangement, this is so only because of assurances given by Canadian authorities that American regulations will, in general, be observed in regard to American goods and technology. The presence of a large number of American subsidiaries in Canada increases substantially the flow of American components and technical data into the country. This, in turn, binds subsequent Canadian exports dependent on these components and technical data to American foreign policy objectives, in spite of the fact that official Canadian trade policy with Communist countries is not itself restrictive (apart from strategic goods).

Under the well-known United States Trading with the Enemy Act, Foreign Assets Control Regulations as well as Cuban Assets Control Regulations specifically apply to exports of foreign affiliates and subsidiaries controlled by Americans abroad, even when they make no use of American components or technology. The curious feature of the Cuban Assets Control Regulations is that they do contain a legal exemption for American subsidiaries to trade with Cuba in cases where United States dollars and United States transport are not involved in the transaction. But this exemption has been nullified in practice through a request by American Government officials for "voluntary compliance" with the regulations. Through the use of such an informal administrative technique, it does appear that American subsidiary companies have voluntarily complied and do not trade with Cuba.

Under the Sherman Act and under Section 7 of the Clayton Act, combinations and takeovers involving American firms both within and outside the United States are subject to scrutiny and prosecution by the United States Department of Justice. This intrusion of American anti-trust law has been subject to substantial criticism in other countries besides Canada.

Examples could be cited where these American regulations have operated contrary to national policy in Canada. The crux of the issue, however, lies neither in the economic cost of exports which have been foregone, nor whether American anti-trust law has had "good" or "bad" effects on the Canadian industrial structure. (My own view is that they inhibit substantially a major program of rationalization of Canadian manufacturing which is urgently needed.) The central issue is the intrusion of American jurisdiction in Canada through the agency of the American subsidiary. The effectiveness of such regulations (as with any set of regulations) is hardly to be measured by the number of "cases" involved – that is, in violations, near-violations or prosecutions – but rather by the way in which they sanction day-to-day behaviour. There is no reason to believe that these laws are being violated by American subsidiaries. An elaborate administrative apparatus encompassing several American Government departments ensures effective enforcement and severe penalties in case of violation.

The United States' balance-of-payments difficulties were met initially by voluntary guidelines issued to American subsidiaries suggesting behaviour to bolster the American balance of payments. When the American balance-of-payments position deteriorated further, these voluntary guidelines became mandatory in January 1968 and the original administrative machinery for surveillance was turned to the purpose of regulation and control on new investment and retained earnings of subsidiaries.

As the pressure mounted on the Canadian dollar, due in part to the behaviour of U.S. subsidiaries, Canada entreated the United States for exemption, and such exemption was granted on condition that Canada give assurances that these regulations would be observed in regard to dealings American subsidiaries might have with third countries. Once more, as in the case of the "open border" arrangement, exemption from American controls was bought at the price of conformity with American policies.

The concessions that are made from time to time by the American government are administrative in character and are not intended to compromise their claims to primary jurisdiction. In the light of this recent experience, Mr. Ball's prognosis of an "expanding area of common political decision" can already be regarded as an accomplished fact, although the phrase itself has about it the air of a polite euphemism. It is the Americans who do the deciding and the Canadians who hold the decision in common.

From the weight of the evidence it is clear that the term "multinational corporation" is a misnomer. This type of corporation, at least its "multinationality," is compromised by the legal obligations and directives of its home government as well as the control of its corporate parent. The political tension which it engenders in a country such as Canada arises in part because of these overlapping and conflicting jurisdictions.

Effective policies to deal with this entire range of issues have only recently begun to be put forward in Canada. The Watkins Report[12] published in February 1968 remains the major set of proposals before the Canadian Government with some important additions and amendments suggested by the more recent Wahn Report. These are presently being considered by the Canadian cabinet for a foreign investment code which may be issued within the next few months.

The Watkins Task Force recommended that a special agency be created *recommend dollar* to co-ordinate policies with respect to multinational corporations, now dealt with separately by a number of government departments and agencies. Its functions would include the collection of substantially more detailed information than is available at present; it would review licensing agreements with the aim of reducing restriction to a minimum; it would examine market-sharing and international commodity agreements; and it would review taxation procedures to prevent hidden tax evasion. These are the characteristic areas for wide discretion by foreign oligopolists.

Some parallel measures were also recommended to deal with domestic, large corporations, particularly in the area of disclosure of financial and performance data. The relative inefficiency of the Canadian industrial structure, however, requires other broad measures such as a reduction of the tariff and the rationalization of industry through the encouragement of selective mergers under government auspices. The Task Force recommended the creation of a Canada Development Corporation to aid in the financing of industrial rationalization programmes. By retaining a certain equity in these schemes this Corporation would thereby provide a Canadian presence, particularly in industries with a high degree of foreign control.[13]

It was intended that the Canada Development Corporation should become a focal point for the mobilization of entrepreneurial and management skills as well as for Canadian capital. Larger projects could be undertaken both in resource development and in secondary industry.

Tax incentives were also recommended by the Task Force to encourage wholly-owned American subsidiaries to offer their shares to Canadians. This would facilitate financial disclosure (such wholly-owned subsidiaries are not required at present to publish their financial statements); it would extend the range of investment choices for Canadian investors; and it would broaden the capital market in Canada. The presence of even a minority interest of Canadian shareholders would loosen the close control of the parent firm over its wholly-owned subsidiary and provide a further concrete basis for super-

---

[12] *Foreign Ownership and The Structure of Industry*, (Ottawa: Queen's Printer, 1968).
[13] One example of what is intended can be provided by the refrigerator industry in Canada. Seven of the nine firms in the industry are American-controlled, virtually duplicating the number of firms in the United States ("the miniature replica effect"). Most plants in Canada produce between 40,000 and 60,000 refrigerators per year when the most efficient level of output would be about 200,000 units per year. Ideally, therefore, the Canadian market should be supplied by about two large firms in order to achieve the lowest unit cost. Rationalization of the industry would proceed on a voluntary basis, providing, of course, that American anti-trust legislation is countermanded for these American subsidiaries.

vision by the Canadian Government in the name of the Canadian shareholders and the broader national interest.

Finally, it was recommended that the American balance-of-payments guidelines and controls to subsidiaries be countervailed by Canadian guidelines made operative by the necessary surveillance machinery.

The issue of American extraterritorial jurisdiction in this country continues to disturb many Canadians as a major factor which compromises their sovereignty. Diplomatic representations and negotiations between Canada and the United States on the issue of extraterritoriality have so far not produced general solutions to the problem.

The report entitled, "Canada and the United States, Principles for Partnership," issued under joint Canadian and American auspices in June 1965 (the Merchant-Heeney Report) recommended that American subsidiaries in Canada be exempted from American extraterritorial legislation. The investigations of the Watkins Task Force, however, revealed that there was no early prospect for such an exemption to be implemented by the American Government although specific concessions on trade with China have recently been made. Such a general exemption would have been the best solution to the problem. Alternatively, concerted international action might be considered but with this prospect still in the distant future, the Task Force had to turn to second-best solutions. In the case of export controls, it recommended the creation of a Government Export Trade Agency to purchase goods from American subsidiaries on behalf of the trading corporations of Communist countries after such an agency had established that there were no Canadian-owned companies available to supply these goods and that only American law inhibited the export of these goods by such a subsidiary.

Should such an agency be established it would, in my view, very likely not have to be used. The problem with Canada's efforts in the past to solve these issues has been the sole reliance on "quiet diplomacy." We have been negotiating essentially to achieve administrative concessions rather than basic political solutions. In Canada, the road to Washington is paved with weak intentions. Thus Canada has traditionally brought few solid counters to the negotiating table and has neglected to avail itself of relevant legal instruments to cope with the intrusion of foreign law. American diplomats in these negotiations would point helplessly to their laws, which in effect tied their hands, while Canadian diplomats had no parallel backing of their position on their own Statute Books. The creation of effective legal and administrative instruments to countermand American extraterritoriality would move this issue to the conference table in a new framework for negotiation.

The same may be said of the proposal to block American anti-trust legislation in Canada. The Task Force recommended that legislation be enacted to prohibit compliance in Canada with foreign anti-trust decrees (modelled on The Netherlands Economic Competition Act of 1956). Such a conflicting legal obligation may deter American courts from extending their jurisdiction abroad.

If the issue of extraterritoriality is to be placed once more on the agenda of diplomatic negotiations between Canada and the United States, Canadians might avail themselves of the full complement of legal instruments to support their position. The paramount objective would be to remove any ambiguity regarding primary control in the Canadian economy of some $40 billion (for 1968 at market prices) of American long-term investment.

The Wahn Report issued in August 1970, *(The Eleventh Report of the Standing Committee on External Affairs and National Defence Respecting Canada – U.S. Relations)* retraces substantially the itinerary laid out by the Watkins Report.

The main recommendations that are reaffirmed include: a central government agency (the Canadian Ownership and Control Bureau) to co-ordinate and supervise all Government activities with regard to foreign corporations, measures to bring about greater Canadian equity participation in foreign firms (up to 51 percent with certain qualifications), stringent laws to countervail American extraterritorial jurisdiction over U.S. subsidiaries in Canada, and the Canada Development Corporation. There are also some important new proposals which highlight in retrospect the omission of the Watkins Report: future takeovers of Canadian business could not take place without the consent of the Canadian Ownership and Control Bureau and "key sectors" of the economy would be identified, "where no further takeovers would be allowed."

The Wahn Report improves on the Watkins Report on the issue of extraterritoriality. Instead of a Government export trade agency, the Wahn Report proposes a simpler solution namely, that such subsidiaries be made subject to existing public utility regulations applicable to railroads and telephone companies; that is, they be required to sell to all credit-worthy customers to the extent that products are available. This would be supervised by the central agency, the Canadian Ownership and Control Bureau and would avoid the creation of an additional agency. This is yet another demonstration that the seemingly insoluble issue of American extraterritorial jurisdiction *is* capable of solution. Our pious pleading in the past for administrative exemptions on an *ad hoc* basis was a testament only to our impoverished imagination and to our acquiescence in satellitic status. To wrap up the package, the Wahn Committee recommends that any company that continues to be subject to extraterritorial control be taken over by a federal government trustee for the duration of this jurisdiction.

A carte blanche policy towards foreign investment has been followed in Canada till now. Except for restrictions on the takeover of financial institutions and newspapers, Canadians have made a virtue of the massive American expansion into their country. Their passivity has been shielded by an ideology of laissez-faire and a faith in the necessarily benevolent consequences of the operation of the free market. This ideology left them unconcerned if not unaware, of the massive shift of decision-making power in their economy to the board rooms of New York and Chicago and the government offices in Washington. A market mentality created a political perspective in which the loss of independence was hardly perceived.

But the new world of the multinational corporation has shattered this vision of built-in harmony bequeathed by Adam Smith. Global oligopolies have far more discretionary power to use in their own interests and against those of the particular host country, than had been imagined. The chief matter of concern is the deployment of the new technology which is the *raison d'être* of these corporations. Control over this technology – its disposition, the distribution of its benefits, its social consequences — becomes an increasingly vital national interest in its own right. Loss of even partial control can hardly be a matter of indifference. The economy is the home of the new technology and the appropriate agency of control today (whatever the speculations about a distant future) is the nation state, still the major locus of power in our society. The fine nexus of co-ordination of interdependent technological systems, the elements of uncertainty about these new and very significant processes, the safeguards required — all of these questions converge on one issue, the locus of power in the economy. In Canada, the lesson is slowly being perceived as political economy replaces traditional economics.

Chapter 14
Foreign Investment in Canada:
A Review*[1]

Grant L. Reuber

Much of the recent discussion in Europe and elsewhere about foreign investment has been foreshadowed in Canada where foreign investment has long
been enshrined as a controversial issue of public policy.[2] In part, Canadian
concern reflects little more than zenophobic or nationalistic sentiment. In
part, it reflects frustration stemming from our failure to achieve more fully
the national aspirations of self-sufficiency and international importance held
out at times in the past for this country.[3] In part, too, this concern reflects
the view that the economic progress associated with foreign investment is
incompatible with the development of a distinctive nationalism.[4] In addition, foreign investment is seen as a serious threat to political sovereignty
and cultural independence, raising such questions as the following: How
much scope remains for independent political and social action in a country
that has as much foreign ownership and control as Canada now has? To what
extent have the U.S. and other foreign governments used, or might they use,
the economic power of their investors to promote their own political, social,
and economic ends? And to what extent might foreign investors, aided and
abetted by their home governments, exert political pressure within Canada in

*An earlier version of this paper was presented to the Economics Club of the University of Guelph in
the winter of 1970-71. The editor is grateful for the time that Dr. Reuber took to update and revise
the paper.

1 For a survey of the issues within a broader context see Harry G. Johnson, "Survey of the Issues,"
   (mimeographed, 1970) — a paper that has been drawn upon at several points in this review. The
   author also wishes to acknowledge the valuable comments and suggestions on an earlier version of
   this paper made by R. E. Caves.
2 An excellent review of European concerns and various suggestions whereby governments might
   help to foster domestic enterprises capable of standing up to competition from large multinational
   corporations controlled by U.S. residents is provided by Christopher Layton, *Cross-Frontier Mergers in Europe* (Bath: Bath University Press, 1971).
3 In introducing the tariffs giving rise to the National Policy in 1879, the Minister said, "the time has
   arrived when we are to decide whether we will be simply hewers of wood and drawers of
   water; ... The time has arrived when we must consider whether we will allow matters to remain as
   they are, with the result of being unimportant and uninteresting ... or (whether we) will rise to
   the position which I believe Providence has destined us to occupy."
4 In the words of Professor George Grant: "Those who want to maintain separateness also want the
   advantages of the age of progress. These two ends are not compatible, for the pursuit of one
   negates the pursuit of thy other. Nationalism can only be asserted successfully by identification
   with technological advance; but technological advance entails the disappearance of those indigenous differences that give substance to nationalism" G. P. Grant, *Lament for a Nation* (Toronto:
   McClelland and Stewart, 1965) p. 76.

order to advance their private interests even if these do not coincide with Canada's national interests? Finally, there is doubt about the economic benefits of foreign investment, about the possibilities for increasing the benefits relative to the costs of foreign investment and about the benefits the country would lose if it had less foreign investment.

In addition to these general concerns, it should be recognized that opposition to foreign investment in some quarters is also based on little more than the straight-forward self-interest of particular groups in the community. In the business world these comprise local capitalists and competing labour groups whose profits, earnings, and power are impeded by strong competition from abroad. In the political world, politicians and officials similarly find their power inhibited by having to deal with foreign investors who are less firmly within their grip and whose horizons frequently are international rather than national. Protectionist opposition to foreign capital is exactly analogous to protectionist opposition to imports and similarly is sometimes manifested by cloaking vested self-interest in articulate nationalism.

The issue of foreign investment largely boils down to two questions, one empirical and the other political. The empirical question is concerned with the total net economic benefits in terms of income and employment that Canada derives from foreign investment and how changes in present policies are likely to affect these benefits. The political question consists of two parts. Is there a positive or a negative relation between the economic benefits arising from foreign investment and Canada's social and political development? And if there is a negative relation, how much economic benefit are Canadians prepared to trade off to achieve their political and social goals more fully?

Size, Growth, and Leading Characteristics

Before addressing these questions further, it will be useful to review briefly some of the main features of foreign investment in Canada in recent years. The various components of the capital account of the international balance of payments are shown in Table 1 for the decade ending in 1970. Several points may be especially worth noting:

(a) Total net capital inflows (column 9) declined substantially during the period from an average level exceeding $1 billion in 1960-2 to about $.5 billion in 1968-70.

(b) The most rapid increase in capital inflows has been in net portfolio investment (sales, purchases and retirements of Canadian and foreign bonds and stocks through financial markets, column 4) increasing from an average of about $.3 billion in 1960-2 to $1.2 billion in 1968-70.

(c) Direct investment (i.e., investment directly by one company in another without passing through financial markets) by foreign companies in Canada increased somewhat over the decade – from an average of $.6 billion in 1960-2 to $.7 billion in 1968-70 (column 2). The most significant change, however, has been an almost three-fold increase in direct investment by Canadian companies in foreign enterprises – from an average of about $80

Table 1

The Capital Account for Canada's Balance of International Payments, 1960-70

Millions of Dollars

Year	Direct Investment in Canada	Direct Investment Abroad	Portfolio Transactions	Other Capital Movements in Long-Term Forms	Resident Holdings of Foreign Bank Balances and Other Short-Term Funds Abroad	Nonresident Holdings of Canadian Short-Term Paper	Other Capital Movements in Short-Term Forms*	Net Capital Movement	Allocation of Special Drawing Rights†	Net Official Monetary Movements
1960	+670	− 50	+ 217	+ 92	+ 60	+ 56	+269	+1,194	...	− 39
1961	+560	− 80	+ 312	+138	+ 142	− 58	+206	+1,220	...	+ 292
1962	+505	−105	+ 294	− 6	+ 92	+ 4	+200	+ 984	...	+ 154
1963	+280	−135	+ 471	+ 21	− 259	+ 43	+245	+ 666	...	+ 145
1964	+270	− 95	+ 645	−	− 527	+169	+326	+ 788	...	+ 364
1965	+535	−125	+ 546	− 92	+ 140	−140	+425	+1,289	...	+ 159
1966	+790	− 5	+ 325	+ 57	− 603	− 12	+251	+ 803	...	− 359
1967	+691	−125	+ 473	+316	− 259	− 47	−530	+ 519	...	+ 20
1968	+590	−225	+1,063	+226	− 401	− 85	−712	+ 456	...	+ 349
1969	+655	−255	+1,832	+ 25	−1,604	+250	− 87	+ 816	...	+ 65
1970	+760	−215	+ 661	−392	− 376	+236	−441	+ 233	+133	+1,663

*Includes errors and omissions.
†Means Not Applicable.

Source: D.B.S. *Quarterly Estimates of the Canadian Balance of International Payments,* Second Quarter, 1970, Table VIII, p. 31.

million in 1960-2 to $230 million in 1968-70 (column 3). Subtracting out-flows from inflows, one finds that *net* direct flows into Canada declined slightly.

(d) Short-term capital flows (columns 6 through 8) together with other long-term capital movements (column 5), comprising such items as assessments to international agencies, inter-governmental loans, receipts under the Columbia River Treaty, export credits and bank loans, have played a major role in determining the net movement of capital into Canada. Moreover, these items have fluctuated much more from year to year over the period than long-term direct and portfolio investment.

Table 2

Percentage of Total Book Value of Long-term Capital Employed in Canada Controlled by Nonresidents, Selected Years 1926-67

	1926	1948	1961	1963	1966	1967
Manufacturing	35	43	59	60	57	59
Petroleum and Natural Gas	–	–	72	72	74	74
Mining and Smelting	38	40	59	59	62	65
Railways	3	3	2	2	2	2
Other Utilities	20	24	5	5	4	5
Total of Above Industries and Merchandising and Construction	17	25	33	34	34	35
(U.S.)	(15)	(22)	(26)	(27)	(27)	(28)

Source: D.B.S. *Daily Bulletin,* February 13, 1970; D.B.S. *Quarterly Estimates of the Canadian Balance of International Payments,* First Quarter, 1966; and D.B.S. private correspondence.

The figures shown in Table 2 relate to the control of Canadian industry by nonresidents. As the figures indicate the share of the value of long-term capital controlled by nonresidents (for the most part, defined statistically as nonresidents owning at least 50 percent of the equity) increased rapidly from 1948 to 1963 when ownership totalled about one-third of the major sectors shown. Since the early 1960's this figure has not increased very much, if at all. About 80 percent of nonresident control at present is accounted for by U.S. residents. Since 1948 the relative importance of European direct investment has increased significantly. It is also noteworthy that during the sixties, as opportunities for investment in Europe and elsewhere have become relatively more attractive, Canada's share of all forms of long-term international capital flows has decreased very substantially relative to the share of total world capital flows coming to Canada in 1957-60.

There is, in addition, the question of take-overs of Canadian firms by foreign companies, which evokes a particularly emotional response in some quarters. Reasonably satisfactory data are available only for the period 1945 to 1961, which coincides with the period when the nonresident control over Canadian companies grew most rapidly.[5] During the period 640 foreign mergers occurred, compared with almost 1200 domestic mergers. These figures may be viewed in relation to a total population of firms in 1961 in

[5] G. Rosenbluth, "The Relation Between Foreign Control and Concentration in Canadian Industry" *Canadian Journal of Economics,* III (February, 1970), p. 28.

Canada of about 100,000 and in the U.S. of 1,200,000. In terms of such characteristics as age, size and industrial distribution, the firms taken over in foreign mergers differed somewhat from those taken over in domestic mergers, but one may view these differences as not particularly large nor significant. On the other hand, foreign mergers had a significantly heavier concentration in vertical and conglomerate mergers, compared to horizontal mergers, than domestic mergers. In addition, the median profit rate of firms acquired in foreign mergers was, if anything, less than that of firms acquired in domestic mergers and the percentage of firms incurring losses when acquired through each type of merger was about 20 percent, though somewhat higher for domestic than for foreign take-overs.

How has foreign control been related to industrial concentration in Canada? An examination of this question for the period 1954-64 indicates that "there was no visible trend in concentration, that there was on average a decrease in the importance of foreign control among the leading firms (in various industries) and that there was no apparent association between the change in concentration and the change in foreign control."[6]

Finally, it is interesting to note that on a per capita basis Canadians invest more in the U.S. than U.S. residents invest in Canada. In 1967, for example, per capita investment by Canadians in the U.S. totalled $208 and by U.S. citizens in Canada it totalled $141. Moreover, total per capita direct investment assets held by Canadians in the U.S. totalled $107 compared with $85 held by U.S. residents in Canada. Many Canadian investors have evidently found it more profitable to invest in the U.S. than in Canada. One of the main conclusions to be drawn from this is that given the size, growth and profitability of Canadian investment abroad, Canadians have a substantial stake in maintaining an international environment that is favourable to foreign investment.

Stabilization Policy

With such large and variable flows of international capital, two questions arise concerning the stabilization of Canadian income and employment. (i) To what extent have outside disturbances in international capital flows forced adjustments on the Canadian economy and, if so, how difficult has it been to offset unwanted consequences of these disturbances through domestic policy adjustments? (ii) To what extent has the existence of highly mobile capital flows impeded or enhanced the effectiveness of domestic instruments of stabilization policy — monetary, fiscal, exchange rate, and debt-management policies?

Most of the evidence available relates to the period when Canada was on a flexible exchange rate system from 1951 to 1962, though some additional work has been done on the period since 1962.[7] On the first question, the

6 These data are presented and described in Grant L. Reuber and Frank Roseman, *The Take-Over of Canadian Firms, 1945-61, An Empirical Analysis*, Economic Council of Canada, Special Study No. 10 (Ottawa: Queen's Printer, 1969). The data cover only those foreign and domestic mergers coming under the jurisdiction of the Combines Act.

7 Richard E. Caves and Grant L. Reuber, *Capital Transfers and Economic Policy, 1951-1962* (Cambridge: Harvard University Press, 1971). For an examination of evidence since 1962 see R. E. Caves and G. L. Reuber, "International Capital Markets and Canadian Economic Policy Under Flexible and Fixed Exchange Rates, 1952-69," (mimeographed, 1971).

evidence indicates that autonomous changes in capital flows were fairly readily accommodated by corresponding changes in the current account without requiring major policy adjustments or significant disturbances in the rate of capital formation out of domestic savings. Moreover, the different types of portfolio flows tended to be mutually accommodating with an above-average long-term inflow typically associated with a below-average short-term flow, so that in aggregate the forces operating on the balance of payments tended to cancel each other out. In addition, for the period 1951-62, foreign capital flows in aggregate tended on balance to have a stabilizing rather than a destabilizing influence on the balance of payments and the exchange rate.

Comparing direct investment with portfolio investment, one finds first of all that portfolio investment posed a substantially greater adjustment problem than direct investment which, under average conditions, was fully accommodated through automatic income adjustments. Secondly, direct investment flows on balance changed domestic employment in the same direction as the change in the flow — raising employment when inflows increased and vice versa. Portfolio inflows which arose because of changes in U.S. interest rates had the same effect. But when increased portfolio inflows arose because of other outside disturbances they were probably deflationary and increases in short-term portfolio inflows were nearly always deflationary.

The evidence available on the second question posed above indicates that highly mobile international capital flows considerably increase the leverages of some types of stabilization policy and substantially reduce the leverages of other types, depending on whether exchange rates are fixed or free to respond to market forces. Thus, foreign capital flows have not so much altered Canada's ability to pursue independent stabilization goals as they have conditioned the manner in which the various instruments of policy need to be deployed so as to achieve these goals more effectively.

Over the years there has been concern about two main issues as far as stabilization policy is concerned: first, to what extent does a country that imports as much capital as Canada retain any ability to pursue independent stabilization policies; and secondly, to what extent does stabilization policy become totally absorbed in coping with the effects of foreign capital flows, leaving little or no scope for meeting domestic objectives? The evidence available suggests that concern on both scores is misplaced. Posing the counterfactual alternative of no capital flows, with or without exchange rate adjustments, the evidence available indicates that Canada's ability to pursue an independent stabilization policy has not been impaired by capital flows. Moreover, foreign capital flows have not imposed unwanted adjustments on the balance of payments or Canadian income and employment to a significant degree — they have not, in other words, converted the Canadian economy into the thirteenth reserve district of the U.S. as sometimes suggested.

Income and Employment Effects

Leaving aside stabilization questions, what have been the effects of foreign investment on the real income and employment of Canadians in the aggregate and how have these effects been distributed among various sectors and regions of the economy? In order to assess these questions, it is helpful to consider portfolio and direct investment separately.

Portfolio Investment

Portfolio capital imports represent a transfer of savings from foreigners to Canadians. Such flows are highly sensitive to changes in the differential between interest rates in Canada and interest rates in the U.S. as well as to exchange rate adjustments, assuming a flexible exchange rate.[8]

Portfolio capital imports are economically profitable to Canada so long as the cost of such capital is less than the domestic opportunity cost of capital reflecting the marginal productivity of capital and the marginal rate of time preference in Canada. Estimating the domestic opportunity cost of capital poses a host of very complicated issues that cannot be pursued here. If one is prepared to accept that interest rates represent a reasonable approximation to the opportunity cost of capital, then the market mechanism tends to ensure that portfolio capital imports on balance are economically beneficial to the country. This is because borrowers will only borrow from abroad when (a) the return on the project for which they seek foreign capital exceeds the cost of borrowing, and (b) the cost of borrowing abroad is less than the cost of borrowing at home.

This picture is subject to several qualifications however. For one thing it assumes well-functioning capital markets that are relatively free of market imperfections such as a lack of knowledge and information, unwarranted allowances for risk and uncertainty and the absence of monopolistic powers on the part of borrowers and lenders. For another, given a rising supply price of foreign capital, increased capital inflows based solely on private cost considerations might result in an excess inflow from the standpoint of society.[9] On balance, neither of these concerns seems likely to be very important because of the close integration of capital markets in Canada with those abroad, especially in the U.S., and because of the elastic response of international capital to changes in interest rate differentials. [10]

A more important qualification relates to future debt servicing payments. Unlike direct investment and portfolio investment in stocks, portfolio bond investment — which comprises the larger portion of portfolio investment — entails a fixed obligation to repay interest and principal which, in the face of changing economic circumstances, may be either a heavier or an easier burden than expected. During the depressed 1930's, for example, the

---

[8] Caves, Reuber, *Capital Transfers, op. cit.,* p. 90, provide estimates of the elasticity of capital flows with respect to changes in interest rates ranging from 6 to 11 for long-term portfolio capital and from 6 to 8 for short-term capital. The estimates of the elasticity of capital flows vis-à-vis exchange rate changes range from 6 to 33 for long-term portfolio investment and 13 to 108 for short-term investment.

[9] This is because the supply curve facing individual borrowers, each of whose transactions by themselves is small in relation to the capital market, will be seen as completely elastic; in aggregate, however, the supply price of capital will increase as all borrowers simultaneously seek to borrow more abroad. As a consequence, individual borrowers will consider the average cost of capital to them rather than the marginal cost which is relevant from the standpoint of society.

[10] For empirical evidence see Duncan M. Ripley, "Some Determinants of Canadian Municipal and Provincial Bond Flotations in the United States," *Review of Economics and Statistics*, 52 (November, 1970) pp. 417-426.

heavy foreign portfolio borrowing undertaken by Canadians during the more prosperous 1920's became a very onerous burden on the economy.

As far as the distributive effects of portfolio investment are concerned, such inflows have a beneficial effect on labour and other noncapital income and an adverse effect on incomes derived from capital. Moreover, by enhancing the supply of capital available in the country and thereby reducing capital costs from what they otherwise would be, investment in more remote and less favourably placed areas is made economically feasible. In addition, by keeping capital costs down foreign capital inflows make feasible more longer-term projects, such as investments in public utilities, housing, urban renewal, and the like, for which interest charges, because of the length of the pay-back period, are an important cost.

Direct Investment

To the extent that direct investment simply provides for a transfer of capital from abroad through a different institutional channel, its income and employment effects in aggregate and on various sectors of the economy are much the same as portfolio investment. The controversy about direct investment stems mainly from two additional characteristics: first, the degree of nonresident ownership and control frequently associated with direct investment, in many cases within the context of a large multinational enterprise; and secondly, the extent to which direct investment constitutes a transfer not only of capital but also of a package of auxiliary factors, including technology, management, and market access, that otherwise either would not be available at all to the Canadian economy or would be available only at substantially greater cost. Both of these characteristics give rise to the possibility of a variety of "external" economies and diseconomies, that is, benefits and costs to society that are not reflected in private valuations.

Before examining these effects, it will be helpful to review some of the hypotheses that have been advanced to explain the flow of direct investment to Canada and in the world more generally. Although this remains open to considerable uncertainty, it seems apparent that there exists no one unique determinant but several determinants of direct investment, the relative importance of each varying with time and circumstance. The various hypotheses that have been advanced may conveniently be grouped into four interrelated categories: the rate of return expected on investment compared with the cost of capital; the financial liquidity of both parent and subsidiary firms; the increase in sales prospects in the host country in relation to plant and industry capacity (the familiar investment accelerator relationship); and a series of longer-term strategic considerations. The first three of these categories correspond to hypotheses that have been posed and empirically tested to explain domestic investment in plant and equipment. Some evidence has been found to support the view that these factors also help to explain foreign direct investment flows.[11] The fourth category of determinants noted above emanates from the literature on industrial organization and

---

[11] Alan K. Severn, "Investment and Financial Behavior of American Direct Investors in Manufacturing," (mimeographed, 1970). Guy V. G. Stevens, "Capital Mobility and the International Firm," (mimeographed, 1970).

includes several related notions. Among the strategic factors that have been emphasized are: the desire to hedge against foreign exchange risk;[12] economizing on transactions costs;[13] protecting and extending existing investments and markets;[14] competition for market shares among oligopolists;[15] the desire to provide an assured source of raw supplies for the future and possibly to deny them to competitors;[16] government policies through tariffs, subsidies and trade restrictions designed to foster import-displacing and export-oriented investment; the economics of new product development, beginning with exports, then expanding gradually through investment in sales and distribution facilities, assembly and finally full production;[17] and the influence of product-differentiated oligopoly in horizontal direct investments and oligopoly, whether differentiated or not, in vertical direct investments.[18]

This latter framework, developed particularly by Professor R. E. Caves, emphasizes the similarity between international and domestic merger activity in markets that are geographically separated. Successful horizontal foreign investment requires that the investing firm have some special advantage in the form of knowledge, production or marketing skills, access to markets or access to inputs which (i) can be drawn upon in the new location and offers sufficient advantage to overcome the extra costs of producing in a foreign location and (ii) is tied to the actual process of production and distribution, thereby implying a higher return via direct investment than through licensing or some other form of exploiting the asset. Vertical investment is associated with oligopoly and the incentives to reduce uncertainty and competition. An important feature of this explanation of horizontal direct investment is that capital flows tend to equalize profit rates in the same industry across nations rather than across industries within the same economy. Moreover, this explanation is consistent with the observed tendency for national corporations to invest in each others' markets and with the tendency for an excessive number of relatively inefficient-sized firms to overcrowd smaller markets — tendencies evident in Canada as well as in other countries.[19] Some of the strategic factors emphasized by other writers can readily be fitted into the foregoing framework.

[12] R. Z. Aliber, "A Theory of Direct Foreign Investment," in Charles P. Kindleberger, (ed.), *The International Corporation: A Symposium* (Cambridge: The M.I.T. Press, 1970) pp. 57-90.

[13] J. C. McManus, "The Theory of the International Firm," (mimeographed, 1971).

[14] John H. Dunning, *Studies in International Investment* (London: George Allen & Unwin, 1970) pp. 67-8.

[15] S. H. Hymer, *The International Operations of National Firms: A Study of Direct Investment* (M.I.T. doctoral dissertation, Cambridge, Mass., 1960).

[16] Maurice Byé, "Self-financed Multi-territorial Units and Their Time Horizon," International Economic Papers No. 8, (London: Macmillan and Co., 1958) pp. 147-78.

[17] Raymond Vernon, "International Investment and International Trade in the Product Cycle," *Quarterly Journal of Economics*, 80 (May, 1966) pp. 190-207.

[18] Richard E. Caves, "International Corporations: The Industrial Economics of Foreign Investment," 38, *Economica* (February, 1971) pp. 1-27. By horizontal investment is meant investment to produce the same goods and services as the firm already produces. Vertical investment, on the other hand, either produces inputs for existing production processes or absorbs the output of these processes.

[19] See, for example, H.C. Eastman and S. Stykolt, *The Tariff and Competition in Canada* (Toronto: Macmillan of Canada, 1967) particularly Chapter 4; H. Edward English, *Industrial Structure in Canada's International Competitive Position* (Montreal: Private Planning Association of Canada, 1964); Ronald J. Wonnacott and Paul Wonnacott, *Free Trade Between the United States and Canada* (Cambridge: Harvard University Press, 1967) particularly pp. 235-245.

The empirical evidence available for Canada, though limited, lends some support to this picture of the determinants of direct investment. First, there is some evidence of a significant relationship between direct investment and (i) Canadian GNP and (ii) long-run interest differentials which may be viewed as a proxy for the relative rate of return on investment in Canada and the U.S. – admittedly a very inadequate proxy.[20] This evidence also indicates that direct investment is related to developments in particular industries, such as the petroleum and mining industries. A second set of evidence emanates from an examination of foreign investment in the take-over of Canadian firms from 1945 to 1961.[21] Year-to-year variations in take-over activity were significantly related to: (i) merger activity in the U.S., assumed to reflect changing attitudes to mergers and various strategic considerations as well as variations in the circumstances in the investing country conditioning the operations of the parent firm; (ii) the supply of internally-generated funds in Canadian corporations, assumed to reflect changes in corporate liquidity and credit conditions in Canada; and (iii) the number of business failures in Canada, assumed to reflect changes in economic conditions and in the supply of firms for sale in Canada. Variations in take-over activity across industries during this period were associated with: (i) the initial distribution across industries of foreign and domestically controlled firms, which may be assumed to reflect various strategic factors referred to earlier; (ii) variations in internal cash flow across industries, again assumed to reflect corporate liquidity and credit conditions; and (iii) the level of tariff protection by industry. A third range of evidence is provided in a number of studies primarily concerned with the effects of Canadian tariffs. This evidence indicates a significant and positive association between the level of tariffs, on the one hand, and the level of foreign investment and control, on the other.[22] It further indicates that the degree of foreign control among industries is positively related to differences in the degree of product differentiation found among industries as well as to differences in the rate of growth among industries.[23]

Economic Benefits and Costs of Direct Investment

The net economic benefits (total benefits minus total costs) of direct investment are equal to: the productivity of the imported capital - the direct cost of the imported capital + the "external" benefits of the imported capital - the "external" costs of the imported capital. The first two parts of this equation refer to the direct benefits and costs of foreign investment and are reflected in the calculations of individual investors. "External" benefits and costs here refer to benefits and costs that are experienced not by the private investor but by society as a whole; they depend on indirect spillover effects and do not enter into private investors' decisions.

[20] Caves and Reuber, *Capital Transfers, op. cit.,* p. 90.
[21] Grant L. Reuber and Frank Roseman, "International Capital Flows and the Take-Over of Domestic Companies by Foreign Firms: Canada, 1945-61," (mimeographed, 1970).
[22] E.g., Thomas Horst, "American Participation in Canadian Markets: A Multinational Firm Approach," (mimeographed, 1970); Eastman, Stykolt, *op.cit.*, Chapter 4.
[23] Eastman and Stykolt, *op. cit.*, Chapter 4.

Both the direct and indirect benefits of direct investment are distributed to the public in several ways. One way is through tax payments to various levels of government, since under existing double-taxation agreements between countries the host country is able to tax the profits of foreign enterprises, thereby capturing a substantial share of the earnings on foreign capital and the rents earned on the package of auxiliary factors. These benefits may manifest themselves, secondly, through a lowering of prices and an improvement in the quality of output in the host country or in higher incomes to local factors of production. And thirdly, these gains may appear in the form of increased productivity and output. In order to capture the benefits of foreign investment as fully as possible it is important to have a good set of tax laws and an efficient tax administration. In addition, it is important to maintain a highly competitive economy. To the extent that market impediments such as tariffs and collusive agreements reduce competition, they prevent the benefits of foreign investment from accruing as fully as they might to local residents.

Two fundamental points need to be emphasized in this connection. First, if foreign-controlled forms simply replace the output of domestic firms, charging the same prices for outputs and paying the same prices for inputs and maintaining production and employment at the same level, no gain accrues to the domestic economy except through the collection of taxes on the returns on the capital and auxiliary factors provided by foreign firms. Secondly, if through tariffs and subsidies foreign firms are induced to produce products locally that otherwise would be imported more cheaply from abroad, the benefits gained through tax revenues may be partly or entirely illusory. Quite conceivably the economic costs of the tariffs and subsidies to the economy may exceed the tax revenues collected from the foreign enterprise. This result, of course, is a consequence of the tax and subsidy policies adopted by the host country and not of foreign investment as such.

Such evidence as we have suggests that the marginal productivity of equity capital in Canada in recent years has averaged about 15 to 20 percent.[24] The cost of foreign equity capital has been on the order of 7½ to 10 percent as indicated in Table 3. Most of the difference between the rate of return on equity capital and its cost has been paid to Canadian governments as taxes of one kind or another. To what extent this has been offset by the tariff and subsidy benefits accruing to foreign firms is impossible to say at present.

Two additional points relating to the cost of foreign direct investment are indicated by Table 3. Not only is the rate of return on U.S. direct foreign interest now less than in the early 1950's but also it is now quite comparable to the rate of interest on industrial bonds. Moreover, the figures available indicate that the rate of return on U.S. direct investment in Canada has on average been significantly below the rate of return on U.S. direct investment in other countries.[25]

[24] These figures are indicated by three types of evidence: (i) given tax rates on profits in excess of 50 percent and interest rates on bonds on the order of 7½ to 10 percent, a pre-tax rate of return on equity of 15 to 20 percent is implied; (ii) data collected from business firms under various auspices suggest pre-tax rates of return frequently in excess of 15 percent; and (iii) direct estimates, based on a Cobb-Douglas production function and empirical evidence on labour's share of output, suggest rates of return on the order of 15 percent.

[25] Figures on rates of return are subject to a number of qualifications, some of which are mentioned by Brash, *op. cit.*, pp. 9-10.

Table 3

Rate of Return in U.S. Direct Investment in Canada, 1951-68

Net Earnings as a Percentage of the Book Value of U.S. Direct Investment

Average for	Manufacturing	Mining and Smelting	Petroleum	Other	Total
1951-55	13.7	12.0	1.8	9.9	10.7
1956-60	10.1	7.4	4.6	7.8	8.1
1961-65	9.2	9.3	5.0	7.7	7.7
1966-68	8.5	11.3	6.0	7.2	8.0

Source: Donald T. Brash, "United States Direct Investment in Australia, Canada and New Zealand: Costs and Benefits," mimeographed, 1970, p. 10.

An alternative approach indicates that under the full employment conditions prevailing from 1950 to 1956, *net* foreign investment had added about 3¼ percent to Canadian GNP in 1956. The contribution of gross foreign investment would have been greater. Without foreign investment the growth in per capita GNP from 1950 to 1956 might have been about 20 percent less than it was during this period.[26]

As in the case of portfolio investment these gains in income and employment have favoured labour and other noncapital factors, longer-term investments, the frontier areas abundantly endowed with natural resources, regions that are relatively short of capital and areas that now are marginal from the standpoint of investment. It has also benefited those who are the beneficiaries of the increased government revenues made possible by foreign investment.

Even the strongest critics of foreign direct investment in Canada concede that it has resulted in increased income and employment.[27] Nevertheless, leaving aside noneconomic considerations, they maintain that the economic costs are substantially greater than frequently suggested and that with changes in policy these costs might be reduced and the net benefits of foreign direct investment might be increased. These criticisms for the most part focus on a variety of "external" effects which it is suggested are quite costly. Other commentators, on the other hand, have suggested that the benefits of foreign investment are even greater than suggested by the direct benefits referred to earlier because of various "external" benefits that have been underrated. Evaluation of these "external" costs and benefits raises a host of complicated issues on which there is relatively little empirical information and which can only be very briefly reviewed here.[28]

The "external" costs of foreign investment that have been mentioned by various writers include the following: the stifling, or alternatively the excessive promotion, of exports; the distortion of import markets; the failure to develop local research activities satisfactorily; centralization of philanthropic

[26] Rudolph G. Penner, "The Benefits of Foreign Investment in Canada, 1950 to 1956," *Canadian Journal of Economics and Political Science*, 32 (May, 1966) pp. 172-83.

[27] E.g., Kari Levitt, *Silent Surrender* (Toronto: Macmillan of Canada, 1970) "Twenty years of unprecedented intake of American capital, technology, know-how and marketing connections have probably resulted in increased income and employment," p. 118.

[28] For two excellent theoretical discussions of some of the issues in question see Caves, *op. cit.*, and Harry G. Johnson, "The Efficiency and Welfare Implications of the International Corporation," *The International Corporation, op. cit.*, pp. 35-56.

activities in the parent's head office and concentration of these activities in the home country; the inadequate effort made to train and develop local managerial and technical talent and drawing off to other countries the best talent that is developed; the stunting of local capital markets by failing to issue more securities locally or, conversely, the failure to bring more capital from abroad and relying too heavily on local savings; the repatriation of excessive sums in interest, dividends, fees, and commissions of various kinds — a penalty that is compounded by phoney pricing practices followed within companies; the lack of co-operation with governments and government policies; the inability to develop strong local firms in the face of competition from foreign firms; the ever-present threat posed for Canada's balance of payments — and the list could readily be extended. The two areas of criticism that have perhaps been most emphasized in recent years are the failure of foreign subsidiaries to make more purchases locally and the deleterious effect of foreign subsidiaries on the development of indigenous entrepreneurship.[29]

There undoubtedly are grains of truth in many of these allegations. What is uncertain is whether they add up to a mountain or a mole hill. The empirical work that has been done suggests that, broadly speaking, the performance of foreign-controlled firms has been as good (or as bad) as that of locally-controlled firms. For example, the performance of nonresident controlled firms is similar to that of resident-controlled firms with respect to exports, imports, and research activity. Such limited data as are available indicate that nonresident controlled firms may be somewhat more efficient than resident-controlled firms. Perhaps the most important conclusion that these studies indicate is that many of the alleged inadequacies in the performance of foreign-controlled firms are primarily determined by the size and circumstances of the Canadian economy, including government policies on tariffs, competition, taxes, research, and education, rather than by ownership and control per se.[30]

As far as "external" benefits are concerned, there seem to be two major possibilities. The first is in the training of labour and management which then becomes available over time to the economy generally, assuming that the foreign firm finances such training and that the skills in question are in demand in the economy. The second is through increases in productivity in domestic firms arising because these firms are induced to emulate more efficient practices in foreign firms.[31] Here too, little is known empirically about how important these considerations may be in Canada.

In the absence of satisfactory information about the "external" costs and benefits of foreign investment in Canada it is impossible to say how these considerations on balance modify the picture of the net direct benefits given earlier. It is also virtually impossible to say anything with any assurance about how, in general, the *net* benefits of foreign direct investment might be increased through policy measures designed to increase total bene-

[29] For two excellent discussions of these and other questions pertaining to the economic behaviour of subsidiaries of international corporations see: Donald T. Brash, "United States Direct Investment in Australia, Canada and New Zealand: Costs and Benefits," (mimeographed, 1970); A. E. Safarian, *The Performance of Foreign-Owned Firms in Canada* (Montreal: Private Planning Association of Canada, 1969).

[30] Safarian, *op. cit.*, Chapter 9.

[31] These points are elaborated by Caves, *op. cit.*

fits and reduce total costs. In order to do so it is necessary to spell out empirically not only how proposed policies are likely to affect the benefits and costs of the current level of investment but also how they are likely to affect the level of capital flows. Finally, in the absence of information, it is not possible at present to say anything useful about how the benefits and costs of conventional direct investment compare in general with the benefits and costs of alternative methods of acquiring the capital and auxiliary factors normally associated with direct investment.

Some Common Fallacies

Of the many fallacies that have been expounded on this subject, only five will be considered here.

1. A key fallacy implied in many critical comments, is that foreign investment is a zero sum game in which a gain to the investor represents a loss to the host country. This is implied, for example, in such comments as "all the profits from U.S. investment in Canada are flowing into U.S. hands." This proposition ignores the gains accruing to Canadians through (i) net tax payments, and dividends on shares held, directly or indirectly, by Canadians in foreign-controlled companies; (ii) increased earnings, lower prices, improved quality, higher productivity, and increased employment opportunities.

2. A second and related claim is that the annual outflow of profits combined with principal repayments at some time in the future is bound to result in serious balance of payments difficulties. In some formulations this argument is extended to suggest that foreign investment leaves the host country in time with the dilemma of choosing between balance of payments difficulties or an increasing alienation of its capital stock to nonresidents. This dilemma is alleged to be inevitable since the rate of return on the foreign stock of capital is almost certain to be greater than the rate of growth of the host economy.

These arguments pose an irrelevant comparison. It is no more relevant to compare the annual outflow of dividends with the annual inflow of investment than for a person to compare the amount he is paying out in interest this year with the amount he is prepared to borrow. His interest payments obviously reflect the amounts borrowed in previous years; what he borrows this year reflects his estimate of the benefits relative to the costs of borrowing money for some particular use in the future. Similarly, the dividends paid to nonresidents reflect payments on an accumulated stock of outstanding claims and have little or no connection with how much net benefit Canada will gain from the capital it imports this year. This gain, moreover, is not reckoned in terms of balance of payments effects but rather in real income and employment effects for the economy. If the gain is positive in terms of real income and employment there is little more to be said. Only under highly implausible assumptions is it feasible to make a case against foreign investment in Canada simply on balance of payments grounds — especially for a country with a flexible exchange rate.[32]

[32] These circumstances are elaborated in Johnson, "The Efficiency and Welfare Implications of the International Corporation," *op. cit.*, pp. 53-4.

174

Two further points are worth noting in this context. First, well over half of the share of profits earned on nonresident equity is collected in the form of corporation income taxes and foreign dividend withholding taxes. Hence, payments in dividends abroad are more than matched by government receipts. Similarly reinvested earnings by nonresident enterprises are more than matched by government receipts. In either case, the host government is provided with revenues at least as large as those received by nonresidents that either directly or indirectly can be applied to investment controlled by local residents if the government wishes to do so. Secondly, given the decrease in the size of both dividend payments and annual capital inflows relative to Canada's GNP and external payments, Canada's capacity to carry its external debt is now greater than ten years ago.

3. The third proposition is the claim that foreign firms finance their expansion in Canada largely on the basis of Canadian-controlled funds. The figures cited to support this myth reflect a basic misunderstanding of the data. The myth rests on the assumption that internally-generated cash flows from the retained earnings and depreciation and depletion allowances in foreign subsidiaries should be regarded as Canadian-controlled funds. But this makes no more sense than to regard the assets giving rise to these flows as Canadian-controlled assets! The same definition of "control" used by the statisticians to define foreign subsidiaries must obviously be applied equally to both internally-generated funds and the value of the assets which generate the funds. The fact that internal cash flows are not transferred back and forth across the border every year in no way detracts from the fact that they are foreign-controlled funds, by the statistician's definition, in exactly the same way as funds raised by the firm by borrowing and equity sales abroad. Both sources of funds together reflect foreign-controlled financing of investment in Canada. On this basis, the figures available indicate that in 1967 foreign-controlled funds financed 81 percent of the investment of foreign subsidiaries in Canada; 19 percent was financed by funds raised in Canada.

4. The fourth proposition frequently implied and sometimes stated is that foreign direct investment will flow into Canada unabated even if substantially less favourable conditions are provided to investors. This argument is usually linked to the abundance of natural resources in Canada and rapidly growing demand for these resources in the U.S. as well as elsewhere. There is no reason whatever to believe that Canada now has or ever will have anything approaching a monopoly on investment opportunities as this proposition implies — even in resource industries. In recent years, in fact, investment opportunities in Europe and elsewhere have become more attractive relative to investment opportunities in Canada and Canada's share of international direct investment flows has decreased substantially. Moreover, the evidence cited earlier indicates that investors are sensitive to economic conditions and do respond when conditions change.[33]

---

[33] One report alleges that as a consequence of the government's action blocking the sale of Denison Mines in 1970, 85 percent of drill contracts in the uranium exploration field were cancelled. European experience also provides evidence that attempts by one country to regulate foreign investors have resulted in a diversion of foreign investment to other Common Market countries.

5. Finally there is the proposition that foreign direct investment has not added to the stock of capital in Canada but has simply been a substitute for domestic investment. This question has been examined in detail for the period from 1951 to 1962 when capital imports were particularly large.[34] This evidence provides no reason at all for believing that foreign investment was a substitute for domestic investment; instead foreign investment complemented domestic investment. For the period as a whole every $1.00 of new direct investment from abroad was associated with $2.00 of additional domestic investment. In periods of recession this latter figure fell to $1.50 and in boom periods it rose to $3.00.[35]

Noneconomic Considerations

Although many of the economic aspects of foreign investment remain open to considerable doubt, there is much more doubt and uncertainty about its political and social aspects. These latter aspects, it seems fair to say have caused considerably more concern than the economic aspects. Hence, it is particularly unfortunate that much of the discussion of the noneconomic aspects of foreign investment has amounted to little more than a series of bald assertions with little or no analytical or empirical content.

One of the first questions to contemplate in considering noneconomic arguments about foreign investment is whether the alternative held out to the present situation assumes a major reduction in nonresident ownership and control — say on the order of at least 10 percentage points over a decade — or merely a marginal reduction of a few percentage points. This is also an important question when considering the economic consequences of foreign investment but it is especially important in considering the noneconomic consequences since many of these are deeply rooted in our society, can only be modified slowly and are unlikely to be much affected by marginal adjustments in present ownership and control patterns.

On past performance at least, Canadian governments, presumably reflecting the priorities of the Canadian population, have not been prepared to take the radical steps necessary to bring about major changes in nonresident ownership and control patterns, evidently because of the substantial economic costs and adverse distributive effects that such steps would probably entail. Nor do many persons outside government circles advocate particularly radical steps.[36] Most suggested changes in policy imply slow and marginal adjustments and it is within this context that it seems realistic to examine the various noneconomic aspects of foreign investment.

A second major point to be recognized is that many of the alleged noneconomic problems of foreign private investment are not attributable to investment as such, even though it serves as one of a series of transmission belts, but are questions of intergovernmental relations and co-operation. There is little reason to believe that these problems, such as the extraterritorial extension of U.S. laws to Canada via subsidiaries, will be attenu-

---

[34] Caves and Reuber, *Capital Transfers, op. cit.*, Chapter 4.
[35] *Ibid.*, pp. 265-7.
[36] E.g. *Foreign Ownership and the Structure of Canadian Industry* (Ottawa: Queen's Printer, 1968).

ated significantly by a marginal reduction in foreign investment and trade. Indeed, to the extent that such a reduction implies more, rather than less, government intervention in private decisions, it may entail greater rather than fewer problems of inter-governmental relations.

Thirdly, there is the question of whether there is a positive or a negative relationship between the economic benefits made possible by foreign investment and Canada's social and political development as an independent state with a clearer identity internationally. If one is considering marginal adjustments in foreign investment, then this question is much less important than if one is considering major adjustments since the noneconomic consequences of marginal changes in foreign investment seem unlikely to be very significant either way. In any event, it is apparent that in fact very little is known about this question at present and that in principle either outcome is feasible. Following one line of argument, one may assume a negative trade-off and then pose the question of how much "nationalism" Canadians should be willing to purchase by foregoing economic benefits.[37] Alternatively, one may argue that national development is closely linked to raising the level of per capita income in the country, thereby providing the wherewithal to invest more resources in the intellectual, cultural, and social development of the country as well as in the sharing of international responsibilities. Moreover, in order to reduce the long-standing drain of many able Canadians to the U.S. the evidence suggests that it is important to narrow as much as possible the continuing gap in real per capita income between Canada and the U.S. In addition, a richer country is likely to have a larger reserve of resources to see it through a period of difficult political relationships with its neighbours than a poorer country. On the face of it at least, it would be hard to argue that Canada is now less of an independent state with less power internationally than it was twenty years ago. To what extent this is attributable to foreign investment is highly uncertain however, nor is much known about how the political and social aspects of the country would differ if Canada had had a significantly smaller inflow of capital during the past two decades.

A fourth consideration of major importance within this context relates to regional nationalism and regional attitudes to foreign investment. As indicated below Provincial Governments generally have been more favourably disposed to foreign investment than the Federal Government. Moreover, there is considerable evidence that many Provinces would strongly resist any measures by the Federal authorities to restrict foreign investment to a significant degree. In these circumstances one may question whether such restrictions, which would result in much federal-provincial dispute, would be likely to foster national unity and the social and political development of the country.

Fifthly, it is sometimes argued that there are certain key sectors of the economy where it is necessary to preclude or to restrict foreign investment, such as banking, communications, and transportation, in order to maintain resident control and ensure political and social independence. Here again the argument is based mainly on assumption and assertion rather than analysis.

---

[37] Along the line of the analysis developed by Albert Breton, "The Economics of Nationalism," *Journal of Political Economy*, LXXII (August, 1964) pp. 376-86.

It is not obvious, for example, that a country like the United Kingdom which allows extensive foreign banking operations suffers politically and socially compared to Canada which does not.

Finally, from a political standpoint, it is apparent that our bargaining position vis-à-vis the U.S. is greatly strengthened precisely because of the large volume of U.S. investment in Canada. By investing heavily in Canada over many years, the U.S. has not only given up a wealth of hostages to the future but also it has provided a strong and direct incentive for politically powerful groups within the U.S. to exert pressure, directly and indirectly, on the U.S. government to adopt policies that are more favourable to Canadian interests. The large volume of U.S.-owned assets in this country, in other words, both strengthens the hand of Canadian negotiators and provides a powerful local lobby in Washington with a strong incentive to promote many Canadian interests. One may seriously question, for example, whether Canadian automobiles and parts would have been exempt from the recent 10 percent U.S. surtax on imports if Canadian production facilities had been mainly owned and controlled in Canada.

Recent Canadian Policy on Direct Investment

Canada continues to rely heavily on foreign investment and the degree of nonresident ownership and control over domestic industry is greater than in any other industrialized country. Over the years the Canadian economy has remained among the most open in the world to foreign investors. At the same time there has been a steady trend during the past decade towards exercising more control over foreign firms and reducing the dependence on foreign direct investment. Some of these measures have taken the form of incentives of one kind or another to strengthen resident-controlled firms relative to nonresident firms and to encourage nonresident firms to perform according to standards that are regarded as being more clearly in Canada's national interest.[38] In addition, measures have been introduced to increase financial disclosure by all larger companies and in 1967 the government issued "guiding principles of good corporate behaviour." Finally, the government has imposed direct restrictions in a number of cases such as requiring all applicants for radio and T.V. licences to be Canadian citizens and inhibiting investment in Canadian newspapers and financial institutions. And recently the Government has intervened directly to prevent American control of a major uranium mine and an oil company.

At present a Task Force is at work within the Federal Government reviewing Canadian policy on foreign investment. Whether further regulations and restrictions emerge from this review and what form any changes in policy may take remains to be seen. One of the most important and interesting features of Canadian policy at present is the apparent difference in

[38] E.g. in 1960 tax incentives were introduced to increase investment in local enterprises; in 1961 the Industrial Development Bank made special provision to assist firms that otherwise might sell equity to foreign firms; in 1962 incentives were provided to encourage research activities in Canada, in 1963 special depreciation allowances were made available to firms, 25 percent of whose equity was owned by Canadians and whose directors were local residents; in 1971 tax reforms were introduced to foster increased resident ownership and control and the Canadian Development Corporation was established with the same purpose in mind.

attitude toward foreign direct investment between most of the Provincial Governments and the Federal Government. Most of the steps taken to promote greater local control and the restrictions placed on foreign control have been Federal measures. At the same time, many Provincial Governments have been actively encouraging more foreign investment, in some cases providing incentives to enhance the inflow. Moreover, Provincial Governments have resisted Federal measures that might reduce inflows of foreign capital.

In addition to the difficulties posed by widespread ignorance about the answers to many of the relevant questions that arise and by conflicts of interest between different political jurisdictions, developing an explicit national policy on foreign investment is made more difficult still by the highly heterogeneous nature of foreign direct investment, and the wide diversity of circumstances prevailing among firms in the same industry and among different industries. Aside from general requirements about providing information and broad guidelines for corporate behaviour, it is extremely difficult, if not impossible, to frame a comprehensive national macro policy to cope with what at bottom is a micro phenomenon, many of the costs and benefits of which can only be sensibly evaluated at a micro level. Thus a general policy runs considerable risk either of being very loose and ineffective in achieving whatever combination of objectives is sought or, alternatively, of imposing constraints that do have some bite but do more harm than good because the policies, being general in conception, are geared to some bogus or dimly-perceived norms that are approximated only rarely in actual fact.[39]

Just how difficult it is to assess circumstances within an industry as well as the operations and performance of large multinational firms included in the industry is well illustrated by the recent *Report of the Royal Commission on Farm Machinery*.[40] Interestingly enough, in this industry one of the leading multinational corporations is an indigenous Canadian firm, for all practical purposes controlled in Canada. By itself this apparently has provided little or no protection against the oligopolistic practices followed by the industry at the expense of Canadian interests.

There is little doubt that, other things being equal, most Canadians favour domestic over foreign investment and that there is much genuine concern about the implications of the present level of nonresident control over Canadian industry. At the same time, it is widely recognized that Canada continues to reap substantial economic benefits from foreign investment.[41] Moreover, it is far from clear what new policies can be devised that will abate the concern about foreign investment without also incurring sub-

[39] Thus, one finds in countries, such as Mexico, which have adopted relatively stringent policies, that the requirements set out in fact are frequently more honoured in the breach than in the observance. *Ad hoc* exceptions condoned by not enforcing the law abound together with a variety of legally-ordained exceptions. The result bears little or no resemblance to the prospect of a finely-tuned, clear and rational policy framework carefully designed to minimize costs and maximize benefits, as sometimes held out by the advocates of a detailed and explicit national policy on foreign investment for Canada.

[40] Royal Commission on Farm Machinery, *Special Report on Prices* (Ottawa: Queen's Printer, 1969) and *Report of the Royal Commission on Farm Machinery* (Ottawa: Queen's Printer, 1971).

[41] It is interesting to note that the main recommendation advanced by Kari Levitt to arrest the disintegration of Canada as a nation under the impact of foreign investment, as she sees it, is the development of a new value system in which there is less emphasis on the individual, in which a lower priority is given to being wealthier, having more leisure and having more luxuries, in which greater emphasis is given to submerging private values and tastes to national values and tastes and where "the desire to control and shape the conditions of life within a community" is given higher priority. *op. cit.,* pp. 152-3.

stantial economic costs — costs falling primarily on many of the poorer areas and the poorer members of the community. It is an open question, furthermore, whether the economic losses resulting from such policies will not do more to harm than to enhance Canada's national development. Simply adopting new policies in response to felt urges, more or less on blind faith, runs a high risk of incurring economic losses and of hampering rather than advancing Canada's development as a nation.